P9-CKS-220

A *WALKING* LIFE

A WALKING LIFE

RECLAIMING OUR HEALTH AND OUR FREEDOM ONE STEP AT A TIME

Antonia Malchik

Cover design by Kerry Rubenstein
Cover image: Frimages/iStock

Da Capo Press
Hachette Book Group
1290 Avenue of the Americas, New York, NY 10104
www.dacapopress.com
@DaCapoPress

Printed in the United States of America
First Edition: May 2019
Published by Da Capo Press, an imprint of Perseus Books, LLC, a subsidiary of Hachette Book Group, Inc.

Print book interior design by Linda Mark

Library of Congress Cataloging-in-Publication Data has been applied for.

ISBNs: 978-0-7382-2016-1 (hardcover), 978-0-7382-2017-8 (ebook)

LSC-C

10 9 8 7 6 5 4 3 2 1

For the parents who have shaped my path:
Papa, Olga, Babushka, Dedushka; Mama, Bob,
Grandma, Grandpa; Liz and Tony.
And for Ian, who walks beside me.

To walk is by a thought to go;
To move in spirit to and fro;
To mind the good we see;
To taste the sweet;
Observing all the things we meet
How choice and rich they be.

—from "Walking," THOMAS TRAHERNE
(circa 1636–1674)

CONTENTS

THE FIRST STEP

> My guide and I are leaving Africa the way our forebears did during the Pleistocene—on foot. . . . It was that primordial diaspora that made the world ours, that made us truly human.
>
> —PAUL SALOPEK, January 21, 2013, first dispatch from his multiyear Out of Eden Walk

A STORY WAS WALKING WEST.

In the damp, early hours of September 5, 2015, young men began appearing in the tiny Austrian town of Nickelsdorf. Exhausted and footsore, they were walking the last stretch of an epic, heartbreaking journey through a nondescript parking lot that led off the road. Young women came behind them, then families, and, finally, those in wheelchairs.

All of the people streaming into Nickelsdorf were war refugees. They'd come from cities that had been centers of culture and commerce for thousands of years before the Roman Empire was even thought of, cities that were shaped by centuries of conquest, tradition, and progress; and they came from rural soils that had given birth to the first human agriculture.

Bethany Bell, a reporter for the BBC, had been waiting for this story for months, through late August and early September 2015. She reported on the migrant crisis as wave after wave of Syrian war refugees piled into the train station in Budapest, Hungary, hoping to cross the border into Austria. Along with journalists from *The Guardian*, *The New York Times*, *Le Monde*, *Deutsche Zeitung*, and publications from all over the world, she waited while the governments of Germany, Hungary, and Austria bent to xenophobia, nationalism, and the strong countering wind of human compassion, wrangling back and forth about what to do with the now-countless refugees fleeing the war that was devastating their homeland.

When word filtered to Budapest that Germany would accept the people and their attendant needs, some of the exhausted thousands waited for buses, but others did what any one of us billions of humans might do in their situation: they stood up in the darkness and drizzle and began walking. A hundred miles from Budapest, they crossed the border into Austria.

Along with reporters waiting at Nickelsdorf, the Red Cross stationed itself to greet the refugees. They handed out food, clothes, and water. But what the people wanted most was shoes. Their footwear by that time had become worn-out and inadequate to the monumental task they were given. In between interviewing refugees, Bell took pictures of bedraggled shoes and a prosthetic leg abandoned on the pavement. Another pile of donated shoes waited to be put to use: teenagers' tennis shoes, women's dress shoes, high-top children's sneakers, black rain boots, polka-dotted rain boots, pink rain boots with red hearts. Aids we use to help us navigate this world on our feet.

Bell described the scene that Saturday morning in 2015 as imbued with an unexpected sense of hope, despite the horrific causes of the refugees' arrival. "Which country are we in now?" the young men asked. On being told they were in Austria, they cheered. The families came much more slowly, far behind. "I want my son to grow up in a place without war," an engineer told Bell of his decision to leave his beloved Damascus with his teenage son.

A sense of hope, said Bell, and, she told me, "for me there was something deeply human in it. For all the things we create for ourselves, the homes we build, the lives, sometimes you just have to walk away."

Walking is both our first step and last resort when fleeing war or persecution. Our feet don't need access to gas stations fed by fuel pipelines, or electric rails, or even roads, all the manufactured boundaries that structure how we maneuver through our physical space. The highways are bombed, the trains aren't running, and suddenly questions of borders and gridded networks of transportation lose relevance. A refugee doesn't have the luxury of restraining his step with respect to political margins. Through our feet, we are reminded that the planet is a whole thing, and that we are animals evolved to traverse it with a sure step and elongated spines.

HUMANS EXIST WITHIN moments and days, the short spans of our lifetimes, in which we see our homes and communities, our national borders, as immovable realities. We forget how wide-roaming our species has been across this living planet, how often violence or starvation or environmental devastation has uprooted us and driven us out, how many miles we've walked in search of hope or adventure or safety, how very large our story is when told by the way we amble across the earth, set loose by the freedom of our feet.

Walking is essential to our physical health and creativity, to children's brain development, to mental well-being throughout our lives, and to our understanding of our place in the world. Walking is not, can never be, just about burning calories or counting steps. It's an ancient act evolved over millions of years and is deeply integral to our sense of belonging, both physically and psychologically.

But driven by a combination of a car-centric culture and an insatiable thirst for productivity and efficiency, we have been designing walking out of our lives for nearly a hundred years. Losing walking might seem the stuff of science fiction, but the fact is that most Americans lack access, time, and often the desire to walk even the bare recommended minimum of thirty minutes a day. We're busy people. We have things to do and places to go, and we need to do those things and get to those places fast. And we think about walking so little that it might *seem* arbitrary, a small, creaky, slow thing in a world of big human concerns and urgent human needs, but the stark truth is that if we lost our ability and right to walk, the results would be devastating. The loss of walking as an individual and a community act has the potential to destroy our deepest spiritual connections, our democratic society, our neighborhoods, and our freedom.

Walk, perambulate, saunter, tread, stroll, amble, hike, trudge, wander: for decades the act of walking has been consigned to the realm of art, a place for poets and physicists and philosophers to wander and think. But walking extends paths into every aspect of our everyday lives, from how our bodies and brains have evolved, to how democracies function, to how we manage and mitigate our health as we rush headlong into a future where digital technology seems destined to manage our lives at levels increasingly intertwined and microscopic.

This is not a path we are predestined to choose. We can change the course of our mobility. And we need to.

This book will explore walking's role in many areas of human life—health, creativity, spirituality and grief, the structure of our communities—and it will explore the ways in which we've lost some of these things (health, creativity, community) at the same time that we've begun to lose walking. It will also describe how we are beginning to reclaim our birthright as a bipedal species and the benefits we gain from our singular form of movement—the visible benefits, but more importantly, the unseen ones.

At its core, this book is about deep human connection. Connection to one another, to the planet, and to our own selves. We evolved as creatures who traverse the earth on two feet at a rate of about three miles an hour. That is the speed at which we learned to hunt, use tools, gather food, raise children, exchange goods, form tribes and societies. It's the speed at which we muse, think, ponder, soul-search. We have always walked the planet. It's who we are.

It's only very recently that large masses of us have taken to moving at other paces and connecting in other ways, and neither our bodies, our minds, nor our societies have adapted to these shifts. We may not for a very long time.

There is no reason, either, why those changes should be permanent. With all our human ingenuity and self-knowledge, we're perfectly capable of creating lives and infrastructure that include walking as a primary means of daily locomotion and interaction, without giving up the ability to travel across the globe at a faster, more mechanical pace. In doing so, we could find that we reconnect to much of what many people feel they've lost over the past hundred years or so: a sense of community, a feeling of time as an expansive, friendly gift rather than an anxiety-inducing taskmaster, and the sheer luxury, the almost pure animal pleasure, of moving through the world under the power of our own miraculous bodies.

IMAGINE THERE IS a path before your feet. It's firm and clean, broken by tree roots and rocks, sprinkled with golden larch needles, or perhaps red-orange maple leaves, or it's a noisy city sidewalk packed with fellow humans, or it's soft with white chalk exposed by millennia of passing feet. Pick the landscape that speaks most to your sense of place, of home. This path is anywhere, nowhere and everywhere. It leads through space and through time.

Now stand up and move as if to stride forward. Before your foot even lands on the ground, your step vibrates in response to millions of years of human evolution. Your hips shift weight onto the foot still pressed on the ground, while your knee works as a pendulum to swing forward. A sensory system made of tiny bones and organs in your inner ear maintains your connection to the gravitational pull of the planet, keeping you upright. Another sensory system gives you a keen awareness of how and where your body is moving, telling your foot, before it lands, how heavily to fall, while at the same time providing feedback to your brain so that you can adapt to the terrain you're in the process of traversing.

There's a lot going on when we take a step. And most of us do it unwittingly, sometimes thousands of times per day if we're lucky. Each of those steps is a falling forward, taken with the knowledge that the ground will catch us before we tumble. Walking is often described as an act of faith, but faith, I think, is the wrong word. It is closer to an act of trust, the kind that comes from a decades-long relationship made strong through the fractures and strata of experience. Faith is given to that which we can never, in this life, know for certain. Trust is given to that which has proven itself. And this relationship, of our bodies and our motion with the planet that gives us life, has developed not over decades or even millennia, but over so many millions of years it's beyond the stretch of human imagination. We step forward in complete trust because we know exactly how our footfalls will be met.

THROUGHOUT THIS BOOK, I will refer more than once to the concept that bipedal walking is what makes us human. This claim begs the question: where does that leave those whose disabilities mean they can't walk, or can't walk without support? Considering how long we live and how dependent an increasing number of us are on complex medical technology to do so, where does that leave all of us?

The definition of "human" has never been consistent. At various points in history it has left out women, African Americans, Jewish people, Christians, non-Christians, enslaved people of any race or ethnicity, the mentally disabled, the physically disabled, and countless others. To clarify: The idea that "walking makes us human" applies not to any individual's claim to humanity, but to a scientific classification that helps to categorize our species. We are not chimps or gorillas or macaques; we are *Homo sapiens*, defined in part by our habitual bipedality. Our evolutionary shift to that habitual bipedalism, says world-famous paleoanthropologist Richard Leakey, is what makes us human, but it's also just the beginning of our shared story.

Walking itself can mean different things to different people. We stride, but we also roll and shuffle and tap. Walking gets us places under our own power, or with whatever assistance is necessary to do so, and we do that in whatever way our bodies direct. And although the words and descriptions used in this book most often assume an able-bodied person, I have come to think of walking as more than a form of transportation; it is a manifestation of being as fully present in the world as is possible for each individual. The words we use as stand-ins for walking are due, I hope, for expansion, opening a door to this wider reality.

SEVERAL YEARS AGO, while I was living in semirural upstate New York, I sat in the children's section of a Barnes and Noble, watching my kids play at the Thomas the Tank Engine train table. I had about an hour before my two-year-old needed her nap, and we had to get groceries before that. We were out of milk, among other necessities. My then five-year-old son tried to coax his sister into sharing her engines, but gave up after she threatened to bite him. I closed my eyes, riding on the never-ending exhaustion that comes with parenting small children, and thought of how badly I didn't want to take them grocery shopping.

It wasn't the shopping itself that made me balk; it was the location. The grocery store was immediately across the street from Barnes and Noble. If I could take my kids by the hand or put them in a stroller and walk there, the door-to-door trip would probably have taken five minutes. But I couldn't walk there. It was, in fact, impossible for anybody to cross the five lanes that separated the two stores' parking lots, at least legally and safely. There was no crosswalk, no crossing light, nothing to indicate that the designers of this road had ever contemplated using it for anything but cars. Getting to the grocery store was an ordeal that began with persuading my kids out the door and back to the car, buckling them in their booster seats, buckling myself, starting the car, cursing the hundred-degree weather and broken air conditioning and the fact that I hadn't found shade to park in, reversing out of our space, navigating the traffic between Barnes and Noble and Lowe's, waiting at the traffic light, parking again, unbuckling the kids, telling them sharply to stay put until I'd gotten our grocery bags out of the trunk, picking up my daughter and holding my son's hand, and proceeding warily through the busy parking lot to the store's front doors, where they would fight over who got to push the child-sized cart without the wonky wheel. The entire process would be punctuated with stabs of pain in my lower back as I twisted to buckle them in their seats and folded myself behind the steering wheel.

It was insane.

The store was right there. If there hadn't been so much traffic exhaust from the road, we probably could have smelled the grocery store's bakery from the bookstore. If we could have walked, the grocery store visit would have been an organic, nearly pleasant side trip in our morning. Instead, it was a car-dependent nightmare.

OVER THE PAST hundred years we have designed and built a world in which most of us no longer have the time or desire to walk, although as far as desire goes, one might ask—when did we ever, except for the Stoics, poets, and the elite? Most of humanity has always walked, but "going for a walk" has generally been a luxury for those with both enough time and enough calories. Now, the converse has become true: the ability to walk as a way of life—to work, school, social events, food, and services—has become the luxury.

After several years of driving my children across the road from Barnes and Noble to the grocery store, and to everywhere else we needed to go, I finally moved my family back to Montana, where I was born and raised, a fifth-generation descendant of homesteaders on my mother's side. We returned to my hometown, where walking and its offshoots are a way of life. We gave up one of our two cars without regret, and our kids slowly learned that they could get places on their own two legs, without being buckled into a car seat, and more importantly they learned that doing so was a lot more fun than driving, that a walking life gave them far more freedom over their own mobility. The lessons of our previous car-dependent life, though, stuck with me, and in my work I returned repeatedly to its consequences, not just for myself but for all of us.

When we walk, time slows down, and our multitasking brains rest and reconnect with our creative selves. When we walk, we become something we've forgotten during centuries of technological revolution and the race to make our lives ever more efficient and productive—we become more human. And in walking we find the space to ask ourselves a question that perhaps we've been avoiding, one that, in part, I wrote this book to explore: What does that mean?

THERE ARE MANY stories in these pages, and many of them have a solitary component, an essence of aloneness. But in each of these, that aloneness is offset by human bonds. Our walking stories nearly always hold these connections, even when they're unacknowledged. In her memoir *Wild*, Cheryl Strayed recounts a solo journey she took hiking the Pacific Crest Trail to process her mother's death and her own broken sense of self and self-worth. The point of the journey is Strayed alone, but the lingering memory of her story, for me, was how many people helped her along the way, how many connections she made through the simple act of others' spontaneous generosity. Even when we are solitary, we do not walk alone.

Toward the end of his nonfiction book *On Trails*, Robert Moor ends up in Morocco trying, with two guides, to map a trail that would be a kind of extension of the Appalachian Trail—separated by the vast Atlantic Ocean but linked geologically by the rocks underfoot, ranges and dirt that had, millions and millions of years ago, been part of one gigantic land mass. Musing on the connections and misunderstandings between people of different cultures, different value systems, and what he calls the problems of "connection without fellow feeling," he wrote: "We can travel at the speed of sound and transmit information at the speed of light, but deep human connection still cannot move faster than the (comparatively, lichenous) rate at which trust can grow."

As our digital world connects us more quickly every year but without much depth, we find ourselves dizzy, addicted, confused, not sure how to keep up—or if we should keep up—and wondering how the speed of connectivity is changing who we are as individuals and societies. These connections are, though, still new and still shallow. To balance them, to learn how to develop them and live with them, we need to allow ourselves the deeper connections that are built, step-by-step, over lifetimes and as physical beings in the physical world. To answer an hour on social media with the irreplaceable delight of walking out our own doors and breathing in this wild world while we wander. The trust we build with one another still occurs, despite all our technological advances, at a human pace.

IN 2013, JOURNALIST Paul Salopek embarked on a decade-plus, twenty-one-thousand-mile journey on foot to trace the ancient migration of humanity from our cradle in Ethiopia's Great Rift Valley to Tierra del Fuego in Chile. He set out to rediscover that human tempo, the motion at three miles an hour that has defined the way we narrate and interpret landscapes for tens of thousands, perhaps hundreds of thousands, of years. A pilgrimage, in a way, to answer what it means to be a human traversing the world at a walking speed and on his own two feet. Salopek is chronicling his journey in regular online Out of Eden dispatches for *National Geographic*.

I've become drawn deeply into his journey, not just because of the walking or the luxury of time and space and slowness. The true gift also lies in Salopek's telling of it: we are lesser creatures without our stories, whether they're told with footprints, or with our words. "Walking has made my legs and heart stronger," he wrote three years into his journey. "But more important, it's limbered up my mind. Spanning nations, continents, and time zones on foot—day after day, month after month—has altered the way I experience life on the planet."

We walk, and dams in our minds begin to crumble; our thoughts find new paths to explore; our prejudices and assumptions about ourselves, about other people, about the world around us, begin to erode, to shift, to blur. Our bodies become alive again and we learn, maybe for the first time since we were little children, what a giddy, vital, physical thing it is to be *alive*.

The story that walked into Nickelsdorf that rainy day in 2015 under the footsteps of refugees was not the transient headline chased by Bethany Bell or any other journalist. It was a human story, *the* human story, and it belongs to all of us.

ONE
TODDLE

"You're conscious now. It means you want things.
You just have to figure out what."
"How do I do that?"
"Go for a walk. See the world."

—*HUMVNS,* Season 2, Episode 5

CONSIDER YOUR FEET. NO, *REALLY* CONSIDER THEM. NOT "Feet are smelly, gross, weird, sexy." Not what feet *mean*; consider what feet *are*. Delicate limbs with the barest hint of a fin's shape; they hold up your body, one at a time bearing your full weight with each step you take. Heel bone rolling briskly toward sensitive arches, landing that weight on a network of metatarsals and steadying for a whisper of a moment on the flats of your toes, holding aloft your entire, complex human form in a beautiful, unconscious balancing act. And then your opposite knee and ankle pendulum forward to land your weight entirely, accurately, on your other foot, starting the whole swaying, miraculous dance over again.

We take thousands of these steps per day, performing an infinity of miracles throughout our lives as long as we are able-bodied. Our feet are one of our most sensitive translators of the world. We give credit for this to our eyes, our brains, and sometimes our ears, but without our feet's ability to read the terrain beneath them, most of us wouldn't go anywhere. They tell our brains and internal balance systems if the ground is icy, rocky, hilly, flat, made of cobblestones or of smooth asphalt. Our feet take a pounding every day of our lives, yet never stop reading the earth with perception that's light and sensitive, like a downy feather floating in a light breeze.

DO YOU REMEMBER learning to walk? Most of us don't. Yet, as infants, learning to walk takes our complete attention. To walk fluidly, we must learn to plan instantaneously: to shift our weight while using feedback from our feet, our eyes, and our internal sense of balance, adjusting to slopes, obstacles, and dangers like ice. There are so many considerations the brain has to weigh when walking that it's a wonder it doesn't take several minutes for humans to accomplish each of our own steps.

Every time we take one of these steps, we fall, catch ourselves, fall again. A "two-beat miracle," Paul Salopek calls it—"an iambic teetering, a holding on and letting go."

When we walk, our ankles and knees work to balance the body's weight over a single foot, allowing the other to release and swing forward. Just before that leg's foot leaves the ground, its knee bends and elastic energy that was stored in the ankle tendons releases. The combination of elastic energy, pivoting, and lifting is what allows humans to walk using comparatively little energy, but the process is complicated. It seems to lean significantly on the brain in ways we're only beginning to fathom, and has so far been almost impossible to replicate with precision.

In 2015, a twenty-seven-year-old single mother named Rebekah Gregory stepped across the finish line of the Boston Marathon and collapsed to the ground. Head on her arms, wearing a blue T-shirt that read "Rebekah Strong," she sobbed from both pain and emotional overload as her trainer lifted her to her feet. Gregory, who had lost the lower part of her left leg as a result of the 2013 bombing of the same marathon, ran across the finish line wearing a bright pink tennis shoe on one foot and a prosthetic limb in place of the other. Gregory's legs had fortunately shielded her then five-year-old son from the worst of the 2013 bomb blast, but after seventeen surgeries to save the left one, and a life of constant pain, she opted for amputation.

Running the last three miles of the marathon—the most her doctors would allow her to do—was an act of strength and resilience. Gregory had not been a runner before her amputation; running the marathon was, as she put it in a Facebook post, a final step in reclaiming her life.

Rebekah Gregory's story is not just about one woman's courage and determination, although it is also that. Nor is it about the technological advances in medicine that allowed her to run at all, although those developments play a role. It is a story about how deeply the act of walking is intertwined with our sense of self, our sense of freedom.

Walking is our first full-body act of independence. Toddlers will gleefully totter away from their parents and then turn back, giggling, knowing that they now have access to unimaginable power—the power to go where they wish under their own steam. As adults, we turn to walking to express our freedom, our frustrations, our goals. When we lose that ability, when it is taken from us, the inability to walk can rock us to our cores. There is a reason that "Will I ever walk again?" is a reliable trope of medical dramas.

"Upright walking is a hallmark of human evolution," said Dr. Jeremy DeSilva, an assistant professor of paleoanthropology at Dartmouth College, in an online course on bipedal walking that I took in 2017. "It was a critical adaptation; a gateway to becoming human."

⁂

SEVEN MILLION YEARS ago Earth's landmasses looked strikingly similar to our present-day geography, although variations that initially seem small snag one's attention, like a child's "spot the difference" puzzle.

The Himalayas were in the process of forming. The land bridge connecting South America and North America was absent. The spray of islands that now make up the Canadian Arctic Archipelago was one solid mass linked to both Greenland and North America.

Seven million years ago, dinosaurs had already been extinct for tens of millions of years, and across the Miocene epoch, up to a hundred species of apes roamed Africa, Asia, and Europe. There was nothing to indicate that one of these species might evolve into a smooth-skinned, relatively hairless creature that in modern times staggers toward the coffee pot first thing in the morning and spends far too much time messing around on the Internet. But seven million years ago, land that is now, roughly, the African country of Chad was covered in dense subtropical forest, and it was home to a creature we have named *Sahelanthropus tchadensis*. Artists' renderings of this species—of whom only skull parts have been found—show it looking far more like apes than modern humans. But *Sahelanthropus*, while not of the hominin* genus *Homo*, had one trait that reverberates in the physiology of modern-day *Homo sapiens*: they seem to have spent at least some of their time up on two legs. This species, says the display of the fossilized skull at the Smithsonian, "took the first steps toward walking upright."

The paleoanthropologists who discovered *Sahelanthropus* in Chad in 2001 can't say exactly what the species' body looked like; they can't say what *Sahelanthropus* ate, nor whether walking upright, as opposed to climbing trees or walking on all fours, was a primary means of locomotion. What they can tentatively say is that they've found yet another link between *Homo sapiens* and our biological ancestors.

*Over the past several years, scientists have changed the term they use to refer to ancient humans and related extinct species from "*hominids*" to "*hominins*." The definition of the family Hominidae, or hominids, has expanded to include orangutans, gorillas, and chimpanzees. While humans are still members of this scientific family, the classification of humanoid species now includes the tribe Hominini, or hominins. The Australian Museum website has a more detailed and accessible explanation of the shift and its reasoning; in the interests of scientific accuracy I use "*hominin*" throughout.

Human evolution is a science that makes tenuous tracks through many links like these, and the evolution of our bipedal walking is one of the most curious areas of the field. It's full of questions and tiny clues: signs of stress below the knee joint—showing that the knee regularly supported the full weight of the body—in *Australopithecus anamensis*, which lived just over four million years ago; a particular curve of the spine that allows bipedal walkers to absorb the shock of foot impact found in *Australopithecus africanus*, a species that lived about two and a half million years ago; and the long thigh bones that enabled *Homo erectus* to stride over the savannah.

As changes in climate encouraged the shift of Africa's subtropical forest to grassland just shy of two million years ago, *Homo erectus*'s unique mode of locomotion gave it a distinct advantage, allowing it to cover greater distances at greater speed than earlier hominins. By the time the species died out about a hundred and fifty thousand years ago—comparatively recently in geological terms, like the timeline of a sneeze in a single human's lifespan—walking upright had given *Homo erectus* longer sightlines across the grasslands and freed up their hands, allowing them to use tools and make weapons, to pick low-hanging fruits, to carry their children, and to develop their prodigious brains. These are among the many gifts left to us, *Homo sapiens*, by those probable bipedal ancestors, along with a tendency toward lower back pain, slipped discs, collapsed arches, and an elegant, loping stride that can take us down the road or across continents.

I TRY TO imagine what those early bipedal steps might have looked like. Was a mature *Sahelanthropus tchadensis* reaching for food? Taking a faltering step or two as she ran away from a predator? A stumbling infant flexing his leg muscles to clamber up a tree? Did our bipedal toddle begin in an even earlier, unknown species?

There are many theories about why we walk upright on two legs, each of them seemingly equally valid, though they remain just that: theories. Bipedal walking is more efficient than quadrupedal walking (even if it is more precarious), which means it uses fewer calories. It also leaves less surface area exposed to the sun, keeping the body cooler. The idea most strongly supported by available evidence, wrote evolutionary biologist Daniel E. Lieberman in his book *The Story of the Human Body*, is that walking upright helped early hominins gather food more effectively "in the face of major climate change," which between ten and five million years ago shrank African rainforests while expanding grasslands.

There is also the compelling theory that upright walking was essential to the development of our massive human brain—not due to the walking itself but because our liberated hands could then engage in increasingly complex tasks, a theory that Charles Darwin himself initially put forward. In his now-classic book *The Hand*, neurologist Frank Wilson explored the idea that the evolution of our hands was what drove the evolution of our brains, not the other way around; neither would have been possible without our ability to maneuver using only our feet.

A more recent iteration of this last theory has to do with humans' ability to turn cognitively complex tasks, which require our full attention, into routine ones, which don't. Over millions of years, hominins have learned to reassign activities like walking, once we've learned how to do them, to a part of our brain where we don't have to consciously think about them.

Research on our ability to absorb, adapt to, and eventually automate complex actions is developing into one of the newest theories about how we evolved to be *Homo sapiens*. It's an evolution that depends, for all our sophistication, on primitive brain circuitry that was initially built tens of millions of years ago. In 2011 a neuroscience team at the University of Rome Tor Vergata used EMG (electromyography, which uses needle electrodes to detect cell activation) to record the activity of twenty different muscles in babies and toddlers. They found that when babies began to take their first steps, the neural networks they used were almost identical to those of rats. Babies' stepping-related neural networks were also found to be similar to those of guinea pigs, macaques, cats, and monkeys, but the similarity to rats' stood out because rats are thought to be the very first mammal to have evolved; we all, in some ways, have rat brains.

Until this study came out, neuroscientists and physiologists had thought that primitive neural networks were abandoned during development, that babies had to suppress the primitive brain to learn to walk. But evolution, as we might have expected, is more frugal than that. "Nature tends not to scrap old hardware," said neurologist and physiologist Dr. Francesco Lacquaniti in an interview about the study; instead that hardware is adapted for new purposes.

I liken this process of automation to that of learning to read: starting out, we have to learn the alphabet, and then each letter's associated sound, or sounds. After extensive effort we begin to link the letter-sounds together to read simple words—"and," "cat," "dog"—leading eventually to more complicated sound combinations like the *ar* in "bark" and the *ch* and *oo* and silent *e* in "choose." Finally, after years of mental labor, we are sucking up the worlds of Ramona Quimby and Captain Underpants after our parents have told us to go to bed.

Like reading, walking shifts almost miraculously until we cease thinking about the efforts we're putting into it and just start doing it. It becomes routine. But by the time we were old enough to build long-term memories, walking was already an unconscious act. It seems to be after that toddling stage, when babies' bipedal walking stabilizes, that more advanced neural networks are laid down on top of the primitive ones.

At what moment this change happens, from conscious, painstaking steps to fluid walking, nobody knows, but at some point our bipedal walking begins to require deeper brain engagement than the four-legged motion of rats. And unlike learning to write or use a fork, walking is not something that most caregivers must diligently introduce to children and teach them how to do. Dangerous and difficult as it is, most of us start out almost compelled to walk. Parents can coax and encourage and invite severe back pain in the lumbar region by holding their children's hands for hours of semi-stable walking, but in the end, as long as they see people around them walking, most kids will haul themselves toward toddling eventually. Modern infants and *Homo erectus* babies likely learned to walk through the same shaky process: an infant pulls herself upright, teeters on her feet, her torso weaving unsteadily; she finally takes a step or two, and then falls, perhaps cries out of frustration or surprise, stands up, steps again, and falls again, over and over and over.

Once on the road to walking, in fact, toddlers take over two thousand steps and fall an average of seventeen times *per hour*. Extrapolated out to six hours of an infant's waking time, that's over fourteen thousand steps and about a hundred tumbles per day. Novice walkers, those just starting out, fall twice as often, an average of thirty-two times per hour. Every hour, every day, all over the world, tiny little humans wobble around bashing their foreheads against countertops, their chins against coffee tables, their whole bodies against any obstacle they don't have the agility to maneuver away from. Their walking is unskillful and, from the perspective of a parent, unsafe. Yet they persist in doing it. Generation after generation, millions of babies push or pull themselves up to standing and learn to walk.

THIS WALKING ISN'T a purely mechanical process; we are not the Scarecrow in *The Wizard of Oz*, staggering forward with our heads full of straw. Our muscles, joints, sensory perception, brains, even our imaginations, are all employed when we take one step, and then another. Deciphering how human walking works requires contributions from seemingly disparate but in fact related scientific fields: neuroscience, physiology, anatomy, biomechanics, physical and occupational therapy, biology, paleoanthropology, evolution, mathematics, physics, geriatrics, pediatrics. While each field has its own particular perspective, a microscope on human locomotion, we need all of them to comprehend not only why we walk and how we walk, but how, in cases of injury, disability, or age-related diseases like Parkinson's, ceasing to walk affects us in ways that aren't always immediately obvious.

Figuring out how humans walk on two legs, known as locomotion studies, began in earnest during the latter part of the Enlightenment, with the work of three brothers: Ernst, Wilhelm, and Eduard Weber each taught different subjects at the University of Leipzig during the early to mid-1800s, but all three of them were fascinated by human locomotion. Together they drew on anatomy, physiology, physics, and electricity to perform their experiments and advance their theories about how we move through the world.

Nearly two centuries of study on walking and motion have followed the Webers' work. Scientists have used electrical impulses, human cadavers, and in one case beheaded frogs to study locomotion. Today, neuroscientists use EMG sensors to detect activity in nerves that connect muscles to the brain. Physical and occupational therapists focus on how cognitive delay or brain injuries manifest as difficulties in walking, such as with long-term vertigo, or as changes in gait that are noticeable in patients with early-stage multiple sclerosis or Alzheimer's disease. Neuroscientists and geriatrics specialists use a variety of methods, including the relatively new field of optogenetics—in which light is used to activate specific brain cells—to study how it is that age- and cognition-related diseases like Parkinson's lead to difficulties with walking. And paleoanthropologists and evolutionary biologists wander around the long-gone worlds of our precursor hominin species, examining fragments of bone to piece together the story of us.

AT TWENTY MONTHS old, my daughter refused to walk, and nobody could tell me why. "At this point," said the pediatrician, swiveling her chair with her habitual briskness, "I'd be neglecting her care if I didn't recommend getting her evaluated." I looked down at my daughter, wrapped in my arms with her damp, curly hair against my chest. She wasn't a regular snuggler, but had just had to endure being poked and measured and weighed on the chilly metal scale and was fed up with it. Yet all the pediatrician's minute observations hadn't explained why she still refused to walk.

We'd tried treats, pushcarts, standing frames, frustration, and encouragement, but for the most part she resisted. The closest she got was every few weeks or so, when she'd pull herself up to stand at the sofa for a moment, and then glance down and scramble back to the floor. "She's tall," I kept telling people, which was true. "I think she's just afraid of heights." She couldn't talk enough yet to verify this theory for me or anyone else, but every time she stood up, she seemed to me to be taking stock of her head's distance from the ground and finding it terrifying.

The pediatrician stopped her typing and looked at me. "I'm recommending her for an Early Intervention evaluation," she said. "Fear of heights" didn't get me far when the developmental charts and the pediatrician said my daughter should have been toddling around months ago.

Looking back at our evolutionary history, the idea of these familiar developmental charts becomes absurd. I can hardly imagine a *Homo erectus* mother building up a tsunami of anxiety because her daughter walked a few months later than others born at the same time. For most of human history—for most of animal history, no matter what species—being alive has been enough.

But much as I can't imagine a *Homo erectus* mother fretting about her late-walking infant in the way that I was expected to, it's hard to imagine how a child who *continued* not to walk would be able to survive. *Homo erectus*, some five million or so years younger than *Sahelanthropus*, did not have that earlier hominin's protective covering of hair or fur, and was more dependent on the support of social groups—archaeological evidence shows that *Homo erectus* regularly used fire for cooking, warmth, and communal gathering—and on meat for nutrition, which required hunting skills. Once a mother stopped carrying her offspring around, a not-yet-walking child would be more vulnerable to predators, the elements, and starvation.

An adult who could not walk could not easily travel with his tribe. He could not run from predators or chase prey. In many societies throughout history, not being able to walk either from disability at birth or disability in mid-adulthood (from an injury inflicted in battle, say) or old age has been a death knell for a human. "If you're living in East Africa two million years ago and you get a stress fracture," said paleoanthropologist Jeremy DeSilva, "you're going to get eaten." At some point, walking upright became not just an optional mode of transportation for hominins, but essential for individual survival.

HUMANS ARE RARELY prey these days, but our compulsion to walk hasn't changed. Rebekah Gregory decided to have her leg amputated after seventeen surgeries because she had to take pain medication every four hours, but also because she was in a wheelchair most of the time. "That was not okay with me," she told a CBS reporter. Crossing the finish line of the Boston Marathon with a prosthetic leg prompted her to post that she'd gotten her life back, but in an interview she reveled in the everyday changes: taking her son to the movies, walking through the airport without a wheelchair.

The kind of freedom and independence Gregory described seems to be something that humans work toward in the earliest days and months of our lives, long before we learn to walk. A newborn can't even hold his head upright while sitting until about four months after birth, much less control his limbs, but if you hold a baby up with his feet against a flat surface, he'll lift first one foot and then put it down and lift the other, an action that parenting books and pediatricians call the "step reflex." Even fetuses have been observed demonstrating these "stepping responses" while still in utero, a step-like lift of the foot that is thought to be a response to sensory inputs. As with other physical responses like the swimming and crawling reflexes, the stepping response, it's theorized, exists to begin building strength and coordination for later movement.

Although we've long observed the stepping reflex, it's only recently that researchers have begun studying natural infant walking in earnest. While the natural development of infants' language, emotions, and vision have been widely studied over the past several decades, comparatively little research has been done on how infants learn to walk. A strange omission considering that much of the study of ancient humans centers on how we came to walk. What better place to seek an answer than in modern humans who are in the process of learning? If bipedal walking is truly what makes our species human, as many paleoanthropologists and evolutionary biologists claim, the failure to study it in infants leaves a sinkhole in the question of how and why we function as we do. The study headed by Lacquaniti that uncovered the primitive underpinnings of human motion—our underlying rat brain that kicks in when we're learning to walk—only highlights how little we know about both the physical development engaged in bipedalism, and how deeply our brain is involved in the process.

In most studies beginning in the 1920s and continuing through at least 2018, infants were observed not in their homes or outside, or even in laboratory settings that bore some relation to the real world, but simply walking in straight lines on flat mats. Any parent could have told researchers they were on the wrong track. My own offspring, like most children, have only a nodding acquaintance with walking anywhere in a straight line. Babies in particular seem compelled to explore their environments along random trajectories. Their worlds are full of obstacles and distractions, attractions and hazards. Incorporating this reality—an infant's natural environment—is integral to the understanding of locomotion.

There was little in this early research about environmental factors, and nothing about how sensory stimulation and input or social interaction create feedback loops in the brain, building confidence and a complicated sense of balance at the same time. There was nothing, in effect, to reflect the real-world circumstances in which babies learn to walk. Yet these earlier studies defined our perception of walking for decades, until research in the 1980s that focused on the influence of perception and adaptation widened our understanding of walking.

New theories began to incorporate the idea that walking isn't just about motor and brain development but also depends on hearing and sight, balance, social conditions (such as an encouraging caregiver), our ability to adapt instantly to varying terrain underfoot, and motivation. That is, babies and toddlers are motivated to walk when there's somewhere interesting to go.

"Somewhere interesting to go" was exactly what previous studies on walking infants hadn't incorporated. The very first study to examine infants' road to stable walking outside of controlled but unstimulating laboratory settings didn't take place until 2012, in the Infant Action Lab run by psychology professor Dr. Karen Adolph at New York University.

The babies learning to walk in Adolph's study were constantly falling down. Outside of a laboratory setting, falling could put babies at risk of serious injury. Nevertheless, inside the lab or out, "infants behave as if they are determined to face the world upright, despite the costs," wrote Adolph. A feat of perseverance reflected in Rebekah Gregory's determination to cross that marathon finish line, and a mark of evolution that is shaping much of our technological future. If our walking is taken from us, most of us will move heaven and earth to get it back. Because we know, without having to be told, that walking is part of who we are.

PART OF WHO we are, but also really, *really* complicated. In the science fiction show *The Expanse*, which takes place about two hundred years in the future, a relationship that comes up repeatedly is that of *Homo sapiens*' bodies with the planet they evolved on. "Belters," people who live in the asteroid belt and on small outer planets, are generally much taller than Earthers or Martians due to lower bone density, and if they end up on Earth, the planet's gravity slowly crushes them.

In the show, walking on Earth is a challenge for those who didn't grow up on the planet, and it isn't just about the gravity. It's the planet's spin, the open atmosphere, the visual, aural, and gravitational noise crowding into the human brain. One particular scene, in which a Marine from Mars is attempting to walk to the ocean through New York City, demonstrates what kinds of difficulties extraterrestrial humans would face. "You're Martian, aren't you?" asks a man the Marine asked for directions. "That obvious?" she responded. It was the way she was walking that gave her away, the man said, "like the sky might fall in on you, like the ground's gonna bite you."

"Here's what you do," he told her. "Feet planted, in line with your shoulders, back straight. Head down, staring at your toes. Then, raise your chin, slowly, a millimeter at a time, 'til your eyes are locked on the horizon."

"Okay."

"In a couple of weeks, your brain will forge pathways, your inner ear will get the memo . . . you'll be no different from an Earther."

The problems the Martian Marine had are very real, having to do not just with muscle control in an unfamiliar gravity, but with neural information and an ability to "read" one's environment instantaneously. We haven't yet, as a species, faced the sobering challenges presented in *The Expanse* of helping human bodies survive in space or on other planets, but we can in the interim investigate the complexity of walking through another medium: robots.

In 2013 a robot named MARLO, which looks something like an air conditioning unit on top of two oddly shaped pneumatic drills, walked several stiff steps across an engineering department lab at the University of Michigan, propelling itself forward on its own two feet. After stopping the robot from careening into a wall, one of its creators grinned and pumped his fist, saying, "Yes!"

Despite technological advances in all sorts of fields, teaching robots to walk as humans do has remained frustratingly elusive for roboticists and engineers. Each milestone achieved—an ability to step up a stair or two, or success in picking up an object without falling over—is greeted with an enormous sense of achievement, even if the robot's skill and agility can't match that of a toddler. MARLO couldn't at that point step over obstacles, couldn't stop itself from walking into a door, and stumbled badly while walking outside, but still, it maneuvered around on two legs and human-like feet with a springy motion. MARLO was officially the first robot to walk without a stabilizing rod on its own two legs.

Engineers have been attempting to build a robot like MARLO since the 1950s, and the term "robot" itself was coined in Czechoslovakia in 1921: *Robota* (possibly related to the Russian verb for "work," *robotat*) was used by the playwright Karel Capek as a term for "slave work" in his play *Rossum's Universal Robots*. (The "robots" in that case were imagined to be artificial but were made from biological material.) It was only after World War II, when engineering and control systems and computing advanced exponentially, that engineers began working on true robots in earnest, and it was only after that time that they were able to focus on robots that walked, like humans, on two legs. In 1969 a team at Waseda University in Japan built the first computer-controlled bipedal robot; it took an achingly slow ninety seconds to complete each step on a completely flat surface. Between then and MARLO's debut in 2013, bipedal robots have inched forward step by precious step.

MARLO was the first bipedal machine to walk without any kind of external support. In videos, it comes across as hesitant—if one can apply that word to a non-self-aware robot—as well as slow. It runs into walls and falters immediately when its feet sense uneven ground; it has a bit of a saddle-sore swagger, like a cowboy. Still, MARLO can walk in any direction (in addition to other problems, earlier bipedal robots couldn't change direction), and in initial testing was even able to take a few steps on a sidewalk outside before veering off into a garden bed and losing balance.

If you ask a roboticist why it's so hard to get a robot to walk on two legs at all, much less on terrain that varies even slightly from the perfectly horizontal, the answer you'll get points straight back to the fact that human walking is unbelievably complicated. Human babies are built to walk and fall; human brains go through thousands of calculations every second, perhaps more, to navigate the world on two feet. No computer system yet built can replicate the combined neuromuscular and brain activity involved in human walking, and these abilities are limited by more than just processing power—it's also about the complexity of being in the world.*

For a robot, as for a human, taking a step forward doesn't just require legs and feet and knees that bend. Robots like MARLO need a sense of balance and an ability to "see" where they're going. "Vision" is provided through either collections of sensors that interpret physical conditions with every step, and/or a breathtaking amount of information provided by human controllers—where obstacles are, what's up and down, what direction "forward" is.

*For his research on training and teaching a robot soccer team to compete in the robot World Cup (RoboCup), Dr. Peter Stone of the University of Texas at Austin took a different approach. He teamed up with Karen Adolph and used her lab's complex, rich infant walking data to "teach" his robots to maneuver bipedally via a method called "reinforcement learning." Instead of trying to imitate adult walking one programming instruction at a time, Stone decided to give his robots information gleaned from the natural motion of human walking, stumbling and all.

Balance is even more complicated. MARLO's designers enlisted algorithms, which constantly gave the robot information about its posture and position; and an IMU (inertial measurement unit), which used gyroscopes and accelerometers to feed MARLO information about force and angular movement. IMUs, which are also used in satellites, are finely tuned bits of machinery that respond to changes in position and gravitational pull.

Gravitational pull applies just as fully to our own human bodies as it does to robots and planets orbiting the sun, but humans aren't packed with expensive gyroscopes. Why, then, don't we spend *our* lives crashing to the ground when we attempt to stand up and walk?

Our ability to stride the earth with our strange, falling-forward-yet-never-quite-falling motion is dependent on a set of minuscule bones and nerves in our inner ears, which make up a fascinating and vital little organ called the vestibular system. The vestibular is the main driver of our sense of balance. It's what connects us to Earth's gravity, and what engineers attempt to imitate when designing gyroscopes that give robots their own crude balance. When *The Expanse*'s Earther told the Martian Marine that "your inner ear will get the memo," it was the vestibular system he was referring to.

THE VESTIBULAR SYSTEM, in essence, tunes our physical bodies to the planet's center of gravity, a relationship so delicate and precise that it almost feels like magic. It's an incredible realization. When you walk across the room, it's your vestibular system that directs you where you want to go, or keeps you upright if you suddenly change direction. While we walk down the road or run across a field or hike over a mountain ridge or nip up subway stairs, it's as if our bodies are chattering to Earth and listening intently to its responses.

Try this: While sitting down, close your eyes. Turn your head from side to side, and then up and down. It feels like nothing, pointless, a simple, almost unconscious movement. But as your neck bends, your brain communicates with your vestibular system. It knows where your head is in relation to a split second ago, and a split second before that, and, generally, where it is in relation to the rest of your surroundings. When you're walking, this communication is happening continuously, the vestibular system detecting and responding to changes in gravity's pull when we change our position. *You* might be lost in thought, but your brain, so to speak, isn't. It's taking in vestibular cues constantly, reinforced by aural and visual inputs, to keep you directed and upright, to help you maintain the pace you wish to set, and to keep your body from careening into lampposts or traffic.

We tend to be conscious of the vestibular system only when it fails: when we've had too much alcohol to walk straight, or if we try to text on a phone and traverse a sidewalk at the same time, or when we suffer from vertigo. Head traumas can often cause damage to the vestibular system, leading patients to fall or trip frequently, run into walls or doors, or feel constant dizziness. Children who have trouble getting their visual and vestibular systems to communicate with each other might stumble frequently, or crave rocking or swinging motions all the time, or have trouble going up and down stairs. It can take months of targeted physical or occupational therapy to restore vestibular function if it's temporarily lost.

An ability to walk smoothly, if that's physically possible, can be vital to a person's health. The human body is lazy, and gravity works against us. Our bodies tend to want to conserve energy by lying down, sitting, getting places by car rather than walking. I'm acutely aware of this feeling on the days I go to my favorite exercise class and my only desire when walking through the door is that the instructor won't have us do jump-squats after crunches. Once I'm down on the mat, I *really* don't want to get up again, no matter how many torturous sit-ups she puts us through. But we need gravity, need that resistance; we've evolved with it, not in spite of it. It's the human body's ability to push back against gravity and interact with it that strengthens our bones, muscles, and circulatory systems and that helps build the vestibular system's sense of balance and navigation.

It's easy to see how deeply gravity affects our bodies, even without futuristic science fiction shows, simply by examining the damage that occurs when humans live without it. In the dramatically titled book *Sitting Kills, Moving Heals*, former director of NASA's Life Sciences Division Dr. Joan Vernikos detailed decades of research compiled as astronauts returned from space. Problems walking and a tendency to vertigo were some of the most often reported issues. Sixty-six percent of returning astronauts had difficulty walking in a straight line, and 69 percent had troubles like running into walls when they changed direction. "Their sense of balance is out of practice and they walk using short, wide steps, like a toddler," she wrote.

In addition to losing their vestibular sense of balance and fluid motion, astronauts, if they spend enough time without gravity, begin to lose touch with another little-known yet crucial sense that helps us walk: proprioception.

Proprioceptors are specialized nerve endings located in our joints, tendons, and muscle fibers. They communicate with certain neurons in our inner ears to send our brains specific information about our bodies: that a muscle has stretched far enough, or that a knee really, *really* won't bend in that direction.

For a robot, proprioceptors are created with motor controls that measure force and torque. The motor controls then feed that information into the robot's main control system, leading to outputs that measure strain on joints and the force of steps. For humans, proprioceptors are similar to our sense of touch. If you brush ice with a bare hand, your nerves tell you it's cold. If you step on ice with a shod foot, your proprioception tells you it's slippery. Our feet use proprioceptors to tell our brains that we've moved from pavement to gravel or grass; these inputs mesh with other sensory information to constantly adapt our balance. Professional dancers tend to have highly honed proprioception because they have to know at every moment how much strain their joints, muscles, and tendons will take. The same is true for gymnasts—a world-class athlete like Olympic gold medalist Simone Biles has to trust that her body knows where, when, and with how much force she's going to flip, turn, and land her jumps. Conversely, children with a sensory-processing disorder related to proprioception might have difficulty with a variety of common tasks, from controlling their posture (which can make them feel physically insecure and hesitant about trying new physical activities) to using a pencil or holding a cup of water (because they can't get a sense of the pressure and force required to accomplish the task of writing their name or grasping a cup long enough to bring it to their mouths). Proprioception is what's involved in one of the most common sobriety tests used by police—the ability to stretch out your arms, close your eyes, and then touch your nose with a finger.

When they've been living too long without gravity, astronauts find that the proprioceptors in their feet become dulled. Although no case has yet been found in which proprioception disappears entirely, Vernikos theorizes that it's perfectly possible, given enough time without gravity, to lose it completely.

Astronauts are a special case. Almost no human spends that kind of extensive time without gravity. We do, however, spend a great deal of time sitting down, stuck in cars or at desks. The types of sensory losses seen in astronauts have never been measured in your average commuting office worker but can be noticeable at lower levels in people who are, for example, bedridden for periods of time. Vernikos has in fact noted that living without gravity is similar to being immobilized or bedridden. Proprioception becomes dulled, and the vestibular system becomes less nimble. I noticed it myself after undergoing an emergency Cesarean section under full anesthesia and afterward finding it difficult to stand for a few days. Not only were my muscles shaky, but focusing on where I wanted to go also took an extra measure of attention, and staying upright as I moved my feet toward a bland, boring hospital wall made me acutely aware of how unsteady

I was maneuvering the world on two spindly pegs perched on inadequate platforms.

As these systems develop throughout our lives, they affect far more than our ability to run up and down hills. While we're learning to walk, constantly stimulating our vestibular system, we're at the same time strengthening neural networks in our brains that seem to be key to our later abilities to learn and solve problems.

Since at least 2007, we've seen more and better research on the links between regular, moderate exercise—walking in particular—and the health of our brains. "Nothing," wrote Vernikos, "speeds up brain atrophy like immobilization." This is especially true of children, whose brains are still growing, synapses still snapping and firing and linking up with all sorts of wonders within our neural networks. We develop our vestibular systems and our cognition in tandem with our walking. Walking creates and maintains the systems that allow us to navigate on foot for the rest of our lives, while at the same time building the systems that allow us to learn. It also seems to be essential to *keeping* our minds agile. As we age, regular walking becomes highly correlated with brain health: people over seventy years of age who walk two or three hours a week have been found to retain the mental sharpness of people several years younger, while those who walk less have been found to be at higher risk of dementia.

This link is one of the conundrums of walking that gnaws at anyone who, like me, gets a little curious and starts digging into this prismatic subject: how and why is walking linked to our cognitive health? We're not sure, but we know that it is. Walking, seemingly so distant from sitting in a classroom learning multiplication tables or keeping a mind sharp as we age, is integrated both with how we learn and how our brains stay healthy.

The vestibular system's development through infancy and childhood contributes to that brain development as we grow into adulthood. As with proprioception-related sensory integration disorders, children born with conditions that cause vestibular impairment—such as cerebral palsy, genetic disorders like Usher syndrome, or certain immune deficiency disorders—have trouble figuring out where their bodies are in relation to the space around them, leading to mis-wired or missing feedback loops as the hippocampus (the part of the brain that controls both long-term memory and spatial navigation) develops. These spatialization problems can manifest later as learning difficulties related to memory, concentration, and reading. And vestibular impairment doesn't just affect those with genetic conditions. There are plenty of other causes of vestibular deficits, including neurotoxicity, such as occurs with children exposed to high levels of lead, and brain injuries at any age.

A definitive review on cognition and the vestibular system extensively examined studies going back to the early 1980s that found measurable differences in various types of cognitive performance in children with vestibular impairment. If a pre-walking baby suffers "complete vestibular loss" due to, say, meningitis, translating into difficulties learning to walk, the baby may grow to be physically unstable, leading to delays in reading, writing, and fine motor skills. Children born with an otolith dysfunction (the otolith is part of the vestibular structure) such as Ménière's disease, which can cause vertigo, tinnitus, and a feeling of pressure in the ears, will walk later than children whose function is within normal range, and will move cautiously and rigidly. They are unable to build strong internal representations of space, leading to difficulties in mental scanning—creating mental images from inputs such as a verbal description—and in areas of learning like mathematics that require mental visualization and rotation of three-dimensional objects.

In the United States, and in several other countries, adults tend to think of learning as something like a mechanical process that submits meekly to rote instruction. But, like walking, learning is an organic, messy process full of mistakes, one that requires a rich sensory environment in order to thrive.

In order to learn, we need to use our whole bodies, not just our brains, eyes, and ears. Not only do we get bored and fidgety if we sit for too long, our attention wandering out the window, but our brains also require vestibular stimulation to build comprehension of spatial relations, comparisons, and a sense of our place in the space around us. "The body," French philosopher Maurice Merleau-Ponty once wrote, "is our general medium for having a world." To fully engage their minds, children need to move, to run and tumble and throw their bodies around. Finnish teenagers consistently have some of the highest standardized test results in the world, and it doesn't seem to be mere coincidence that, rather than being pushed to rote-learn subjects like reading at younger ages, their early childhood education is all about creative, hands-on, full-body play.

Problem solving and reading, to take two of the most highly valued educational attainments, require both mental effort and an ability to sort, order, and review various tasks and lessons. They require, essentially, imagination, and much imaginative capacity is built in early childhood as the vestibular system and the hippocampus form synapses together that help us interpret the three-dimensional world. When you're walking, your entire body sends your brain cues that tell it how far away an obstacle is, or that you need to slow down for a steep hill. Healthy proprioception allows us to steer and maneuver our bodies confidently, while a healthy vestibular system is needed to hone navigation-related skills and to develop our innate understanding of up and down, or near and far. Being able to categorize where we are in space in relation to unconnected objects affects our later ability to categorize how other things relate to one another, like numbers. We aren't, after all, born knowing that numbers are sequential and comparative, that the number two is greater than the number one; that thirty-seven is twelve less than forty-nine, and so on.

In the cautious language typical of peer-reviewed scientific journals, researchers noted that "much remains to be learned" about vestibular loss, walking, and cognition, while adding that occupational and physical therapies such as sensory integration—a therapeutic approach that views children through the lens of how their neural networks organize sensory information—can go a long way toward helping children develop balance, stability, cognition, and a firmer sense of their own bodies in the space around them.

Research on children's walking and brain development is also beginning to inform the other end of life. Parkinson's disease, seemingly a disease of the brain, usually manifests first as problems in gait. A slow walking gait in a cognitively unimpaired elderly person often foreshadows later dementia. And, conversely, elderly people who walk regularly seem to be at less risk for dementia and Alzheimer's.

How we learn to walk and move and balance ourselves—falling down that seventeen or so times an hour as an infant—is tied to the fact that we are, like it or not, earthbound creatures. The unique gravity and movement of Earth is pivotal to how we've evolved and to how we transport ourselves under our own physical power. While our vestibular system tunes into the planet, our proprioceptors talk to the brain, and they work together to stand up and send us out into the world, allowing us to explore it on our own two feet.

By its very nature, evolution demands that we acknowledge our connection to our environment, and that environment includes planetary forces beyond what we can see, smell, and touch. As paleoanthropologist Richard Leakey has indicated, when he and his team in Turkana find yet another fossil in the sprawling human family tree, they are not finding missing links between humans and our evolutionary drift from other mammals, but instead links that tie us ever more deeply to the natural world.

PIECING TOGETHER THE transition from climbing to sporadic bipedal motion to full-time upright walking is a driving question for many paleoanthropologists and evolutionary biologists. If we come to understand *how* bipedal walking developed over millions of years, we may also learn *why*. We are still learning how we evolved in a particular environment, and how this environment has shaped us physically, socially, and psychologically.

Indeed, how it continues to shape us. Research from several different fields, from anthropology to urban planning, is building a strong case for the theory that the way ancient hominins walked their territory gave them—gave us—the ability to intertwine spatial cognition with social cognition and a sense of self: the cognitive demands of foraging for food and caring for uniquely helpless infants later translated into brainpower that could be used for developing social behavior, including a sense of community.

These are complicated ideas that, like the vast subject of walking itself, have opened up unexplored territories for future research. The potential for our built and natural environments to shape our psychological states is immense. Both the environment that surrounds us and our ability to move securely through it are integral to our confidence and stable sense of self. "Our minds map our bodies and the world around us," stated one study's authors. "Who we are is where we are." And, they might have added, who we are is *how we move* in where we are.

OUR WALKING IS so rich, so complex that once you become conscious of what's involved in it, it's impossible to ever again toss off the phrase "I'm going for a walk," or watch an infant learn to toddle, without giving thought to how truly extraordinary that ability is. Ask any parent standing a few feet away, arms outstretched, cheering on their newly toddling baby as he takes those first hesitant steps, following an evolutionary imperative that remains mysterious. "Good job!" we say. "Look at you!" And then they fall, and we kiss their ouchies, and they try again. Before we know it, we're accumulating gray hairs and reaching for their hands as they try their best to run out into traffic, across parking lots, over ledges, down stairs, up boulders, into our arms. They begin to walk, and they are free to explore the world, to risk their bodies a hundred times a day—all without their parents' protection, if they're fast enough.

Until MARLO the robot and its cohorts can walk indistinguishably among a human crowd, the ability to stride the earth on two feet will remain our own particular trait, a sign and driver of our humanity.

TWO
MARCH

Our insistence on belonging, community, and human connection is one of the greatest acts of courage and resistance in the face of oppression.

—MARIA POPOVA, Brain Pickings

"THE NEED TO BE TOGETHER, TO BE HUMAN . . . IS SO INCREDIBLY big right now, more than ever before," said performance artist Marina Abramović in a 2016 interview. The "public is so tired to look at things," she added while discussing the pervasiveness of technology in our lives. "They want to experience something different." Abramović responded to the need she perceived by curating participatory performance art at the Benaki Museum in Athens, Greece. Museum visitors turned in their cell phones and their watches and, after slow-walking (for about three hours) and counting lentils (which could take up to six hours), they lay down on the floor to experience being, simply being, in the presence of others.

The Benaki Museum performance took place in 2016, at a time when Greece was in the midst of an economic meltdown and a refugee crisis, yet 53,000 people took Abramović up on the invitation. "The need of this kind of exercise," she said, "was incredible." It was as if people knew that when all the human-constructed institutions of finance and border politics collapse back into meaninglessness, they will be left with one thing: the power to be together. The presence of community and one another. When the shit hits the fan, when everything we've been taught to rely on is proven too feeble to withstand trauma and crises, we walk out our doors and turn to one another.

❧

"Social connection is a fundamental part of the human operating system," wrote cognitive neuroscientist John Cacioppo in his book *Loneliness*. We marvel at the interconnectedness made possible through the spread of the Internet, but the truth is that we have been living with a far more complex system for at least tens of thousands of years. Our ability to pick up subtle cues as we talk to another person, navigate varying social dynamics in different cultures, and maintain our own webs of relationships throughout our lives all results from evolutionary pressures that required *Homo sapiens* to rely on one another.

"No one can deny that competitiveness, envy, hatred, cruelty, and betrayal are all aspects of human nature, and that these negatives are all well represented in human history," wrote Cacioppo. But "if such ruthlessness were, in fact, the defining essence of human nature, we would never have evolved our way out of the rain forest, much less the grasslands of eastern Africa. . . . the driving force of our advance as a species has not been our tendency to be brutally self-interested, but our ability to be socially cooperative."

❧

Walking is insinuated into these interpersonal relations from the very beginning of our lives, from those first steps we take as wobbly toddlers, opening up our field of vision and throwing ourselves into a wide new arena of interactions with strangers and caregivers alike. It's insinuated even more deeply than that, into our lives as early hominins and in the development of our communities, societies, and governments. "Once we became bipedal, bonding and social interactions [took] on a totally different value," Richard Leakey once said. "I do not believe bipedal primates could have survived unless they had, in addition to being bipedal, changed the way they think in terms of . . . social networking and social connections."

It was from these pressures that groups of hominins began to form lasting communities, a social organization that relies on interdependence and trust to function. This evolutionary interdependence extends into all aspects of our lives, even into areas that we think of as unrelated, including economics. Proponents of free-market capitalism commonly refer to Adam Smith's 1776 book *The Wealth of Nations* (the full title of which is *An Inquiry into the Nature and Causes of the Wealth of Nations*) as a textbook, almost a bible, for an economic ethos that says humans will do their best, most productive work, and benefit society, only in their own selfish interests. But what Smith actually recognized was that it is just as much a part of human nature to act in the interests of one's community. Social conscience, morality, and the law were, he thought, the frameworks within which individual agency would work best.

Smith, who taught moral philosophy at the University of Glasgow during the mid- to late-1700s, developed a network of theories related to the social contract and the failings for society of an economic system run by monopolies and rentiers, along with a theory of justice that he never had a chance to write out in full. He saw people's moral judgments as being formed not out of selfishness but out of sympathy for others. In his lesser-read book *The Theory of Moral Sentiments*, he wrote that "how selfish soever man may be supposed, there are evidently some principles in his nature, which interest him in the future of others, and render their happiness necessary to him, though he derives nothing from it except the pleasure of seeing it." It was justice, not solely self-interested activity, that Smith saw as underpinning the foundations of a strong society. Selfishness was clearly, for him, not the same as self-interest.

This jaunt into eighteenth-century economics might seem like a tangent, but misinterpretations of Smith's work have informed many leading American policy makers for over a hundred years, and have led to a consciousness that mistakes selfishness for social good. That ethos of selfishness, or believing that the individual is solely responsible for his or her own welfare, and his or hers alone, underpins a culture in which we have forgotten the kind of give-and-take interdependency that is at the very heart of human societies. This misperception pervades public policy driven by devotees of novelist Ayn Rand's "virtue of selfishness" and economist Milton Friedman's faith in the power of utterly unfettered markets to solve all human problems.

By contrast, Smith understood that every human acts only within the bounds of the wider society, an organic system that requires a conscious adherence to social norms and agreed-upon (and enforced) laws that allow maximum economic freedom *within those bounds*. He understood that our actions and choices have an effect on other people near and far, and that moral judgment assumes that we act in accordance with that knowledge. Smith understood, in other words, the kinds of connections, bonds, restraints, and expectations that form communities.

Once, our communities were simple networks of close-knit tribes, but in modern times we don't have to be related to people, share ideals or political inclinations with them, or even *like* them to be part of the same community. The word "community" itself has almost become a cliché, a buzzword, a symbol of something we yearn for, a nostalgia that is almost primal. What we're imagining, though, is not some idealized 1950s suburban lifestyle, but a sense of connection that lies at the heart of our evolutionary history.

COMMUNITY IS BOTH possible and necessary because of our evolutionary interdependence, but also because we share space: air, water, soil, roads, towns, cities, landscapes. In particular, our physical communities are made of spaces in which we interact, mingle, and strive to get along. Public spaces are where we greet our neighbors, watch out for kids on bikes, walk to work, give strangers directions, and bump into people because we're typing "<<hugs>>" in response to a friend's breakup news. We do these things on sidewalks, in alleys, on side roads and footpaths, and in public squares and parks. These tiny, everyday acts are crucial to both building and repairing a life quality that many—perhaps even most—people feel they've lost over the last century: a strong sense of community, defined by a quality that in research circles has been termed "social capital." In other words, neighborliness.

The academic idea of social capital has been around since at least the 1920s, although obviously community and neighborliness have been around for much longer than that. It was only when we began losing these things that we had to find ways to define and quantify and study them: how often people greet one another, how accessible amenities like libraries and coffee shops and grocery stores or markets are to all the public. How trustworthy we think our fellow citizens are. How many times a day people nod "hello" to each other and answer "Pretty good," truthfully or not, to a tossed-out "How you doin'?" How comfortable people feel stopping by a neighbor's house to beg an emergency cup of sugar. These muffled beats of everyday life contribute to the strength of our societies in far more ways than we realize. Dr. Cletus Moobela, a senior lecturer at the University of Portsmouth's School of Civil Engineering and Surveying, wrote that relatively high social capital has been shown to increase productivity and prosperity; decrease rates of depression, suicide, heart attacks, and cancer; reduce crime, child abuse, and drug abuse; and even make government agencies more responsive and efficient. It's also characterized by high levels of trust and civic engagement. Both rampaging kids and the cranky neighbor who yells at them to get off the lawn are strengthening their community's social fabric; our problems come because we are so often unaware of the role these interactions play in ensuring our community's long-term vitality. Essentially, we don't think nodding hello twenty times a day or asking to borrow a cup of sugar matters much in the grand scheme of things, which leads us to dismiss their value both for our community and for ourselves.

I would hazard a guess that many people feel that the everyday interactions of everyday neighbors don't, in fact, make the slightest bit of difference to the state of the world. It's human nature to long for greater meaning, to long to *do* something, something that feels profoundly consequential to the world at large. But when those opportunities come, it is exactly the previously existing social capital that will determine how well a community fares. When disaster hits, for example, we don't have the time to learn which of our neighbors needs help, or which of our community leaders can be trusted to organize rescues and responses. That knowledge and trust is built in the everyday, sometimes joyful but sometimes mind-numbing aspects of community life. The PTA fundraisers, the fire hall's spaghetti dinners, the boring planning board meetings; but also the passing exchanges with the librarians and coffee shop patrons and the retired teacher whose door we knock on after every major snowstorm.

In Chicago in 1995, a heat wave killed 739 people—"One of the most unexpectedly lethal disasters in modern American history," as New York University sociology professor Eric Klinenberg called it. But just as mysterious as the number of deaths, Klinenberg wrote, was the way in which they were distributed. While the two hardest-hit neighborhoods were the poorest and most racially segregated in the city, so were the neighborhoods with the *least* number of heat-related deaths. Two neighborhoods in particular, he noticed, were located next to each other and looked similar on paper, but suffered very differently from the heat wave.

In Englewood, which residents described as "bombed-out and abandoned" due to decades of losing jobs, restaurants, and grocery stores, residents had retreated into their homes during the heat wave, many eventually dying in what were essentially brick ovens. Englewood's death rate was the highest in the city.

The neighboring suburb Auburn Gresham, however, had never lost its core. It had restaurants, churches, stores, and community clubs and organizations. It was a place where "people hung out on the street," and residents told Klinenberg that during the heat wave they'd known whom to check up on. Despite its being known as one of the worst neighborhoods in Chicago, Auburn Gresham paid a far lower toll for the heat wave than wealthier suburbs across town.

Seventeen years later, in 2012, Hurricane Sandy ravaged New York City. Afterward, Klinenberg found that, as in Chicago, neighborhoods with lower levels of social capital—places where people lived but didn't necessarily interact with their neighbors or community—took much longer to recover after the storm. Having been through that storm myself, though further upstate from the city, I was acutely aware of our dependence on others, from our generous neighbor and his gas-powered generator to the daily crowds from nearby towns and villages who flocked to the YMCA looking for heat, light, and showers.

Cities like New York will have to adapt to climate change and rising sea levels and more powerful and frequent hurricanes using strategies like sea walls, flood gates, and managed retreats. But community resilience and social capital are going to become more important than ever for survival. "Increasingly," Klinenberg observed, "governments and disaster planners are recognizing the importance of social infrastructure: the people, places, and institutions that foster cohesion and support."

ONE OF THE single greatest factors in building that social capital, and in learning to trust and rely on one's neighbors, is a community's walkability. The everyday dynamics that walkable neighborhoods provide also ensure the regular connections to the rest of humanity that each of us desperately needs. These interactions can be small, often almost inconsequential (that borrowed cup of sugar, say), but our brains have evolved to look for our tribes, our communities, and our neighbors to remind ourselves that we're not alone.

Infrastructure is essential to building that social capital. While some forms of urban development can encourage social capital, others don't, and the main difference lies in whether they facilitate physical interactions among people: pedestrian-oriented designs such as accessible public spaces, sidewalks, and houses with front porches, among other features intended to bring people in contact with one another, contribute highly to a community's social capital. Gated communities are the only design factor that negatively affects social capital.

A town in which getting to the grocery store or the coffee shop and friends' houses is supported by walkable, accessible infrastructure has exponentially more opportunities for people to see and greet one another, to help one neighbor and be forced to be civil to yet another whom we don't like. "Mrs. So-and-so is such an old bag," we might grumble after our habitually grumpy widowed neighbor objects to our trash bin being out a day longer than allowed. But during the next snowstorm we're still out shoveling her sidewalk because we know all about her hip replacement and that her son isn't coming home for Christmas this year, and that she lets us pick her excess apples every September, and that she's lonely. Neighborhoods high in social capital are gritty. Messy and imperfect. But coping with that messy neighborly life makes for strong communities.

Gated communities, an extreme version of sequestered suburbia, are by contrast usually formed with the intention of reducing vulnerability to crime by restricting access. Edward J. Blakely and Mary Gail Snyder, who published the book *Fortress America: Gated Communities in the United States* in 1997, wrote that the social exclusion these neighborhoods foster can be dangerous for the cohesion of nearby communities: "without social contact, the social contract that underpins the health of a nation will be damaged. . . . We no longer speak of citizens, but rather of taxpayers, who take no active role in governance, but merely exchange money for services." Actual, in-person, face-to-face contact and interaction with all varieties of people is an essential ingredient for functional communities. And while gated communities are often built in the interests of security, sociology and urban planning researchers have found that crime rates are no lower in these neighborhoods than in their surrounding communities. The International Foundation for Protection Officers, an organization that promotes support for and professional development of security officers, found that crime in a brand-new gated community usually dips slightly in its first year, but rises to the level of the surrounding community after that—gates, the authors wrote, turn out to be no more effective than a well-run Neighborhood Watch program.

The very fact of living in a gated community tends to increase residents' fear of crime and of "others" outside the walls, Blakely noted. Gated communities present an idea of safety and trustworthiness, but in fact undermine both through their absence of rich daily interactions across a community's varied social fabric. If you don't regularly see your neighbor's son at the corner store, would you be less inclined to help him with jumper cables or accept his offer to mow your lawn? It's much easier to make assumptions about people based on the way they dress or walk when you've never had the chance to knock the sharp, shiny edges off your relationship, when you barely know each other.

Trust is the bedrock of human societies, and it is in the building of trust, and the testing of it, time and time again and over many years, that societies thrive. We lose more than we realize when we sacrifice walkable communities for car-centric, far-flung suburbs or gated neighborhoods. It's not only the community fabric that unravels; we also forgo the incredible, almost miraculous, capacity for empathy that human beings have. We compromise the ability to see that most people, no matter their faith or religious affiliation or lack thereof, have similar values and similar ideas about what matters in our lives, what the essential truths are that drive us. We forget what makes our societies work, how we negotiate this shared space, how we turn shared values—and conflicting values—into compromise and policy. The loss of trust can unmoor a society.

Imagine Boston in December 1773, before the United States existed but after the settlement had already become a city. Imagine it at nighttime, cold enough to see your breath, the air sharp with frost. A group of men dressed in costumes that mimicked the clothing of the nearby Mohawk tribe slipped down the dark, cold streets. The men were a restrained bunch, yet their quiet motions contained riotous hearts, convictions that over two centuries later still lend an aura of glory to one of America's nascent narratives: a destructive protest otherwise known as the Boston Tea Party.

Numbering somewhere between thirty and a hundred and thirty (accounts vary), the men had a short time earlier been among a crowd of thousands of people—seven thousand according to some records, five thousand according to others—converging on the white-steepled Old South Meeting House to hear Samuel Adams speak. He, and those who gathered to hear him, had been waiting for the Massachusetts governor's decision on whether he would allow ships laden with tea to leave Boston Harbor without paying tax to England. The governor refused, insisting that the *Dartmouth*, the *Eleanor*, and the *Beaver* could neither land nor leave the harbor unless the taxes were paid. The crowd, incensed, swarmed the streets.

A few men, members of Sons of Liberty, a secretive semi-military political group, slipped off to change into costumes to hide their identities and then gathered again, aiming for the boats and their cargoes of tea. Running down Hutchinson Street to Boston Harbor, the men snuck onto the *Dartmouth*, the *Eleanor*, and the *Beaver*. Three hundred and forty-two chests of tea, over 92,000 pounds in total, were cracked open and their contents dumped overboard. The next day, the men returned to make sure any still-floating tea was fully submerged, preventing salvage.

The lead provocateurs in the Boston Tea Party had not, as far as history is able to tell us, spent the evening intending to start a revolutionary war, but they were very consciously engaged in that most ancient of democratic processes, a right older than the right to vote: the protest. The physical placement of their bodies in the public space as an almost-last act against a government's refusal to listen to—to trust—its citizens. The right to gather on the public streets either in protest or celebration, or for countless other reasons, is an often-overlooked but vital right enshrined in the US Constitution's Bill of Rights. It's in plain sight, part of the comma-heavy First Amendment: "the right to peaceably assemble."

In the American imagination, the Boston Tea Party has a mythic quality, one single bright moment of rebellion against a repressive government, but in truth it is only one of thousands, at least, of marches, protests, riots, and rebellions that humans have participated in ever since *Homo sapiens* began to form more complex communities. Protests have always been an essential ingredient in functional societies, whether or not they lead to change, much less revolution. The Boston Tea Party could have ended with its participants meeting one of the many unpleasant deaths that have awaited rebels and protesters over the centuries, except that America won its revolutionary war, and so we are left with stories of victorious heroes rather than executed traitors. The revolt, though, came from the same places that protests and riots have throughout history—perceived injustices, last straws, and a longing for freedom snarled with demonstrable inequities.

When British subjects living in the American colonies petitioned King George III for redress of grievances with regard to taxes on tea, they had a right to expect an answer. Redress of grievances had been laid down as a British ruler's obligation ever since King John's signing of the Magna Carta in 1215. King George III's refusal to entertain those petitions was at the root of the Boston Tea Party's rebellion: the populace assembled, and then they protested, and then they marched. They threw tea in Boston Harbor, yes, but physical, communal protest was their first act against a government that no longer saw itself as accountable to its citizens, ending in the revolution that overthrew it.

The new government had a new constitution and a bill of rights that Americans today still hold as nearly sacred. First among these rights is what Burt Neuborne, a professor of civil liberties at New York University, calls the "life-cycle of a democratic idea: born in a free mind protected by the two Religion clauses"—freedom from imposed religion as well as the freedom to practice religion—"communicated to the public by a free speaker; disseminated to a mass audience by a free press; *collectively advanced by freely assembled persons*; and presented to the government for adoption pursuant to petition."

In the 1800s even the British House of Lords argued that "rioting is an essential part of our constitution," and America's own Thomas Jefferson said in 1787 that unruly mobs "tended to hold rulers accountable to the true principles of their institutions and to provide the medicine necessary for the sound health of government."

Until the mid-1900s, the US Supreme Court repeatedly struck down municipal and state requirements that protests and marches obtain approved permits in advance, citing that inviolate First Amendment right to assemble. The court eventually shifted because the collective right to assemble had begun to be conflated with the individual right to free speech, a weakening that many constitutional scholars have argued is unwarranted. Free speech and association have their place, but assembly is something different. Protest marches that adhere to the restrictions of permits and regulated times and places can never truly have the same effect as the swell of energy and, often, outrage, that brings tens of thousands of people to their feet as they march along at the pace of humanity's craving for justice, forcing governments to reckon with the people they are beholden to.

The right to free speech is in the end an individual rather than a communal right—an important distinction. The right to assemble is, along with the right to petition, the only first amendment right that requires more than one person, and it is in that collective action that people build the capacity to influence those in power.

THE MOST FAMOUS protests in history serve to illustrate both protest's power and the fragility of the relationship between people and their governments: Parisians yelling of bread and storming the Bastille in 1789. Gandhi's march to the salt mines to protest British colonialism in 1930. Cesar Chavez leading striking farmworkers to walk four hundred and sixty miles to Texas's capital in 1966. Martin Luther King Jr.'s 1963 March on Washington advocating for civil rights.

More recently, the importance of physical mass protest has been stressed in the face of growing authoritarianism worldwide. In a passionate, hard-headed piece titled "Prepare for Regime Change, Not Policy Change," Turkuler Isiksel, a professor of political science at Columbia University, wrote that "the only democratic, nonviolent practice capable of deterring the autocrats is the sight of endless crowds marching: vociferous, tenacious, disciplined citizens claiming ownership over their constitutional liberties and defending the integrity of their political institutions. Erdoğan [the president of Turkey who was elected on a platform of reform in 2014 but who quickly turned to authoritarian practices like quashing the free press and jailing political opponents] was never so rattled as he was by the Gezi Park protests that quickly spread all over the country; Putin experienced the only real challenge to his regime during the street demonstrations of 2011 and 2012." While these protests failed in the face of violent crackdowns from authoritarian leaders, mass protest itself has not died out completely, and their failures only served, wrote Isiksel, to prove the necessity of protesting early and often when authoritarianism begins to take hold.

In an interview about the 2017 television adaptation of her 1985 dystopian novel *The Handmaid's Tale*, the writer Margaret Atwood discussed this understanding via a crucial scene in the show's third episode, in which the main character and her best friend attend a protest march that goes south quickly, with law enforcement firing live ammunition into the crowd: "The point at which you know you're under totalitarianism is when a peaceful protest crowd is fired upon," she said. "But when you have a full-out shutdown, then there aren't any more protests because people know what will happen. Or there's such overwhelming protests that it can't be controlled."

Gilead, the fictional post-America country depicted in *The Handmaid's Tale*, is an authoritarian regime ruled by fear and violence. The government's most effective tactic, underpinning its use of torture and swift executions of dissidents, is to make its residents feel isolated and alone. In those conditions, as citizens of autocracies and dictatorships have found repeatedly throughout history, personal fear becomes rampant. Human beings are biologically obligated to connect with people they can trust; when that becomes impossible, it's a simple step to individuals becoming chronically terrified.

Walking together, even without protest, can be a way for people to combat this isolation. In *The Handmaid's Tale*, some of Gilead's most oppressed residents, the handmaids, find some of their only freedom—and their only opportunities to probe for authentic, trusting connection with one another—in their daily walks. It is in walking together that we can explore freedom of thought along with freedom of movement and cautiously form social bonds, even under governments in which trust is a rare currency.

This truth is part of my own family's recent history.

Born in 1945 in Russia's Ural Mountains and raised in Leningrad, my father was a child during Joseph Stalin's last years in power, and lived until he was nearly thirty under a system of government that restricted, and often forbade, free thought and action. For a few months in 1991, when I was fourteen years old, my family moved from Montana, where my father had emigrated with my mother in the early 1970s, back to the Soviet Union. By that time, Soviet president

Mikhail Gorbachev had already done much to weaken the Iron Curtain and ever-so-slightly loosen restrictions on Soviet citizens' actions, which allowed my father to return and help open a telecommunications business.

Much had changed during the seventeen years my father had spent as an American citizen. What hadn't changed was people's love of walking. While walking was in many ways a necessity (very few people in the Soviet Union owned private cars), it was also one of the few ways people could explore intellectual and political ideas without risk of reprisal.

"My friend Pyotr—Petya—and I, we walked all [over] canals, all over bridges, talking about art and literature and girls," my father told me as we walked some of those same canals and bridges. "We walked for hours, all day." My father, Petya, and several of their other friends loped all over Leningrad's canals and islands discussing their latest smuggled Beatles album or the forbidden Aleksandr Solzhenitsyn manuscript their families might have read in secret the night before. Years later, my father took my mother, a visiting graduate student from America, on some of those walks, and to do that he had to rely both on his knowledge of the city and his trust in his friends—when they met in 1967, my mother joined my father and his friends by sneaking away from her student group, which was illegal.

Walking gave my father and his friends the space to explore disallowed thoughts and ideas, to shape their own political and social identities within the confines of the system they lived under, and to build social capital in a world where so much true community had been broken, crushed, and strip-mined. They couldn't protest, they couldn't act politically outside Communist Party guidelines without putting themselves and their families at risk, but they could think, and they could walk, and they could learn to trust one another. Even in an unfree country, walking can make freedom more than an illusion.

The more isolated people feel, the easier it is to control them through fear, which is one of the reasons the right to collective protest is so essential to the functioning of a democracy. Dr. Zeynep Tufekci, a professor specializing in the intersection of technology and society at the University of North Carolina at Chapel Hill, wrote in her 2017 book *Twitter and Teargas: The Power and Fragility of Networked Protest*, that repressive regimes control populations by tapping into and warping a human's deep need for belonging: "fostering a sense of loneliness among dissidents while making an example of them to scare off everyone else has long been a trusted method of ruling."

Protesting for or against a cause with like-minded people shows without a doubt that a person is not alone in his or her deeply held beliefs. While online organizing has been effective at connecting far-flung groups, including people who live more isolated lives in places with lower population density, there is a certain amorphous quality to that form of human contact. It's hard to gauge which online connections are authentic, or even if the connections being made are with real people. A Twitter hashtag related to a political or social question of the day that seems to be getting an enormous amount of attention online comes across very differently when you find out that the majority of the activity comes from a few thousand or million fake bot accounts run by a computer based in Macedonia. True protest still requires, as Martin Luther King Jr. once said, "the sound of the marching feet of a determined people."

Politicians aren't unaware of this power, which is why they so often attempt to restrict it. In response to nationwide Black Lives Matter protests as well as the long-term 2016 prayer camp at Standing Rock in North Dakota, at least thirty US state legislatures mooted, and in some cases passed, proposals in 2017 and 2018 that restricted the freedom of assembly. Some laws banned the wearing of face masks or hoods while participating in protest; others sought to eviscerate the collective energy of assembly by loosening definitions that allow a legal protest to be considered an unlawful riot; and still others moved to give drivers legal immunity when they run over protesters who are obstructing a public road or highway. This last law is particularly disturbing in light of the death of Heather Heyer, a young woman who, while protesting a white supremacist march in Charlottesville, Virginia, in August 2017, was killed by a self-proclaimed white nationalist who drove his car into the crowd of counter-protesters. It also takes on significant weight when considering the amount of public space that has been given over to roads and the movement of traffic over the last century, leading to the question of how peaceable assembly is possible when public space is inaccessible or nonexistent. For protesters, obstructing traffic is often the only option when exercising the right to assemble.

THE POLITICAL PATHS walked by protests are unformed, often unpredictable, but one place they all seem to lead to is the intersection of individual empowerment and civic engagement. Gandhi's march to the salt mines has, like the Boston Tea Party in the United States, claimed a crucial place in the history of India, though Britain didn't pass the Indian Independence Act until seventeen years later. The March on Washington took place nine years after the US Supreme Court had declared school segregation to be illegal, and it was another five years before the Fair Housing Act was passed. Protest isn't, in the end, necessarily about breaking systems and seeing immediate change enacted, enticing as that prospect is: it's about something less easily defined, speaking directly to people's yearning for political agency, especially in a system in which they feel personally powerless.

One of the most memorable protest movements to fully inhabit the spirit of the ancient right to assemble was the prayer camp established in 2016 at Standing Rock in North Dakota. The camp was set up to resist the oil pipeline being built through sacred burial sites and under the Missouri River, the Standing Rock Sioux tribe's sole source of clean drinking water.

The massive, months-long resistance drew early initial attention not through a protest but through a two-thousand-mile relay run. Several members of the Indigenous youth group Rezpect Our Water and members of the International Indigenous Youth Council (IIYC) ran from North Dakota to the US Army Corps of Engineers office in Nebraska, and finally to Washington, D.C., to deliver a petition with 160,000 signatures opposing the pipeline. "The run," said Danny Grassrope, one of the IIYC members who ran anywhere from forty to eighty-one miles per day for the relay, "brought me back to my spiritual being." Grassrope said that he didn't expect so many people to show up for the run because the participants were "just bringing awareness."

He didn't know, said Grassrope, that so many people would join them to resist the pipeline, nor that the relay run would lead to a massive gathering focused on prayer. Terrell Iron Shell, another member of the IIYC, said that there were fewer than ten members when the group started, but in their act they ignited a movement.

The IIYC also, perhaps, didn't expect the sense of camaraderie that grew up over the months that the protest camp worked to feed activists, heal from confrontations with police while staying nonviolent, and build a community brought together through common goals and common hardships. Writer and founder of *YES!* magazine Sarah van Gelder wrote of Standing Rock's sense of community: "There's a rightness to these connections, and to the feeling that people here will help you when you need it." Layha Spoonhunter, a twenty-six-year-old who arrived at the camp from Wyoming, told a reporter from Canada's CBC News that living in the camp had given him "something of a spiritual reawakening." Many participants spoke of feeling politically empowered in a way that no other activism could rival.

Tribal members living on Indian reservations in the United States have seen an unimaginable amount of tragedy; at Standing Rock, said Danny Grassrope, something seemed to shift. Suicide rates are higher for Native Americans than other groups of Americans, with many pointing to a combination of poverty and hopelessness as the main cause. Suicides among young people, kids and young adults aged fifteen to twenty-four, are particularly high, about three and a half times the national average—the Oglala Sioux Pine Ridge Reservation alone had to declare an emergency after seeing fourteen youth suicides from August 2014 to April 2015. But Grassrope saw one entire six-month period go by without a single suicide attempt, which he credits to the support and sense of purpose at the Standing Rock water protector camp. He hopes that the collective strength demonstrated at the prayer camp can show young people a different way forward, breaking the cycle. "People got to know they weren't alone," he said, "even in their own personal fights."

This empowerment seems to be universal to protest, even if the immediate policy outcome of the action is failure. "If ten thousand people camping at Standing Rock to protect the Missouri River could not stop the siege of the Dakota Access Pipeline," asked poet and professor Layli Long Soldier, "then what does it take? What more?" The answer to this question may take years to emerge, but the most famous protests in history serve as a lesson in the "something more" being the long-term social capital and political empowerment built through the act of protest itself. One of the most powerful moments shown in the ABC News documentary of Standing Rock was of a silent prayer march the water protectors undertook the day after a confrontation with police during which many were attacked or jailed. Four hundred people walked in complete silence to the police line, where the leaders offered water and mutual prayer to police standing on the other side of barbed wire. "Something I'll never forget," said Terrell Iron Shell of that march. "Because of how together we were, how unified we were." It took a lot of work, Grassrope told me, to recover from the violence inflicted on the water protectors, to gather at the camp again and remind everyone of their commitment to nonviolence and prayer. But it is in that kind of collective work, both in the resistance and recovery and in the hour-to-hour or day-to-day solidarity, that the deeper human potential of protest can be realized. In a way, said Grassrope,

"I felt like we were successful. We gave people grounding and gave them hope."

A protest can perform, for its participants, some of the same work that everyday neighborliness does, creating interconnectedness and civic engagement, satisfying the craving to be together that performance artist Marina Abramović noticed. "Protests have always had a strong expressive side, appealing to people's sense of agency," wrote Tufekci in *Twitter and Tear Gas*. "For many, taking part in a protest is a joyful activity, and often provides a powerful existential jolt—especially if there is an element of danger and threat to the safety and the well-being of protesters, as there often is." In many ways, Tufekci writes later, participating in a protest, especially a long-term one lasting days or weeks, gives participants the sense of community and belonging that many feel is lacking in our everyday lives.

The sense of affirmation and solidarity that protests give also creates the space for individual acts of heroism from seemingly ordinary people. One of the most memorable images to come out of the Black Lives Matter movement was of a graceful young woman, the end of her long black dress flipping outward slightly, lifted, most likely, by a breeze. She stands with the straight, unslouching posture of a ballet dancer. Her shoulders and arms bare, her gaze fixed straight ahead, she seems not to notice the two policemen in riot gear approaching her with heavy weaponry and plastic handcuffs. In an essay on the event that she later published in *The Guardian*, she wrote, "I wasn't afraid. I was just wondering: 'How do these people sleep at night?' Then they put me in a van and drove me away."

Ieshia Evans's still, unmoving presence against the might of the Baton Rouge police force prompted media comparisons to another solitary protester who'd made a stand in 1989: the unknown man who stood in front of a line of government tanks that had been sent in response to illegal protests in Tiananmen Square in China. Dressed in a white shirt and black pants and carrying a grocery bag, the man had no weapon with which to combat the tanks except his body, his feet. As the tank drivers switched direction to maneuver past him, he repeatedly shifted his position.

The photographs of "Tank Man" are among the most iconic images of the twentieth century. They were smuggled out of China by the journalists who captured them, one of the photos in a box of tea, another after being retrieved from its hiding place in a toilet, where *Newsweek* photojournalist Charlie Cole had hidden it before police raided his room and destroyed two other rolls of film. The Chinese government also forced Cole to sign a confession stating that he'd taken photographs during martial law, punishable by imprisonment.

One lone, unarmed protester so intimidated a government that to this day images of "Tank Man" are almost unknown in China. The same is true of the 1989 Tiananmen Square protests, which lasted weeks; little is known of them in China today.

Putting one's physical body in a public space as an act of petitioning one's representative government for change is dangerous, is unpopular with those who see little wrong with the status quo, and can also be a sublime, powerful act. It is in these kinds of mass acts that citizens both demand attention from a government that has refused to hear their individual voices, and begin to find their political identities. The iconic pictures of Tank Man and Ieshia Evans are powerful in part because of their solitary quality—one human being standing unmoved in the face of government oppression—and because the quality of stillness these undaunted protesters exuded. They were there, though, because the collective energy of assembled protesters had brought both them *and* militarized government response to that place and time. Mass, collective protest had created space for the power of their stillness and assertion of their rights.

❧

SOCIAL MEDIA IS often thought of as the new ground for political and social activism. But while it's easy to create a social movement on Twitter or Facebook, translating that into actual policy change is very different. The Gezi Park protests in her native Turkey, Tufekci wrote in *Twitter and Tear Gas*, grew from nothing into a massive movement within days, demonstrating the power of organizing using digital tools. "However," she wrote, "with this speed comes weakness, some of it unexpected . . . the ease with which current social movements form often fails to signal an organizing capacity powerful enough to threaten those in authority." A year of organizing and direct advocacy for change, which the city and bus company refused to agree to, led to the thirteen-month-long Montgomery bus boycott sparked by Rosa Parks's resistance, and the civil rights movement took a decade to get to the March on Washington—time Martin Luther King Jr. and his colleagues spent forming and deepening social connections, strengthening and testing the fiber of their movement. In contrast, mass protests like Occupy Wall Street formed rapidly but then, lacking that underlying resilience created over time and through building trusted networks, often lost focus, direction, and, most importantly, their potential to effect change.

Online activity can also deepen social division rather than build society-wide cohesion: an analysis of 2017 Twitter activity by researchers at the University of Washington found almost no crossover between users promoting hashtags related to Black Lives Matter and those promoting hashtags related to Blue Lives Matter. Online echo chambers are old news at this point, but the interesting part came when the researchers looked at the intersections between those hashtags and the data released by Twitter tracking the activity of particular troll factories in Russia. The most active accounts *on both sides*—posts with the most retweets and responses tagged either #blacklivesmatter or #bluelivesmatter—came from Russian troll factories, meaning that foreign actors sought not to promote any particular cause in America, but to sow division, distrust, anger, and even hatred. "There are paid trolls sitting side by side somewhere in St. Petersburg," wrote Dr. Kate Starbird, one of the paper's authors, on (appropriately) a Twitter thread about the findings, "hate-trolling each other's troll account, helping to shape divisive attitudes in the U.S. among actual Americans who think of the other side as a caricature of itself."

These findings make one of the strongest arguments I've yet read for getting to know our communities, and one another, in person again, face-to-face. And they also, perhaps, show why many movements, while forming contacts and strength online, eventually move into the physical realm, and why it's vital that they do so. From the millions donning pink "pussy" hats during the worldwide women's marches in 2017, to white supremacists and their opponents gathering across the United States later that same year, fervent believers march together to show one another both that they are not alone and that they're real people. That desire is instinctive, innate, and powerful, no matter what the political or social cause.

In February 2018, seventeen-year-old Jaclyn Corin survived the mass shooting at Marjory Stoneman Douglas High School in Parkland, Florida, in which a gunman killed seventeen people. Along with other friends "sharing intimate accounts of their horror," Corin, who was the junior class president, wrote about her experience on Facebook and Instagram, begging for change in a culture where mass shootings are all too frequent. Due to her and her classmates' online advocacy, the #NeverAgain hashtag spread across the globe almost overnight. But knowing the speed of the news cycle and the ephemeral nature of social media, Corin also began organizing two hundred fellow students for an almost immediate journey to lobby their state legislature in person. "The news forgets very quickly," she said. "And if we were all talk and no action, people wouldn't take us as seriously." While Corin and her fellow teens are naturals at using social media, they are also aware of the necessity of a mass physical presence for political and social action, embodying the spirit of the "assembly" clause of the Constitution's First Amendment.

During the 2017 protests against Russian president Vladimir Putin, opposition leader Alexei Navalny made extensive use of social media to draw worldwide attention to official corruption, resistance, and authoritarian crackdowns on anyone opposing Putin's government, but the opposition itself took place on the streets. President Putin compared the protests to what he termed dangerous Arab Spring–style movements that led to coups in countries like Egypt and Ukraine. Perhaps making the president's point for him, in a protest attended by thousands that February, one marcher held a sign bearing the words of an opposition leader who'd been gunned down two years previously: "Our only chance left is the street."

What does social capital have to do with all of this? Everything. Society is run as a communal act, something we form together even when we disagree. Generation after generation, democratic governments and the populace must learn to recalibrate their relationships, to rebalance power, to remember what is expected of representation and of citizenship. Generation after generation, people have had to fight for their rights and to have those rights protected. Nobody, not even billionaires with heavy-hitting lobbyists and dreams of libertarian utopias, forms or builds government alone. Walking and walkability, the choreography of daily life, build trust between neighbors and communities, and through that, research has shown, people significantly increase their civic engagement while at the same time strengthening their ability to understand one another.

Effective protest requires not just the right of the people to gather, but accessible public spaces in which gathering is possible and citizens who understand what those rights are. "Public 'streets and parks . . . [from] time out of mind, have been used for purposes of assembly. . . . Such use of the streets and public places has, from ancient times, been a part of the privileges, immunities, rights, and liberties of citizens,'" stated a US Supreme Court ruling in 1939 that upheld the right to assemble on the public streets, striking down a municipal requirement that such gatherings require a previously obtained permit.

"From time out of mind." "Since ancient times." "The privileges, immunities, rights, and liberties of citizens." These are powerful words, drawing on the lessons of history. When state and local governments began restricting the right to assemble to certain times and places, which they did in the United States starting in the 1800s, and when the Supreme Court started allowing these regulations to stand starting in the mid-1900s, those actions had very real consequences for democracy.

Protesters in authoritarian countries such as Russia and Turkey have been arrested by the hundreds, if not the thousands, and their rights of assembly removed. Just as chilling for the future of democracy, perhaps, is the case of Spain in 2014. In answer to a blanket ban on protests of any kind, as well as marches or assemblies in front of Congress, activists resorted to protest by hologram. Eighteen thousand people sent in holograms of themselves protesting, which were projected in front of Congress on a loop for several hours while activist leaders gave speeches, also via hologram.

Is this, combined with the uncertain reality of online comments and petitions, our future? What government institution would respond to a hologram protest? Would they care? While click-ready petitions of the Internet age are the perfect form for gathering tens of thousands of signatures quickly, can we truly fool ourselves into thinking they're more effective at swaying an elected representative's vote than a crowd of in-the-flesh constituents presenting their requests and pleas in person? That's aside from more recent revelations that foreign actors, trolls, and automated bot farms pretending to be citizens can not only hack away at societal unity through amplifying divisions, but can also generate millions of online comments aiming to sway public policy one way or another. Online petitions, as one researcher put it, allow more people to speak out but make it "much more difficult for them to be heard."

Digital technology has opened up unimaginable worlds of access and connectivity, but it has also brought into question its own role in undermining the foundations of governments built *by* people, *for* people. The realities of face-to-face contact and in-person mass protests, the tools of centuries of struggle for full citizenship and rights, have become even more essential to grounding us as we navigate through a new era of humans' relationship with technology. Physical protest is an embodiment of the ability to hold our governments accountable beyond our letters and phone calls, even beyond our votes. The right to use our public spaces to remind those in charge of policy that the "demos" in *democracy* refers to us, the people. New eras of protest will have to learn how to combine the ease and speed of online connectivity with the long-term face-to-face organizing that gives physical protest its strength and staying power. The right to assemble and protest might not always be protected by governments, but it is both our first and our final way to hold them accountable.

ULTIMATELY, PEOPLE FUNCTION best when they interact with their communities, when they feel like they belong, when they know their neighbors and neighborhoods, when they have an investment in how their government functions, and, crucially, when they are able to act on that investment. Through building and exercising social capital, we learn once again that "government" is not, or should not be, some distant untouchable power, but simply a larger collective expression of the ways in which we walk through this world together.

Walkability and social capital exist in a direct relationship, each strengthening the other, and that same walkability, the ways in which we perceive walking and have access to walking, has a direct effect on how well our societies function, and for whom.

How our public spaces are created and maintained, how we use them, and who gets to use them without repercussions makes a difference to the health of our neighborhoods, towns, and nations. Walking is both a cornerstone of a functional society, and a deeply political act in its own right.

The movements of state legislatures in 2017 to crack down on protest are part of centuries-long efforts by governments to suppress the power of collective assembly, but their efforts also lean on the erosion of social capital, of human trust. And over the past hundred years the suppression of collective assembly and the evisceration of social capital have been fueled by the removal of public roads and highways from full public access. If there is nowhere to walk, where does that leave us?

CHAPTER 3

STUMBLE

Not TV or illegal drugs but the automobile has been the chief destroyer of American communities.

—JANE JACOBS, *Dark Age Ahead*

IN 2014, A YOUNG MOTHER NAMED RAQUEL NELSON WAS CHARGED with vehicular homicide. The allegation was both heartbreaking and surreal: though Nelson was not driving (she didn't even own a car), she was being charged with her own son's death because the four-year-old had been hit by a driver while running across the road. The man who actually killed her son was given the lesser charge of hit-and-run.

Everything about Nelson's case illustrates the disappearance of walking from the everyday lives of *Homo sapiens* and the twentieth century's claiming of roadways by the automobile. A mother is walking home with her children, crossing a multilane road after a long day. Her small son is struck and dies, and despite the driver's history of reckless driving (it was his third hit-and-run), the mother is charged and threatened with prison for crossing the street. This tragedy, despite its senselessness and horror, is one of over thirty thousand deaths from car crashes in the United States every single year (total *injuries* from crashes regularly top sixty thousand). At least five thousand of those deaths are of pedestrians being hit by drivers.

In a little over a hundred years, we've gone from seeing walking as normal, as ordinary, as *pedestrian*, to seeing it as eccentric, sometimes even criminal. This simple motion, the swing of our feet, has been integral to the making of us for millions of years. And we're losing it.

AT THE TIME of her son's death, Raquel Nelson was jaywalking.

Let's pause here. "Jaywalking" is a term that Americans now accept without thinking. Crossing mid-block instead of at a crosswalk, racing the crosswalk timer once it's begun its countdown (illegal in California), crossing an empty road at a more convenient point than a far-off intersection—all of these acts are lumped under the flaunting of legality termed "jaywalking."

But jaywalking is a recently invented term, a recently invented idea. The very existence of this concept is an insult to the history of public roadways and public spaces. Cars have been around barely more than a hundred years; roads have been around for thousands and pathways even longer. It is only in our recent, automobile-centric history that we've translated "traveling by foot" into "stay off the road." For the first few decades of the 1900s, cars had to share the roadways with bicycles, carts, wagons, buggies, horses, streetcars, trams, and many, many pedestrians. "Before 1920," wrote Peter D. Norton in his book *Fighting Traffic: The Dawn of the Motor Age in America*, "American pedestrians crossed streets wherever they wished, walked in them, and let their children play in them. . . . 'The streets of Chicago belong to the city,'" one judge explained in his 1913 decision fining a driver for knocking over a pedestrian, "'"not to the automobilists."'"*

* Much of the information in this chapter came from Norton's book, speeches, and conversations over email. I owe a great deal to his scholarship detailing the history of jaywalking and how car companies originally sold America on their vision of freedom.

This clearly isn't the case today. Imagine you're about to go somewhere. A thought comes: "I need to go get milk." "I want to run down to the post office." "Let's head to the playground." "I'm going to be late for work." The thought turns into a bodily urge. The feet shift, the hips turn. Even if you're driving, your body knows what "to go" means. It's known for millions of years.

Now erase your city, your town, your highways, from your mind. Imagine there is no fencing, no streets, no signs telling you not to trespass. "To go" wherever it is you're going becomes a vast proposition. The world greets your feet, your eyes, your ears, your swinging arms, just as if you haven't been ignoring this lovely planet for the past century. It's still there, still the world, roaming it is still the birthright of your bipedal body.

Now place a road in your path. Some houses. A church or mosque or synagogue or temple. A market. Shops. Some of these things you have to walk around or through, skirting them, bending yourself around the marks of settled civilization. But your path, your going, is still wide and open, sinuous and weaving, the roads and alleyways no impediment to your walking.

Take a moment to sink into this feeling. Examine your own body and imagine it standing at the edge of the road. Imagine, if you have any kind of impairment, that the road is accessible to wheelchairs, walkers, and people with balance or vertigo or vision issues. That is, no curb to step from, possibly no sidewalk. But imagine also that there are no cars parked along the edge of it and that you can cross the road anywhere and anytime you please. You need to go get milk or the mail, and you just go. There are no streetlights, no traffic to force you to go in hard geometric angles, no wide spaces forbidden to your feet and wanderings.

In this reality, the idea of jaywalking is nonsensical. With or without roads, pedestrians have always had the first right to public space. Walking is how humans get places; denying us this access makes no sense.

Below our freeway interchanges and potholed downtowns hide footpaths and trailways that humans once had intimate communication with. Instead, we now have straight, wide roads that are designed solely to move traffic—cars—as efficiently as possible from one place to another. And for that we can credit a concerted push by the automobile industry in the early 1920s that ended in making jaywalking illegal, setting up a knock-on effect of wider road lanes, faster freeways, and increased limitations on our freedom to get places as and how we wish. If the early years of motoring had turned another direction, our ability to traverse our neighborhoods, towns, and cities might look very different. We might be able to meander, to wander at will, to roam across land that was, once upon a time, simply earth, and that we once simply walked.

Increasing numbers of pedestrian deaths in the years just before and after 1920 at the hands of drivers—especially deaths of children, who still had the right to play in the roads and were expected to do so—led to hard-hitting municipal campaigns focused on errant, obnoxious, and dangerous "automobilists." In the four years after the end of World War I, wrote Norton in *Fighting Traffic*, "more Americans were killed in automobile accidents than had died in battle in France."

Cities, with their vast walking populations and relatively few car owners, fought back. In 1919, Detroit ran a Safety First campaign during which bells at City Hall, a church, a fire station, and every single school tolled eight times twice daily on every day that someone was killed in traffic. In 1922, Baltimore constructed a monument with inscriptions memorializing all children killed in traffic crashes in the previous year. In Pittsburgh the same year, over five thousand people attended a ceremony dedicating a memorial to the 286 children killed in accidents the previous year, particularly singling out those killed by car drivers. Just a few weeks later, Washington, D.C., dedicated a monument to the ninety-seven children who'd been killed in traffic crashes the previous year, in a ceremony attended by a thousand people.

The situation was dire. In 1925, pedestrians made up two-thirds of the dead in cities with populations over 25,000. Cities all over the country were scrambling to figure out a solution, almost none of which involved getting pedestrians off the road. They were focused on driver behavior, vehicle access, and speed. "An automobile is a dangerous weapon," an official from the New York medical examiner's office said. The *St. Louis Star* wrote that drivers were "killers." The police, who saw their job as protecting walkers from drivers rather than the other way around, were generally on the side of pedestrians. A 1926 survey of four hundred and eighty city police chiefs found that 72 percent said driver carelessness was the cause of pedestrian deaths.

IT'S IMPORTANT TO remember that at this time in American history, most people also didn't own cars. Cars were a luxury, not a necessity. People got around on foot and via public transportation. Streetcars were ubiquitous in cities all over the country, from Minneapolis to Los Angeles, and ensured, as public transportation is meant to do, that residents could travel between various parts of town without relying on an expensive private conveyance like a car or carriage. People simply didn't need cars. The automobile industry therefore had to come up with ways to make driving cars desirable, which would make purchasing cars more likely, whether anyone needed them or not. To do that, the image of the car had to change from a deadly menace to a standard machine with preeminent rights to the road.

The main attraction of a personal automobile was always its ability to ferry an individual driver directly from where he was to where he needed to be more quickly than walking or taking a streetcar. The car's selling point was, and remains, speed. But on a congested roadway, speed becomes a moot point. It doesn't matter if your Model T can purr along at thirty miles an hour, or if your Chevy Cruze can go from zero to sixty in under eight seconds, if safety restrictions keep you to ten and crowded streets reduce that to five. The freedom to walk where we need to go and the efficiency demanded by car-friendly spaces are fundamentally incompatible. In those conditions, automobile manufacturers' enticements are limited to the car as a luxury item. If it's a hassle, especially a dangerous hassle, to drive places rather than take your feet and buses or trains, it's impossible to persuade people that a car is necessary to their daily lives.

But car companies like GM and Ford didn't start out with the intention of making an unwalkable world. They and their users—drivers, car owners and enthusiasts, automobile clubs—faced a public relations nightmare as streets became a battle zone, with drivers the lethal aggressors; and they faced a technical challenge in the immovable reality of traffic congestion. The streets of the early 1900s really were a free-for-all. There were no traffic lights, no crosswalks, no acknowledged need for these things. Drivers found it difficult to progress to their destinations, impeded by streetcars, pedestrians, bicyclists, and horse-drawn carts, all of which (or whom) had equal rights of way on the roads.

While the eventual shifts toward traffic control were supposedly made in the interests of public safety, they ended up being ludicrously unjust. Rather than designing cities and suburbs around the theory that it was in society's interest to allow the largest number of people the greatest amount of mobility (which boils down to building heavily pedestrianized cities and neighborhoods served by clean, affordable, efficient, and accessible public transportation), America opted for the opposite: design for cars to move from A to B as quickly as possible. To do that, governments and automobile manufacturers had to get everyone else off the road. Drivers can't step on the gas if they're constantly on the lookout for weaving bicycles or aimless people on foot.

Jaywalking laws first rolled out in the 1920s with newspaper ad campaigns aimed at the bumbling, foolish jaywalker who put himself, and drivers, at risk. Taken from derogatory descriptions of rural visitors to cities, called "jays," the term "jaywalker" was designed specifically to shame pedestrians. Advertising campaigns from the period displayed artists' sketches of foolish-looking bumpkins ambling across streets and causing havoc.

The industry roped in schools, which began teaching traffic safety, and the Boy Scouts, who handed out "tickets" to jaywalkers, which had no legal force but served to embarrass people walking across the street. A 1924 *New York Times* op-ed described the various types of dangerous, inept pedestrians as "veerers," "runners," and "crabwalkers." Looking down upon the sidewalks, asked the author, do you see the "ordered progress of civilized people?" Or was it more like "hostile bacteria magnified into an internecine Armageddon?"

Slowly, over several years, the idea of streets as public spaces began to erode, and the idea of them as the province of automobiles worked its way up into higher levels of government and urban planners, at first in the name of safety and later in the name of efficiency and order.

Vintage video footage of a 1906 trip down Market Street in San Francisco, a silent black-and-white film created by the Miles Brothers four days before the city's devastating earthquake, shows how free our movement once was: A camera strapped to the front of a streetcar captured, in black and white, twelve minutes of what initially looks like mayhem. But it takes only a few seconds for the mayhem to resolve as an intricate choreography of movement, and it's less like "internecine Armageddon" than it is like the eddies and rapids of a river at the tail end of summer. The streetcar is traveling down the road from 8th Street to its terminus, and traverses a lively snippet of public life on a public road. Bicyclists and car drivers weave around horse-drawn carriages and one another, delivery trucks stop any old place, and pedestrians walk and cross wherever they wish.

There are behaviors we engage in today when crossing the road that are almost completely absent from this 1906 slice of street life. The flick of the head back and forth, back and forth, waiting for the break in traffic that will be long enough for us to cross two lanes or more, or waiting for a car in each direction to take note of the crosswalk and stop for us. In that busy but uncongested 1906 street scene, we don't ever see people peer, birdlike, around the corner at an intersection, the motion we now make to make sure someone turning right at a red light notices us, even when we have a "walk" signal. In 1906, pedestrians meander across the road, walk at a normal pace, hop in front of traffic to jump into a streetcar, stroll, run, and pause, as if they belong on and in this public space just as much as anyone else does. The street has far more men in bowler hats, women in floor-length skirts, and nonchalant children than it does cars.

THIS WAS THE world that people like my maternal grandmother were born into. One of two children in a fairly well-to-do family in Oakwood, Ohio (neighboring Dayton), she had a long and interesting life that included a pilot's license and a flair for race-flying, and a nearly completed PhD in political science, at a time when women were mostly still expected to stay home and look after children. It ended severely constricted in her eighties, though, because macular degeneration took away her ability to drive. She had spent most of her last fifty years in Great Falls, Montana, which has ample sidewalks but whose services and amenities are placed for the distance and convenience of car travel, not for the pedestrian. Once she was unable to drive, there was almost nowhere for her to go.

That wasn't true in 1912, the year she was born. When my grandmother was still a tiny girl in frilly dresses and curly blonde hair, giving no hint of the whiskey-drinking, bull-riding-watching, Oldsmobile-driving elderly lady she would become, the roads were the territory of every traveler, most particularly those traveling on foot, and would remain so for many years after. Our downtowns were not yet ruled by traffic lights and crosswalks, and there was no national interstate system. In my grandmother's childhood, all of the people traveling in the ways shown in that 1906 San Francisco street scene really did belong on the public roads.

Today it's hard for us to imagine what the roads belonging to all users would mean for a person's ability to get around on her own two feet. We walk, consciously or not, in a grid. Even jaywalking keeps us in the hard line of a trapezoid as we seek the shortest, fastest route across the expanse of asphalt where our feet aren't meant to be. Our lives are squared off by sidewalks and intersections. And by 1930, all those people striding and strolling the streets of San Francisco in the Miles Brothers' 1906 film, those pedestrians, would become something else, a strange new entity. They would become jaywalkers, and this shift would foreshadow our long slide into a car-centric reality that steals from us our public spaces, our air quality, our health, and even our lives.

TODAY, IN ALMOST any municipality in the United States, you can get fined a solid amount of money for jaywalking. The law might not always be enforced, but it remains on the books. In Los Angeles, often described as a car-centric dystopia characterized by its long stretches of road and few intersections, meaning fewer places for people to cross the road even semi-safely, jaywalkers can be fined up to $250, and jaywalking laws are strictly, if intermittently, enforced. In Jacksonville, Florida, wide mid-century-era highways linking the downtown to beaches and affluent suburbs carve through low-income neighborhoods. There, even on roads where a crosswalk might be over a mile away, fines averaging $65 are handed out for a multitude of walking crimes, including jaywalking, failing to cross in a crosswalk, and failing to "cross road with shortest route."

In many cities, jaywalking laws have become the barest excuse for excessive force, especially in situations where race seems to be a significant factor in enforcement, as in a 2015 case in Stockton, California, when a sixteen-year-old Black boy had exited a bus and walked only a few steps in the bus lane before being ordered by a police officer onto the sidewalk in a situation that quickly and inexplicably led to violence against the boy. A hundred years ago there would have been no jaywalking law for that young teenager to be inadvertently breaking.

Think about waterways. In many US states as well as Canadian provinces, several European countries, the Philippines, India, and elsewhere, lakes and rivers are public property. That doesn't mean they're always publicly accessible—a lake might be locked in by privately owned land—but in general navigable waters are open for the use of all who can get to them. The small town I live in is built on one end of a lake, and has several state and city beaches and parks on the water's shores, meaning that in the summer all us great unwashed masses can swarm onto the water and kayak up and down the river just as easily as the part-time residents of multi-million-dollar homes lined up along the shoreline. In high summer the lake is packed with motorboats, water skiers, kayakers, paddleboarders, Jet Skiers, parties floating around on huge blow-up rafts, and thousands of swimmers. It's a popular, busy place to be when the weather turns hot and school lets out.

It's also, if you're on a paddleboard or kayak or just swimming across the water, dangerous. Motorboats and Jet Skis often run at high speeds and don't always watch for slower man-powered crafts, or lone bodies crawl-stroking through the snow-fed water. Speed and alcohol result, inevitably, in fatalities and accidents every year. And as with cars and pedestrians, people moving around with only their bodies are the most vulnerable.

Licensing, breathalyzers, and enforcement of lower speed limits could go a long way toward reducing accidents, as well as making parents feel safer taking their kids out on a canoe or teaching them to paddleboard. It would also piss off a lot of people.

That anger would be very close to car companies' and drivers' irritation at early-1900s restrictions on their movement through shared public roads in towns all across America. Yet their solution, of banning foot traffic except on sidewalks and designated crossings, looks absurd when we propose applying them to waterways: should swimmers, kayakers, and canoeing fishermen be confined to the bare edges of every lake simply so Jet Skiers can race across it as fast as they like without the risk of hitting and killing someone? Four million acres in the United States are now devoted to roadways, and in addition we've built about a billion parking spaces; all that public space once open for multiple uses and modes of transportation is now closed off from almost all everyday human activity except driving and parking.

An image by the Swedish artist Karl Jilg, which was commissioned by the Swedish Road Administration in 2014, captures this restriction of freedom perfectly. It's a color sketch of a standard downtown intersection with storefronts and people walking on the sidewalks. Except that, instead of a road, there's a yawning, bottomless gulf next to the sidewalks. A sheer drop-off. A woman walks with a young child, holding him or her tightly by the hand as the child pulls away, the small left foot of perhaps a five-year-old lifted slightly in response to an urge absolutely innate to children, the urge to run, to explore, to bounce and walk and roam. But while one side of the narrow sidewalk shows a plate-glass storefront, or perhaps a café, the other side falls immediately into the lethal crevasse. The mother can't let go of her child's hand because that wide, dark pit is where traffic lives, and probable death.

The pit takes up the majority of the space in the painting, and keeps everyone *not* in a car shunted onto the narrow sidewalks. They can cross the pit only by an even more narrow and precarious wooden bridge—the crosswalk.

If the lake where I live were suddenly closed off to paddleboarders and swimmers and fishermen in canoes in the interest of safety, local residents would raise hell, but later generations would forget that we ever had such gloriously open access. That is what has happened to our freedom to walk; it was taken away and then designed out of our lives, and over the decades we forgot that it was ever a right.

"The people who wanted car dependency," said Peter Norton at the 2016 Live.Ride.Share conference, "told stories that made history the justification of it. . . . To get the *future* they wanted, they had to tell a version of the *past* that they wanted"—an invented past of supposedly inevitable progress and of true freedom always just around the corner. He called the entire hundred years of car fixation "insanity."

Following his research, it's hard not to agree with him. There was nothing inevitable about our current car-dependent state, no reason in the world why our city centers couldn't look like Amsterdam or Copenhagen, where pedestrians roam en masse and at will and more people, including children, travel by bike than by car, and where the infrastructure naturally supports those who travel by wheelchair as easily as it does those who travel on foot. The only difference is that one solitary industry managed to persuade America that its vision of the future should be everyone's vision of the future.

This vision came fully into public view in 1939, when General Motors premiered Futurama at the World's Fair in New York City. A display that attracted 30,000 people per day, over five million viewers in its first summer, Futurama was a sprawling, nearly acre-large construction showing a city of skyscrapers surrounded by layers of hyper-looped highways. The display was meant to depict what the ideal city could look like by 1960. There were no sidewalks, no visible people, no children playing, no real parks, and, as far as I could see, no way out except by car. Sketches and photos of Futurama remind me of the science fiction movie *Dark City*, in which residents who think they're living in a vibrant city with easy access to vast ocean beaches eventually find that they've been kidnapped by an alien race and are in fact stranded on a spaceship somewhere in the galaxy, with no beaches, no way off, and no memory of how to get back home.

Futurama gave 1939 America a utopian, idealized vision of the future: clean, streamlined, no grit, no trash, no traffic congestion, no messy relations between people. Once you built a city in which cars could move smoothly, this vision said, the rest of society will fall into happy, manageable place. Considering the chaotic, compromising work it takes to run even a small town well, much less a city or entire society, one would have to assume that GM's Futurama would be run entirely by computer, or perhaps a benevolent robotic overlord. At the time, it was presented as a city designed to free people from the stress of everyday living—that is, the stress of shared space and life with other human beings. But actually it is a city designed for machines, particularly cars, to realize peak efficiency, not for humans to live a good life.

JANE JACOBS, ONE of the most influential voices in urban planning and transportation of the twentieth century, instinctively understood the flaws of this utopian vision. In *The Death and Life of Great American Cities*, her most well-known and widely read book, Jacobs detailed the true networks, motion, and infrastructure that combine to make great cities possible.* These are interactions, "eyes on the street" in the form of people using and subconsciously monitoring their public spaces, sidewalks and street life full of encounters and meanders, chances for serendipity and neighborliness but also for a human ecosystem that reduces opportunities for petty crime and increases economic vitality. These organically formed neighborhood networks, she wrote, "are a city's irreplaceable social capital."

Jacobs's innate understanding of what makes a city thrive set her directly in conflict with Robert Moses, New York City's infrastructure czar from the 1930s through the 1960s, and the force behind many of the city's major bridges and freeways. Moses was one of the most

* While Jacobs stated outright that her observations on cities couldn't be extended to towns and villages, I'd argue that they can and should. Her reasoning was that cities are full of strangers, whereas smaller towns are not. That is less true than it was when her book was published in 1961, and even those who've known their neighbors since childhood still have to learn to live together. Communities, no matter how small, are formed through the frictions of daily encounters.

powerful and ideological transportation heads of the twentieth century. He was also, as Jacobs saw clearly, one of the most destructive. Moses took GM's idea of Futurama and attempted to turn it into reality. He produced plans that leveled "undesirable slums" and eviscerated older communities, replacing them with apartment buildings that were idealized on paper but sterile in reality, incapable of fostering an enduring sense of neighborliness, all to ram through them the highways of the future: the Cross-Bronx Expressway, among many of New York City's clogged and decaying freeways, was one of his shining achievements, and at the same time that it was destroying neighborhoods in Harlem and the Bronx, it also strangled their residents' access to jobs and amenities in America's most economically vibrant city.

The Cross-Bronx is also one of the most loathsome and frustrating highways I've ever had the misfortune to drive on a regular basis, which is only partly beside the point: one of our car-centric culture's fantasies is that, by building enough highways with enough lanes, traffic will someday be "solved." This solution never arrives—the more and wider highways we build, the more people drive, and the farther out we build suburbs so commuters can hang onto some modicum of quality of life between long, frustrating commutes to and from work. We've reached a point at which all of our thinking about city planning and town design focuses largely on managing the ever-growing traffic of personal automobiles. "Cities," though, wrote Jane Jacobs, "have much more intricate economic and social concerns than automobile traffic. How can you know what to try with traffic until you know how the city itself works, and what else it needs to do with its streets? You can't." A reality that we've often paved over in a century of building for cars.

CITIES AND TOWNS high in social capital have all sorts of unexpected strengths, like poverty-stricken but resilient Auburn Gresham, the suburb that defied expectations in Chicago's 1995 heat wave. And as noted in Chapter 2, this is true of many parts of New York City—the metropolis after Hurricane Sandy was full of stories about tenants hanging power strips outside doors, windows, and fences so that other people could charge their phones, of people traversing six- or eight-floor walkups to check on neighbors, and of strangers helping Staten Islanders clear out rubble and soaked furniture.

These kinds of stories are well documented in natural disasters all over the world. That beautiful, flowing life of the San Francisco street depicted in the 1906 video short? It was ripped apart a few days later in an earthquake that killed 3,000 people and destroyed most of the city. But in the aftermath of that disaster, eight-year-old Dorothy Day witnessed an outpouring of community and selflessness. "While the crisis lasted," she wrote in her autobiography, "people loved each other." It was an experience that would shape the rest of her life and lead her to found the *Catholic Worker* newspaper and Catholic Worker Movement, devoted to helping the most marginalized of society. Her experience of social capital is similar to that of New Yorkers after the terrorist attacks of September 11, 2001, when the community found its resilience through the connections that humans have always, and will always, crave.

In New York, this resilience in the face of disaster would have been far more limited without Jane Jacobs's relentless advocacy. She inspired several successful community-led fights against freeways that would have ripped apart neighborhoods like Greenwich Village and SoHo. Neighborhoods without the protection of voices like hers—largely neighborhoods where people of color lived, whose voices and needs were ignored by those in power—did not fare so well when Robert Moses began enacting his vision, and the combined passion for urban renewal and highway building would leave, as Jacobs wrote, "whole communities torn apart and sown to the winds, with a reaping of cynicism, resentment and despair." A pattern that was imitated across the country, shattering communities and forcing generations of us into a life behind the steering wheel.

I CRASHED MY first car while driving down a highway. It wasn't actually mine; it was my parents', a used Dodge sedan they'd bought cheap and that I borrowed on the days I had my dishwashing job after school. Often we didn't have the money to register it, and we only sporadically paid the insurance. When I crashed it—the second time I'd done so; the first time it was only damaged, not totaled—the lack of insurance resulted in a $3,000 fine, and of course the car itself was a write-off. I was seventeen. I went home that night to sit on my bedroom floor and write shakily in my journal, the moment of impact with the other car and the moment of sliding front-first into the ditch playing themselves over and over whether my eyes were closed or open. It was ten years before I could ride calmly as a passenger, and I'm still an ultra-cautious driver. "You drive like an old lady," friends complain. "That's because I hope to become one someday," I answer.

The day I wrecked my parents' car there were thirty other crashes in our area. I'd been driving to school from an early-morning physics class I took at the community college, and the roads were covered in black ice. "Black ice" is a phrase that chills the eagerness of any driver accustomed to winter. It hides in plain sight, appearing the same color as the roads, deceptive and slick as hell. Hit a patch of black ice at the wrong speed, and all else is up to dumb luck.

Thirty crashes. That was a lot for our sparsely populated area. A high-risk driving day. The number has stuck in my head over the years, partly as self-forgiveness, since the roads were clearly dangerous for everyone. Yet its significance fades when compared to the average number of crashes seen in the United States every year: in 2016 alone, according to the National Highway Traffic Safety Administration (NHTSA), 5,987 pedestrians were killed in traffic crashes. That's among the over 37,000 people killed overall in those same crashes—drivers, passengers, bicyclists, bystanders, and walkers—and the tens of thousands of pedestrians injured.

Raquel Nelson's case shocks because it is so deeply and obviously unjust. Yet we're used to car crashes. They've become such an embedded part of our national psyche that we're barely aware how many people are killed, how many families are destroyed, every year. In 2001, over forty-two thousand people died in car crashes in the United States. From 1994 to 2003—nine years—2,970 people died in terrorist attacks (most of them in the September 11, 2001, attacks on the Pentagon and World Trade Center). Multiply the toll from 2001 by nine, and you have around *142 times* more people dying in car crashes over the same period than in terrorist attacks.

Speed is the most common reason for traffic-related fatalities, whether it's drivers, passengers, or pedestrians who are killed. A person hit by a driver going twenty miles per hour has a 13 percent likelihood of death or serious injury; if the driver is going forty miles an hour, that likelihood jumps to 73 percent. If you're a parent who takes his or her kids to school every morning, these numbers translate into sharp, nerve-wracking realities.

Paired with speed is what Sergeant Cat Brown, a fifteen-year officer with the St. Paul, Minnesota, police department, calls "being tunneled." We lose a sense of perspective and common sense when we get behind the wheel. We tend to think we have more control than we do, but distracted by phones, food, children, sleepiness, anger, planning, or just plain life, *80 percent* of drivers simply don't see pedestrians.

That statistic comes from the drivers who were pulled over by St. Paul police after failing to stop for pedestrians at a legal crosswalk. The aim of the officers was to educate drivers, to remind them that the road is a shared space and that tunneling, losing sight of the fact that the public road isn't solely a conduit for their own personal vehicle, can get someone killed. Including themselves, especially since the advent of smartphones has made driver inattention such a serious issue. "You can't be on your device" when you're driving, Sergeant Brown said in a panel about pedestrian safety and law enforcement training. "You might tweet yourself away."

The fact that we think we can tweet, check Facebook, and tap out text messages while driving is the logical conclusion of how little we understand what we're doing when we shift into "drive." When you add the phenomenon of tunneling to the statistics on speeding and fatality rates, the prospects for pedestrians look dire. An investigation by the business magazine *Bloomberg* found that traffic fatalities rose by over 14 percent between 2008—there were 37,262 deaths in crashes that year—and 2016. Speeding and drunk driving increased only marginally during that period, and it's speculated that smartphones contributed significantly to the rise in traffic-related deaths. But US rules on data collection regarding cell phone use in crashes vary widely by state. Some don't collect the information at all. In some states, using a cell phone while driving isn't even illegal. These discrepancies mean that the National Highway Transportation Safety Administration doesn't have reliable data on how often texting and similar activities contribute to driving-related deaths.

One need spend only a short amount of time at a busy intersection to see how often people are looking at their phones while they're driving. Teaching my own children to cross the street safely, I had to include a firm "Make sure you make eye contact with the driver" instruction, because we have sometimes spent many minutes at a legal, well-marked crosswalk waiting for drivers to look up from the phones hidden in their laps or sitting propped up on a steering wheel. Pedestrian deaths, the *Bloomberg* report found, were up 9 percent between 2008 and 2016, a significant chunk of the increase of overall traffic deaths. The NHTSA might not have good statistics on how often distracted driving leads to fatal crashes, but the indications are anything but hidden.

In a move that's eerily similar to the campaign against jaywalking in the early 1920s, stories about the dangers of pedestrian distraction—rather than driver distraction—as related to traffic deaths began showing up in the public sphere around the time that deaths themselves started to rise. Walking while texting can pose its own problems—an

Australian researcher found that texting while walking actually causes people to "walk like a robot," lurching and stumbling; we're stealing from our ability to walk upright without having to think about it, and directing that attention to our screens. And a walker distracted by her phone might stroll directly into traffic, giving drivers no warning and no time to stop. Even I had to train myself to "pull over" if I wanted to text while I was walking, after too many near misses with other pedestrians on the sidewalk and understandably grudging acceptances of my apologies. But the fact is that people on foot are unlikely to kill other people by bumping into them. A person wielding a five-thousand-pound vehicle can, especially once she reaches higher speeds.

WHAT SHOULD BE most shocking about these numbers is that we accept them as normal. A hazard of modern life, a trade-off for the supposed freedom granted to us by the automobile. That's not even to mention the traffic that people sit in every day in cities all over the country—not an image usually used in advertisements for cars—the air pollution and greenhouse gases afflicting our lungs and the climate, the damage done to neighborhoods and landscapes carved apart by roads as impassable as any wall, or the damage we do to ourselves by getting everywhere we need to go by sitting rather than walking.

For generations of Americans, cars have meant freedom. But that freedom is a mirage, a chimera created by our national imagination and extensive advertising, an unreal construction with very real consequences.

When we read about car crashes in the newspaper, the language that's used to describe them is worlds away from the attitudes of the early 1900s. Instead of speaking of automobiles as "dangerous weapons," we talk about how pedestrians are too distracted. Instead of calling them "car crashes," we call them "accidents," as if there are forces utterly beyond our control that cause our cars to run into the soft, vulnerable bodies of people. Our entire mindset about cars, traffic, risk, and fatalities has been revolutionized from the inside out.

We live in a physical and psychological world that was invented in the 1920s and 1930s and sold to us in the name of efficiency and progress. It is a world that cities and towns all over the country are waking up to and trying to change—like drawing the curtain back on the Wizard of Oz's charade—but it might never have existed in the first place if the automobile industry had lost the battle over speed, once seen as the main factor in high pedestrian fatality rates.

The highway-building frenzy of the mid-1900s led to a vast network whose sole purpose was to allow cars to travel at higher speeds without, theoretically, endangering people: elevated highways, clover-leaf interchanges, bypasses, and in-city streets of four lanes, six lanes, turning lanes, parking lanes, with legal crosswalks set off in the heat-shimmering uncertain distance. But the builders failed to see how damaging the car-centric future would be to the needs of actual human communities.

IT'S HARD TO overstate the effect this initial campaign has had on the structure of American society today. The eviction of pedestrians from the public roads led to easier car travel, which led to increased desire for car ownership and the roads that would support it. It wasn't long before roads were designed not to enable people's movement around their communities but to move car traffic through places as quickly as possible. "The United States is full of cities that have been shaped or reshaped around the car," wrote urban planner Jeff Speck in *Walkable City: How Downtown Can Save America, One Step at a Time*. "Because there have been so many incentives for driving, cars have behaved like water, flowing into every nook and cranny where they are allowed."

These movements, which started as the futuristic fantasies of highway engineers in the 1930s and 1940s, led directly to the creation of white flight suburbs in post–World War II America. Those suburbs wouldn't be possible without highway systems to support them, and those highways would be pointless without the cars they carry. The very structure of most of our downtowns is dictated by early ideas of automobile convenience. Not being able to drive where you want to go, and to park there, is now both anathema and foreign to modern America.

Yet walkable communities are essential to vital, vibrant neighborhoods; they've also been shown to be economically more successful and more resilient. In places where parking is removed and sidewalks revitalized, business owners sometimes object, but studies show that small shops and cafés see upticks in business that can range from 20 to over 100 percent. Pedestrians visit more shops, and spend more time in them, than drivers do. Wandering, meandering, roaming—they are fodder to the creative human brain and meat for human social interaction, but they're also good for the economy.

The original national interstate plan, laid out in 1947 and updated in 1955, leading eventually to the 1956 Federal-Aid Highway Act, showed exactly where freeways would run through city centers. These designs came from highway engineers, who were focused on efficiency and speed—how to move traffic—and completely ignored the impact highways and freeways would have on a city's ecosystem.

Take downtown Detroit, for example. In 1951 it was home to dense housing and vibrant neighborhoods. Today, the Motor City's downtown is dominated by a network of highways, interchanges, and ramps that replaced close-knit historic communities like Black Bottom. Or take St. Paul, Minnesota. In 2016 Black Lives Matter protesters closed down the I-94 freeway there for several hours after the shooting death of Philando Castile, a school cafeteria supervisor, during a routine traffic stop. As with some Black Lives Matter protests elsewhere, the choice of freeway was deliberate. I-94 had been constructed by blowing a ravine directly through the African American neighborhood of Rondo in the 1950s and 1960s. Rondo was once a cultural hub of St. Paul, home to thriving local newspapers, a music scene, integrated schools, and social clubs. The community protested against the loss of their neighborhood to a highway, but I-94 opened in 1968, and today, pedestrian overpasses connect Rondo across the racing, always traffic-choked eight-lane freeway. The scars are still there, including the psychological ones; at the Hallie Q. Brown community center, maps show where the land now covered by I-94 once held homes and businesses, some of whose owners and residents are still alive today.

A major factor in the highway system plan for inner cities was getting rid of "blight." What this meant was that lower-income areas, overwhelmingly neighborhoods populated by very few, if any, white people, were razed for the purpose of providing efficient driving access to the suburbs—which were, almost exclusively, white. Once communities were displaced to make space for the highways, their residents moved to locations scattered around the city. Usually, they lacked the political power and financial resources to keep their neighborhoods intact, and up until the late 1960s people of color were legally barred from moving out to the same new suburbs their white neighbors fled to. Even after the Fair Housing Act was passed in 1968, active discrimination and lack of legal consequences for segregation maintained the status quo for decades.

White flight to the suburbs did more than subsidize decades' worth of highways. As Jane Jacobs wrote about so forcefully in *Death and Life*, it stripped Americans of a collective memory that saw roads, towns, and communities as public spaces. It allowed us to begin building larger houses farther away from jobs, schools, and neighbors, and to spend more time enclosed in our own mobile worlds, cut off from air, birds, trees, footsteps, and each other; protected from weather, pollution, exertion, and each other.

It exacerbated racial and class inequities in ways that most people (at least most white people) are completely unaware of. When the interstate system, the pet project of President Dwight D. Eisenhower, was proposed and enacted in the 1950s, it brought higher-speed roads to previously less accessible areas of the country, like my home state of Montana. But it also punched freeways right through heavily populated cities, cutting residents off from their jobs, their neighborhoods, and any access they once had to public transportation.

Seeing these kinds of changes early in his career was what led Peter Norton to pursue research in the history of the car-centric century, to uncover the layers of advertising, anti-pedestrian campaigns, and devotion to utopian efficiency that made it possible, and eventually to write *Fighting Traffic*. Working at the Delaware Historical Society in Wilmington, he spent a summer in 1988 sorting and cataloguing hundreds of old photographic negatives of the city. The differences, he found, between the streets in the photos that he was organizing and the same streets when he walked out the door were stark: "Photographs of Wilmington showed neighborhoods where people walked, and rode buses, streetcars, and 'trackless trolleys' (trolley buses), and had access to an extensive long-distance rail network for longer journeys," he wrote me in an email. All of that changed between 1955 and 1975. The I-95 freeway "erased dozens of city blocks of this not-very-big city. People had lived there," he noted, pointing out what seems obvious but is not necessarily something we think about very often. Wherever you see a highway cutting through a city, *people had lived there*. Hundreds of communities with neighbors and families and all sorts of social capital and interpersonal dynamics. And over and over again, race was a deciding factor in which neighborhoods stayed and which were deemed dispensable. Neighborhoods like the 15th Ward in Syracuse, New York, were razed completely to build elevated highways, and the same thing happened in cities like Boston, Milwaukee, Birmingham, and Minneapolis. "There were a million excuses for kicking them out," Norton wrote, "but there seemed to be no way around the truth that (white) people, who didn't live there and apparently didn't care about the (Black) people who did, wanted that land—and not even because they wanted to *be* there, but just to *get through it* to somewhere else." Wilmington, he stressed, was just one case. There were hundreds of others like it.

Raquel Nelson's Atlanta neighborhood is a legacy of this earlier suburban era. Built at a time when white people were first moving out of the cities, it later became poorer as those with money to do so—again, largely white and middle-class people—moved even farther away from Atlanta, to suburbs with larger lawns and two-car garages.

Nelson couldn't afford a car, so the day her son died she'd taken her kids out the same way she went to work and to the university where she was a student: she rode the bus. To people who rarely use public transport, this sounds simple, but it's not. Very few American cities have comprehensive bus systems that are easy to use, inexpensive, and convenient. Even in Portland, Oregon, long thought of as the American poster child for bikeability (if not walkability) and public transportation, it can take hours and several transfers to get where you need to go. In European cities I've lived in, like Vienna and Moscow, getting around via bus, tram, or subway is considered normal no matter what your economic status. In the United States, a national imagination that sees driving a car as a right and a necessity has led to severe underfunding of public transportation systems all across the country, meaning that the less well off and those who can't afford a car's upkeep are nevertheless dependent on an inadequate public transportation system to get to work, stores, banks, and schools. Getting around Atlanta and its suburbs by bus is an undertaking, and yet it's necessary: the city is built for the convenience of driving, meaning amenities are spread out to areas unreachable on foot. They're served by buses, but poorly.

I imagine Nelson having planned a day that wove in the specialness of birthday preparations with knowing she'd have a job getting her kids along, knowing the three-year-old and four-year-old in particular would be tired, bored, excited, impatient. Eager to run, tired of walking. Constrained, constantly, by the rush of roads and the roaring of buses. Moving yet not free. They went to Wal-Mart, and then she took them out for pizza; they had to wait over an hour at a bus transfer station for the final leg of their day's journey, and by the time the bus got them to their home stop, it was dark.

I've been there, or in similar situations, so many times. The heavy diaper bag dragging my neck out of line, a baby on my other hip. Holding tight to my preschooler's hand as he strains at my arm. He knows about traffic and the dangers, but he doesn't *know*. He gets excited, pulls away, and I have to act fast, grab an arm, a shoulder, anything, before he jumps out into the road.

To do this for hours is exhausting, and I've nearly missed enough times that it makes me freeze as I sit here writing, pen in hand, thinking of the many ways drivers have almost killed my children because I was just that bit too slow, too tired, too slack-fingered in my grip. Or the many ways I might have done it to someone else's child, because I was driving just that bit too fast, too tired, too unconscious of who else might be using the road.

Nelson's neighborhood, and thousands like it, became infected by suburbia's appetite for wider roads that would facilitate pause-free, attention-light driving. It was built with the assumption that people would not be walking anywhere, even to the crosswalk. The neighborhood has sidewalks, but they are skinny and hug the road with no separation, a living image of Karl Jilg's death pit, but with wider, faster streets and fewer places to cross. While Nelson's apartment building was immediately across the street from her bus stop, the closest crosswalk was a quarter mile away. As a mother of young children myself, knowing how eager children are, how fast, how full of energy yet bored by unnecessary trudging, I would have made the same choice she did on a regular basis: cross the road at the bus stop, limiting to a minimum the amount of time spent next to a fast, busy, pedestrian-unfriendly road while carrying bags of groceries and not enough hands to snatch my children back from danger.

After being convicted of vehicular homicide, Raquel Nelson faced a three-year prison term for her son's death; Jerry Guy, the man who killed her son and then drove off, served only six months. Guy admitted to drinking and taking painkillers before killing Nelson's son, and had two previous hit-and-runs on his record, but he did not lose his driver's license.

The charges of vehicular homicide against Raquel Nelson were, on retrial, dropped. She was, nevertheless, forced to pay a $200 fine and to plead guilty to a lesser charge: jaywalking.

This imbalance is familiar to just about any American, most of whom have probably been in at least one minor crash and many of whom have been convicted of minor infractions like driving a few miles over the speed limit or driving with an expired registration, or what should be major infractions like driving while intoxicated. Yet these illegalities are considered unworthy of removing us from behind the wheel; our right to drive is so ingrained that it takes more than the death of a child to lose it.

ROADS HAVE BEEN with us for millennia. Most of us have heard of the marvels of Roman roads, how they ran straight and true, connecting the empire across countries and landscapes like a vast circulatory system. But even in ancient Rome, chariot traffic was considered a nuisance to be heavily regulated, according to journalist Tom Vanderbilt. Excepting the transportation of construction materials for temples or other large-scale public projects, Caesar banned all carts in the city during the bulk of the day. They were allowed entrance only after three in the afternoon.

The long-standing existence of roads is something different from entire societies, entire countries, carved and limited and defined by their devotion to car travel. In America, except in places like New York City and precious few neighborhoods in parts of precious few other cities, we seem to have completely forgotten that it's even possible to get places without driving. A walkable community, which was the norm a bare hundred or so years ago, now seems either quaint or the province of better-off post-Millennials who haven't yet had to make the choice between vibrant city centers and family-friendly mortgage prices.

HOMO SAPIENS TEND to see reality through the perspective of our present moment. We have difficulty thinking through the long-term consequences of our actions, and even more difficulty seeing that present moment through the rich filter of history.

We also tend to view "progress" as inevitable forward movement. But progress is a tricky thing. We can see this in evolution itself, which for our species, as for many others, has not been a clean line of one species of humanoid evolving smoothly into the next. A hundred thousand years ago, many species of humans still existed at the same time; our evolution comes out of a messy tangle of starts and stops, millions of years of various species living, evolving, changing, dying.

Technological and social progress aren't any different. There are all sorts of ways to view the world, to create culture and government—who's to say that the ones we engage in are the correct ones, the inevitable endpoint of progress? Our thinking so doesn't necessarily make it true. Technology, which we also perceive as an inevitable march forward in a single line, is even messier. We add lead to makeup and house paint and water pipes and then discover it poisons children. We create chemicals and bombs to use in warfare, leaving civilians and soldiers alike poisoned and ill, and then use many of those same materials to create household goods, fouling waterways, soil, air, and our own delicate biology. We build nuclear power plants and then find ourselves at a loss for how to cope with the radioactive waste.

This is not a blanket judgment of technology. Human beings have been experimenting ever since we picked up sticks and rocks with our freed hands, and we will continue to do so. The point is that "progress" is a messy ramble, less a clear path through the woods than a process of bushwhacking through a jungle full of dead ends and U-turns and countless life-threatening encounters.

Building a completely car-dependent culture has brought us to one of these dead ends. Instead of increasing our freedom of movement, we've limited it to where and how we construct roads. Instead of opening the planet up to our human experience, we've gridded it out and closed it off. Instead of learning how to make better, stronger communities, we've boxed ourselves into suburban lives that are at the same time disconnected physically and hyper-connected digitally, building out of our lives the wealth of daily interactions that make community-scale social capital possible, while investing in infrastructure that makes us incredibly vulnerable to the vagaries of a planet ruled by nature.

The arrival of self-driving cars—known also as autonomous vehicles (AVs)—to the mass market will eventually change the conversation about driver behavior, but it will also open up, once again, the wider question of our shared public spaces and whom they're for. Will we assume that self-driving vehicles need uninterrupted highways to reach their full potential, and then make the same community-destroying mistakes we did through the highway-building frenzies of the mid-1900s? How will pedestrian safety be programmed into their systems?

In America, cars are associated with freedom. You get in your four-door or your convertible or your truck, and the world is open to you. That's what the car commercials show, and what our national imagination tells us. A teenager's first set of car keys is handed over with a trunkload of independence. The world is yours now, kid. *This* is what defines your freedom, not the ability to vote or drink or live apart from your parents. The ability to drive. And with the ability to drive comes the ability to escape our neighbors, our communities, and our fellow human beings.

AFTER MY FAMILY left Montana in 1991 and settled into Moscow, we took the train to Leningrad to spend time with my father's mother and siblings and to meet my cousin for the first time. There, my father took my younger sister and me on long walks and told us stories of his childhood. His pre-Montana life began to take shape for me, not just in my imagination but physically. The particular cucumber-like smell in the stairwell of my grandmother's apartment building, the bridges my father had illegally jumped from to go swimming in the Neva River, the route to his school, which he'd hated, and to the zoo, where he'd go by himself to feed the elephants. And woven through all of it were the walks he'd later taken with his friends, when they explored the city on foot and the territories of forbidden thought in their conversations.

Many years later, long after Leningrad had become St. Petersburg and the Soviet Union had collapsed, when I was living my exurban life where I couldn't cross the road from the bookstore to the grocery store without a car, I thought back to my father's walks. Even growing up under Stalin, assuming they avoided being shot or sent to the gulag, and later after Stalin died and the gulag was dismantled but free expression still came with severe consequences, people like my father were free to roam, the mind encouraged in movement by the feet. But my children and I didn't have that particular freedom, like so many Americans, living where sidewalks do not exist but busy roads abound. Every errand or outing was predetermined for us, its route mapped and enforced by what was accessible to my station wagon. We could not stray, meander, or wander, and I couldn't help but wonder if our form of movement was beginning to constrain our flexibility of mind.

THIS WAS REALLY the promise dangled in front of us throughout the car-centric century, which was made possible by jaywalking laws and the eviction of pedestrians from the public roads, and initially sold almost exclusively to white America: owning a car and living in the suburbs made life orderly. Not only could you have the perfectly cut dandelion-free lawn and wide roads for your traffic-free drive to work, but you could avoid the painful mess of living among people whose culture and struggles you didn't understand and whose place in society you questioned. You could get in your sedan and drive away from it all, to a world where the difficult questions of justice and equity and reparation and mutual interdependence didn't exist. Or at least, you could pretend they didn't.

But as human beings have had to learn over and over, there is no "away." You can't just send all your convicts to Australia and have petty crime disappear. You can't throw out your plastic packaging and not see it turn up in the food chain. And you can't gate yourself off from people whose race or religion or gender or culture you're not comfortable with, and expect that your community, your family, or yourself will always remain exactly as you wish.

We will never have all the roads we need for everyone to drive everywhere they want in the free, lighthearted way promised by car manufacturers' advertisements. We will never have all the highways and exits and bypasses, all the country roads and garages and parking lots. The city of Futurama is, like all utopias, something that will never come to pass. The question is, even if that utopia were within our grasp, given the gifts that walking has granted us, and how much it still has to offer us and our communities, would we embrace that future? Or do we want something more, a more expansive kind of freedom, a built environment and way of life that can nurture us at every layer of our human selves?

CHAPTER 4
LURCH

In effect, humans have dragged a body with a long hominid history into an overfed, malnourished, sedentary, sunlight-deficient, sleep-deprived, competitive, inequitable, and socially-isolating environment with dire consequences.

—BRANDON H. HIDAKA, "Depression as a Disease of Modernity: Explanations for Increasing Prevalence," *Journal of Affective Disorders*

HOW WELL DO YOU KNOW THIS BODY OF YOURS? NOT THE lumps and rolls and knobbiness and wayward hairs you've been scrutinizing and criticizing since your early teens. The rest of it. How well do you know your heartbeat, its slowing as you fall asleep, its increase as you walk uphill? The tension of your forearms and shoulders as roll your wheelchair to a meeting you're late for? How well acquainted are you with the sagging complacency of your butt and spine after sitting at your desk for hours? Or how your lungs struggle while walking along a busy, polluted road on a hot day?

Have you ever noticed the amount of time your eyes take to refocus on a far-off horizon when lifted from a computer screen? Or the barely noticeable but monumental decrease in overall body tension when you turn your feet from a traffic-clogged street to grass-bordered footpaths under rustling tree leaves? Forget about controlling your body, about body image. How well do you *know* it?

Ask yourself: Can you get from where you are right now to somewhere else you want to go, on your own two feet or in a wheelchair, however you define walking for yourself, using only your body? Make it somewhere within a mile—or about twenty minutes' walk at a moderate footpace—to keep it realistic. Could you do it? Could you do it in comfort, in safety? How about with a small child or energetic puppy in tow?

For far too many, the answer is no. There might be a freeway along your route, or long stretches of highway-like rural roads with no shoulder and no crosswalks. I once walked in San Antonio, Texas, from its picturesque and serpentine River Walk to a coffee shop a little over a mile away. In just a few minutes I'd exited the heavily pedestrianized tourist area near the Alamo and landed on a narrow strip of sidewalk abutting a busy several-lane road that ran under a noisy overpass and through a tangled intersection where several roads met at bizarre and wide angles, making them treacherous to cross. I found the coffee shop in a rundown district of abandoned warehouses and a trash-strewn train line. This route would have deterred any but the most committed pedestrian. It was designed with traffic in mind, not people.

The area you're looking to traverse might have a high crime rate, making walking alone unsafe. It might have a low crime rate, but a person walking might be deemed suspicious, as happened to an acquaintance of mine when she was living in Mississippi. She used to walk across town to her job but got stopped by the police so many times she gave up and bought a used bike instead. They assumed she was either homeless or a prostitute. Who else, they said, would be walking?

Women like my friend face significant barriers to walking freely, from missing infrastructure to active violence to tiresome everyday harassment. "You can't wander lonely as a cloud when you're always checking to see whether you're being followed, or bracing yourself in case the person passing grabs you," wrote essayist Rebecca Solnit, referring to William Wordsworth's famous poem "I Wandered Lonely as a Cloud." "I've been insulted, threatened, spat on, attacked, groped, harassed, followed." Nearly every woman I know inhabits that tension of potential invasion when she walks in a public space.

And both Solnit and my friend are white, as am I, giving us a level of protection that people of color can't take for granted in the United States. In most American cities there are neighborhoods where the color of your skin can signal to its residents that you don't belong. It's a legacy of our highway-building and suburbia crazes that these neighborhoods also tend to be quieter, more tree-covered, calmer, and wealthier, as well as predominantly white.

The consequences of living with structural racism are apparent in cases like those of poet and essayist Hope Wabuke's elderly father, who had a passel of police officers point guns at him while he was walking in front of the Acadia, California, house he'd lived in for thirty years. "To the Acadia Police Department," she wrote in an essay, "my Black father did not fit."

Throughout the twentieth century, we bound our public roads in a labyrinth of laws, guardrails, asphalt, and concrete that removed transportation access from our bodies and placed it behind physical barriers and psychological signs saying, "No Trespassing." What kind of freedom do we actually have if, because of infrastructure, racism, or social norms, we can't get where we need to go on our own two feet?

The consequences of severing the earth from our feet are devastating. A century's worth of building a world for cars rather than people has exhausted, drained, and fractured our lives in more ways than we can possibly imagine. It negatively affects our individual health and erodes our communities; it leads to infrastructure design that perpetuates racial and class divides, and to levels of loneliness and social isolation so extreme they're being studied as a health crisis.

The current generation of children will have shorter lifespans than their parents, a fact that's been statistically shown too often to ignore.

US children are advised to get sixty minutes of active play per day, but only about a third actually do. *Three-quarters* of British children spend less time outside than prison inmates, with screen time, fear of strangers, and traffic being the main factors keeping them indoors.

Diabetes is just one of the severe health conditions whose prevalence has reached a crisis point, and it can lead to a cornucopia of other problems: heart disease, nerve damage, kidney damage, hearing impairment, Alzheimer's. In America in 1958, fewer than two million people had diabetes; today, twenty-six million people do, and another eighty million have pre-diabetes. The rate of obesity-linked diabetes in children—Type 2 diabetes, which was almost unheard of in children before 1990—rose by nearly four thousand cases every year between 2002 and 2005. In children, Type 2 diabetes also turns out to be resistant to common treatments.

Discussions about obesity, diabetes, and heart disease range from finger-pointing about lifestyle choices to admonitions against fat shaming, but we often forget to ask the far more fundamental question: why is it that a simple, low-stress, everyday active lifestyle is out of reach for most of us?

Lack of nutritious food ("food deserts," as Michael Pollan dubbed them) can be blamed for much of this rise. Inactivity, though, plays a complementary role, and it's not due to increasing laziness. What children and adults face is lack of access to the most basic opportunities for health—the ability to step out of our front doors and walk where we want or need to go. Two-thirds of the world's 415 million diabetics live in cities all over the world, many of them unwalkable—Houston, Mexico City, Rome, Shanghai, Johannesburg. Six million British adults get virtually no exercise—forget thirty minutes a day; these adults don't even get thirty minutes a month. In Abu Dhabi, 20 percent of the population aged twenty to seventy-nine already has diabetes, and it has one of the fastest increasing rates of the disease of any city in the world. In Houston, one of America's most car-dependent urban areas, a third of residents are expected to have diabetes by 2040.

And it's deeply affecting our kids, who have declining mobility across the world (this is true even in Scandinavian countries, where active lifestyles tend to be valued more highly than they are in the United States). A study of over eighteen thousand children aged seven to fifteen, in sixteen countries, found that traffic danger is "consistently cited by parents" as the main barrier to letting their kids roam around outside on their own. Traffic concerns, car-dependent cities, and car use by parents make walking as a way of life foreign to many children, but shifting social norms are also a factor. Twenty-eight percent of parents in the study worried about being judged by neighbors if they let their kids play outside alone. It's easy to scoff at this concern, but in numerous high-profile cases in the United States parents have trained their children to walk and play outside on their own, responsibly and safely, only to have a neighbor or stranger call child protective services, putting the parents in danger of losing their children to the foster system due to accusations of neglect or abuse. In my not-so-ancient Gen-X childhood, when parents expected my friends and me to spend summer days roaming around town on our own, this particular fear didn't even exist.

How did we manage to create a world where children can't even go outside and play safely, much less go for a walk? Where even minimal exercise involves specialized clothing, health club memberships, time carved out to spend at the gym, and a level of income that makes it all possible? It seems insane that even those who can afford Fitbits and Apple Watches have to scramble together walks up and down apartment stairs, or even around their bedrooms, to get in the minimum ten thousand steps per day that we're advised to achieve for our health. They simply can't reach that milestone through normal daily walking.

In 1969, almost half of American children walked to school. As of 2009, only 13 percent did. Walking to school was once a defining experience of an American childhood: "When I was your age," the joke goes, "I had to walk a mile on my own two feet to get to school. Uphill both ways." "In knee-deep snow," my younger sister and I often add, remembering a variety of houses our family rented on steep hills in the Montana countryside, and our freezing predawn winter walks to the school bus, walks that shifted slowly to springtime lightness through woods of lodgepole pine and fields full of daffodils, the air acrid with burning slash. It never occurred to us to value these walks; they were just something we did, at least until I got my driver's permit at fifteen. But now, as adults, my sisters and I talk about our walks to school or the school bus as if they were full of the delights of a summer camp. Freedom of movement is inherent in this feeling, that giddy knowledge that you can open a door and step out of it and go . . . anywhere.

While we didn't always have walking at our disposal—some of the houses we rented were in rural areas where there was nowhere to go except onto a neighbor's property, where we promptly got yelled at—we had those walks during the school year, and earlier childhood memories of wandering the sleepy streets of our original hometown, where we lived until I was ten. There, we and our older sister walked on our own to school and to friends' houses; with no telephone in the house until I was nine and no cable television until later than that—ubiquitous Internet and cell phones were still decades off—walking was how we met up with friends, gossiped, explored, played, sold Girl Scout cookies.

That experience has become a rare one. If only 13 percent of American children are walking or biking to school, the other 87 percent are probably walking or biking very few other places, either. That translates into millions of children without knowledge of one of the most basic human experiences: getting places on foot. Our bodies as transportation, as movement, as the eventual answer to the freedom discovered by a toddler walking solidly for the first time. And bound together with the loss of freedom are the physical consequences that eat away at their ability—our ability—to live the most basic of healthy lives. Every minute our children spend sitting in a car instead of moving around on their feet translates to loss of bone density, lower lung capacity, and bored brains.

The boredom of immobility is not the kind of boredom that comes from long summer days lounging under a tree doing little, or the boredom of standing in line at the grocery store. Those types of boredom can prod the brain and release its creative energy. The boredom children face through excessive sitting in cars and in school is different. It's a bodily boredom that finds its outlet in anxious or hyper behavior, outbursts and repetitive motions, kicking, fidgeting, and just plain whining that often lead to diagnoses of attention deficit hyperactivity disorder (ADHD) or attention deficit disorder (ADD) and treatment with medication.

ADHD and ADD are, of course, real issues. The rates of ADHD in US children rose from nearly 8 percent in 2003 to 11 percent in 2011, and many of these children have found relief through medications, public schools' special services, and targeted therapy. But an increasing number of parents, teachers, and medical practitioners are finding that plenty of these children simply aren't allowed to move often enough. Sitting in a car or bus to go to and from school, and then being forced to sit in school for long periods of time, even at kindergarten age, children's bodies are screaming at them to run, climb, jump, roll, tumble, *anything*. The vestibular system, remember, is developed through these crucial early years, through hours of full-body movement. Perhaps fidgeting or hyper behavior, in some of these cases, is simply the result of children helpless to change their situation but trying to answer their bodies' unmet needs in any way possible.

Angela Hanscom, a pediatric occupational therapist and founder of a nature-based development program called TimberNook, wrote, "In order to develop a strong balance system, children need to move their bodies in all directions, for hours at a time." Without this freedom, children not only fidget but also have trouble focusing, paying attention, and retaining information.

The simple act of walking to school increases attention and concentration in students. A survey of twenty thousand Danish children aged five to nineteen found that those who walked or biked to school performed better on activities requiring concentration, with the effect lasting for up to four hours. "We learn through our head and by moving," wrote Niels Egelund, of Denmark's Aarhus University, about the study. "Something happens within the body when we move, and this allows us to be better equipped afterwards to work on the cognitive side." His study was part of a nationwide look at the links between concentration, diet, and exercise in Danish children. The links between walking and biking and concentration were found to be stronger than the link between concentration and diet.

By contrast, a study of British children found that nearly a third of four-year-olds are "not physically ready" to start school. Demonstrating trouble with balance and coordination as well as tasks involving eye-hand coordination, the children couldn't walk in a straight line and had trouble holding a pencil and putting on their own shoes. The researchers pointed firmly to an increasingly sedentary lifestyle, not only from time spent in front of iPads but, importantly, an enormous amount of time riding in car seats. When children get everywhere sitting in a car, and are then forced to sit for hours a day at school, their learning suffers.

Some American schools recognize this need and answer it not by increasing recess time, but by incorporating tools like ball chairs or pedal seats for class desks, or taking short stretch breaks. These solutions are "creative and thoughtful," as Angela Hanscom wrote, "but they won't fix the underlying problem." What children really need is for us to flip the educational time model so that they spend *most* of their time hanging upside-down from monkey bars, rolling down hills, spinning in circles, playing chase, and wandering, meandering, walking. These natural, everyday childhood activities are the best way for children to fully develop their vestibular systems, leading to better balance, core strength, and, later, focus on reading, solving math problems, and thinking creatively.

Dr. James A. Levine, an endocrinologist who teaches and researches at the Mayo Clinic's Arizona campus, spent decades pioneering "chair-release programs" in corporate offices, which he later expanded to innovative schools. In the schools, children were given the option of sitting while learning, instead of being required to. Teachers reported that not only did their students focus better on math and generally seem to be learning more, but also that the students themselves were happier, healthier, and energized instead of exhausted at the end of the school day.

In a Swiss Waldkindergarten—"forest kindergarten"—kids from four to seven years spend all day, every day playing outside, even in winter, and don't learn any math or reading until first grade. Canada is experimenting with a similar program incorporating free play for all-day kindergarten, and in Finland variations on free play are actually required in kindergarten; until recently, kindergarten teachers weren't even allowed to teach reading. The focus is on letting children learn in the best way possible: through self-directed play, using their bodies.

It's not just that getting people, including kids, out of their chairs and car seats improves blood sugar, blood pressure, and, often, weight-related health issues, although Levine has observed these improvements repeatedly; the release is also psychological. "When people get out of their chairs," he wrote in his book *Get Up! Why Your Chair Is Killing You and What to Do About It*, "they blossom as if they finally are free from prison. . . . by getting up, as a first simple step, people start to regain personal power."

THE INABILITY OF teens and young children to walk to school, or to the park or a friend's house, is almost as much of a problem in suburbs as it is in cities with neglected and crumbling infrastructure, but for different reasons. Once flight from cities became popular, suburbs moved ever farther away from urban cores. Not only were they built around car travel, they eventually stopped including sidewalks at all. We've all seen these suburbs, and some of us live in them. I've lived in one or two over the years. Cookie-cutter houses spread acres apart or crammed several to each acre, connected from the house to the road by a driveway but with nothing to connect the houses to each other, and the whole node connected to services and amenities by only a highway or rural road unsafe for anything but car travel. There are communities across the country where it is illegal for children to walk to their bus stops, much less to school, because the roads they have access to simply aren't designed for people. In 2016, at Bear Branch Elementary School in Magnolia, Texas, parents woke up one day to the message that they were no longer allowed to walk their children to school at all. Backed by local law enforcement, the school's principal stood firm behind her rule that students had to either take the bus or be picked up by parents waiting in the "car line." At a school in Tennessee, one father was arrested for objecting to the rule that forbade parents from walking to pick their kids up rather than waiting in a mile-long car line. Teaching children the building blocks of a healthy lifestyle is impossible when the most basic action associated with their most regular activity, walking to school, is presented as countercultural, dangerous, illegal.

In cities, the problem can be safety as much as access. In neighborhoods haunted by crime and gang violence, students describe tactics like changing their route every day in order to avoid being tracked and attacked by gang members. After closing and consolidating many of its city's schools, Chicago expanded a program called Safe Passage, which was aimed at protecting students walking dangerous routes to schools that were now farther away. Instead of having neighborhood schools that they could walk to easily, students were faced with crossing gang territory to get to their new school. Some have lauded Safe

Passage's success by pointing at decreased crime rates, but others have called it a "visual Band-Aid." One Chicago political official said that parents should be able "to hire a driver, use public transit or put their children on a school bus rather than worry about rape, gunfire, fistfights or a long, frigid walk to school." A parent who began driving her four-year-old to preschool said of her three children, "They will ride to school for the rest of their lives, as long as I'm in Chicago," citing gang violence.

And who could argue? When we have neglected our fellow citizens, communities, and cities to such an extent that crime is a defining experience of being outside, the first concern of any parent would be their children's safety. So children learn their first post-toddler lesson about walking: a world navigated on your own two feet is too dangerous to venture into.

Often, sidewalks and crosswalks and parks themselves are narrow or unsafe or in disrepair or simply nonexistent. In Washington, D.C., pediatrician Dr. Robert Zarr launched an initiative called Parks Rx, a program that trains physicians to connect children to nature and aims to prescribe outdoor park time as a treatment for obesity, asthma, and some forms of mental illness. But he also found himself designing a map of all the city's parks, searchable by zip code, because his patients had very little natural access to walking. For his prescriptions to work, he had to come up with ways for his patients to hop off at a park on their way to or from school.

In Denver, city councilman Paul Kashmann was greeted during his election campaign by a young mother who hauled him off to show the lack of walkability near the district school. Some streets had no sidewalks; others had what he calls "Hollywood sidewalks," strips of concrete rolling immediately up from busy roads and not even wide enough for a parent and child to walk side by side, impossible for walking aids or wheelchairs. There are hundreds of blocks of these sidewalks all over Denver. Despite being an extremely walkable city by American standards, only the city's better-off neighborhoods are truly safe for children, attractive for families, and accessible for users with certain disabilities.*

And then there's race. We can tell people to walk for their health: Just thirty minutes a day! It makes all the difference! Walk to the store, walk to work, walk to school. Choose walking over driving; you'll feel so much better! Get your children out walking! Such an easy way to claw back your health and mobility. But that advice, while perfect for many, is hard to swallow when one remembers that Trayvon Martin, a seventeen-year-old Black kid, was doing just that: walking back to his father's home from a store when he was attacked and killed by George Zimmerman, who found his strolling presence threatening in their gated community.

"I've been a black man in America for a long time," wrote writer and tech founder Carvell Wallace in the *Huffington Post*. His essay, "How to Parent on a Night Like This," is about taking care of his daughter and eleven-year-old son while watching the announcement that a grand jury had not indicted Darren Wilson, the police officer who shot and killed Michael Brown in Ferguson, Missouri. Wallace wrote about sending his children to the corner store and wondering "if they'll be attacked walking down the street," a line that tears my heart open as I think about my own children, so very pale-skinned, and the future they have the luxury of expecting by comparison.

---

*After extensive searching online, I returned to Kashmann to ask where the term "Hollywood sidewalk" came from, but he didn't know. Nor did anyone I could find in Denver's public works or transportation departments. An employee in the street maintenance department called back after searching herself and said nobody she asked knew where it came from either, but that it's slang for what's called a "mountable curb." The sidewalks are very real, but the description seems to have introduced itself to the city via wormhole, or perhaps someone dreamed of it. In any case, a "Hollywood curb" or sidewalk is defined in the 2004 City and County of Denver Pedestrian Master Plan as "an attached sidewalk no more than 3 feet in width, with a rolling, not vertical curb."

THESE LIMITATIONS AREN'T just about high-profile cases. The case of Hope Wabuke's elderly father being held up in front of his own home is one of hundreds of situations in which a Black man walking is treated with suspicion. The case of the sixteen-year-old Stockton, California, boy who was accused of jaywalking after having just stepped off the bus is another. Another Black man, this time in Sacramento, was thrown to the pavement and punched eighteen times after being accused of jaywalking, although the police dashcam video showed that he'd actually been crossing the street legally. Nandi Cain, the victim in that case, told a *Sacramento Bee* reporter that he still had nightmares about his arrest, which was done, he said, "for nothing." He told the *Bee*, "I could have kids someday. They could be walking down the street and this could happen to them."

"Walking While Black" is the title of an essay by Garnette Cadogan, one of America's premier literary writers on walking, whose intimacy with the subject began during long walks in his native Jamaica. In Kingston, Cadogan was simply a boy, and then a man, walking. He was like everybody else. In America, he had to learn to rein in his body, to pay careful attention to his surroundings in the same way we do when we're first learning to walk, to diminish his stature and steps in public. In America, he had to unlearn the freedom of walking that should be the right of all. "As a black adult," he wrote, "I am often returned to that moment in childhood when I'm just learning to walk. I am once again on high alert, vigilant. . . . Much of my walking is as my friend Rebecca once described it: A pantomime undertaken to avoid the choreography of criminality."

When I consider the span of humanoid history, millions of years when the planet, our world, was open to our feet, our eyes, our limbs, and our lungs, I can't imagine a condition that feels less like freedom than the one so many of us currently face.

THE PROBLEM GOES beyond the issues of infrastructure, race, gender, and sex to infect the fiber of every private life. The ubiquitous nature of cars and traffic has left us in a situation in which, even where walking is both possible and acceptable, we might be with every step, every indrawn breath, inhaling toxins at high enough levels to be carcinogenic, affecting the health of our lungs, our hearts, and even our brains. Pollution from automobile exhaust goes hand in hand with our industrial reality, and only recently have scientists begun to pin down the long-lasting effects these emissions have on our individual health.

The higher the volume of car traffic we walk near, the higher the concentration of seriously harmful particulates we're exposed to. Los Angeles's air was for decades just about the dirtiest in the country, until cleaner air standards began to break the dual grip of industry and traffic. But geology and geography can make even smaller cities near toxic. In Salt Lake City, doctors have advised women wishing to get pregnant to leave the area for cleaner air. Despite its popular image of clear skies over snow-capped mountain peaks, the city frequently ranks as one of the most polluted in the country due to heavy traffic and industrial activity. Its frequent smog has been linked to preeclampsia, stillbirth, birth defects, and several other pregnancy-related complications, including lower rates of fertility in men.

Salt Lake's famous inversion layer—a weather system in which air pressure traps colder air closer to the ground, keeping pollutants from dissipating—plays a large role in dangerous wintertime particulate levels, but the fact remains that the pollutants have to be there in the first place. Missoula, Montana, is another even smaller city held hostage by its inversion layer for air quality, which improved somewhat when the nearby pulp mill closed its bleaching plant. The inversions aren't going away, though, and traffic is still a main factor in the cities' pollution.

This problem isn't a uniquely American one. A 2016 report from UNICEF stated that around three hundred million children worldwide are breathing "highly toxic air," in places where air pollution "exceeds international guidelines by at least six times." Since children's lungs are still growing, being raised in a polluted environment can permanently reduce lung capacity by 20 percent. "Traffic pollution stops children's lungs growing properly," respiratory toxicologist Ian Mudway, of King's College London, told *The Telegraph* in response to a separate study finding that eight- and nine-year-olds living in cities with "high levels of fumes from diesel cars" have 10 percent less lung capacity than normal. Children are affected even in utero: a 2016 study found that fine particulate matter, of the kind produced by both factories and traffic, is causing nearly sixteen thousand premature births in the United States every year.

Pollution from traffic damages children down to the level of their DNA. A 2017 study looked at the relationship between a type of hydrocarbon specifically emitted by motor vehicle exhaust and the shortening of telomeres in children. Telomeres protect the ends of chromosomes as cells divide throughout a person's life, and are particularly vulnerable to oxidative stress from free radicals and peroxides. As we age, telomeres take a lot of abuse and become shorter—this process takes either a lot of time or a lot of damage. It's not, to put it mildly, something that's meant to happen in children. Yet children all over the world are exposed daily to the kind of hydrocarbon exhaust that will cause it. Add to telomere shortening the significant impacts on cognitive development for children who attend schools exposed to high levels of traffic pollution, according to a study in Barcelona, Spain. Working memory and attention, as well as executive function, were all measurably decreased for children going to school near high-traffic areas. In direct language rarely seen in published scientific studies, the writers found that the association between air pollution and cognitive development "was strong."

Toxic air pollution nanoparticles have been found in human brains in quantities described as "abundant" in a depressing study that examined the brains of people in Mexico and in Manchester in the UK. The magnetite particles found in people's brains—"millions per gram of freeze-dried brain tissue," said one of the study's authors—are extremely toxic to the human brain and have been linked to Alzheimer's disease. The type of magnetite particles found in the study came specifically from industry, power stations, and car exhaust. The study also found platinum, cobalt, and nickel, indications that the heavy metal particles came from a catalytic convertor. Another study, this one published in 2015 in the medical journal *Stroke*, found that adults living near busy roads had increased risk of dementia, and were nearly 50 percent more likely to suffer from—as the journal's title would indicate—stroke. Even small increases in air pollution, the study found, were enough to increase the risk.

Air pollution has even been tentatively linked to obesity itself, in addition to reduced lung capacity, asthma, dementia, and Alzheimer's. The human body simply did not evolve to absorb these types of toxins, and we've gotten to the point at which the popular blog *Lifehacker* posted a helpful guide titled "How to Protect Your Lungs in a Smoggy City." The top recommendation? "Avoid walking or cycling on busy streets." The last point advises readers to exercise in a gym with air conditioning instead of outside.

As we drive—and I say "we" because I drive plenty, too—we create an increasingly hazardous world for anyone who wants to walk, who needs to walk, whose freedom is dependent on maneuvering in the wide, riotous world. Those who cannot afford a car, those whose health or impairment doesn't allow them to drive, those who walk for the sheer joy and pleasure of it, children who long to roam, are all placed at risk. We create a world not only dangerous to our soft human bodies but toxic to our lungs, hazardous to our brains. With every mile we drive, every gallon of gas we burn, we create a world where human beings find it difficult to move around without harm.

After reading this depressing litany, you might be stuck in a quandary. Sitting too much damages your health; driving too much damages your *and* others' health. But walking outside might poison your children and hasten the onset of dementia.

Shouldn't we just give up now? Stockpile HEPA filters and lock ourselves away until someone fixes all these problems?

Tempting. But access to walking isn't just about our health. It's like the earth's fragile, fruitful crust: It holds us together. It allows ideas to flourish and societies to form. The more we bind and smother our world in pursuit of a car-centric culture, the deeper the crevasses will be between our understanding of one another and our knowledge of ourselves.

BRANDON HIDAKA, A medical doctor and PhD, sought to address in his research the dual questions of whether depression in modern societies is, in fact, increasing, as has been speculated, and whether modern life itself might be contributing significantly to its growth. In reviewing decades of published research, he found not only that depression is more common than it used to be (and, sadly, happening earlier and lasting longer than in previous generations), but that it's impossible to ignore depression's entanglement with the knotty web of modern lifestyles. Poor diets, lack of exercise, and decreased exposure to sunlight (the human body makes vitamin D from sunlight, and our sedentary, indoor and in-car lifestyles mean most of us are deficient in this vital nutrient) all contribute. But, importantly, so does the state of our social lives and relationships. "A toxic social environment," wrote Hidaka, "characterized by increasing competition, inequality, and social isolation may also contribute" to depression.

Hidaka's work complements that of John Cacioppo, the cognitive neuroscientist who wrote *Loneliness*, and other research cataloguing the decline of social capital in American society. Urban affairs analyst and senior fellow at the Manhattan Institute Aaron M. Renn wrote of the decline in social capital in Rust Belt communities and its link to widespread despair: "When you have an iPhone but your community is disintegrating socially, it's not hard to see why people think things have taken a turn for the worse." Economic challenges do need to be addressed, wrote Renn, but the real problems are bigger than that.

In a study of overdose patients in McKeesport, Pennsylvania, Katherine McLean, a sociologist at Pennsylvania State University, uncovered a similar theme. Her interview subjects repeatedly referred to erosion of social capital as a factor in their community's problems, though they didn't use that term. "Hopelessness" was pointed to as a cause of heroin use, and McLean found that social isolation went hand in hand with poverty. While a steel mill's closure translated into lack of jobs for McKeesport, overdose patients also pointed out the lack of social activities, effective government, and just plain people. "There is no sense of community here," one of her interview subjects said. "Not one. Not one iota of community here. Not one." Change, said the woman, couldn't be achieved through individual education or treatment, only through community.

THERE IS MORE to the ecosystem of human health than the state of our hearts, lungs, muscles, and body mass index. *Who we are* and *how we feel* have as much impact on our health as whether or not we make it to the gym three times a week and chew our way through an allotment of kale. Depression, anxiety, chronic stress, and other states of the mind catalogued under the term "mental illness" also have, as research increasingly shows, effects on our physical health.

Over and above all of these states rests a fact not just of modern life, but of the state of human existence: we are alone. The endpoint of our lives terrifies many of us with the knowledge that we face it alone.

One might have faith in a god, but at that final threshold no other human being can take our hands and face it with us.

This aloneness haunts us throughout our lives. We wish to be understood, to be *known* by another human being, to connect and connect and connect with others in an unceasing effort to assure ourselves that we are not, in fact, alone. We have friends, we have family, we have coworkers and neighbors, doctors and priests, customers, patients, teachers, students, pets, acquaintances, enemies. People and nonhuman animals who care about us, notice us, know us. And today, we have Alexa, Google Home, thousands of followers, "friends," and colleagues spread over vast distances but reachable with an immediacy that would have staggered past generations. The Internet has connected us so intensively and so well that even I, who was in my mid-twenties before I had a reliable email address and Internet connection, have trouble remembering what it was like back in my childhood, when I walked or rode my bike across town to see if a friend wanted to play. Then, my family's only contact with our overseas relatives was an expensive international call with lots of static about once every three years from a neighbor's kitchen phone; today, my children Skype and FaceTime with our relatives in Russia and their grandmother in England at a moment's notice.

All this overflow of connectivity, and yet we are so, so lonely. Health officials in America, Canada, and Europe have labeled loneliness an epidemic. It crawls through our daily lives leaving a numbness that feels like depression, a disconnection from reality, a hopelessness that requires a human touch, a human voice, a friendly, caring human face, to lift. How is it possible, in the midst of all our connections, that we are lonelier than ever?

Years ago, in the 1940s, long before the Internet and World Wide Web were built, psychoanalyst René Spitz studied the development of infants in two different settings: one group was being raised in an orphanage, where they received adequate food, shelter, and education but almost no attention of the kind they'd get from an attentive parent.

The others were being raised in a prison nursery, where their incarcerated mothers were allowed to hold, nurse, and nurture them. By the age of one, the cognitive differences between the two groups were surprisingly measurable. The babies in the orphanage, who were technically considered better cared for due to the aforementioned food, shelter, and so on, had fallen behind the babies living in incarceration but with access to the touch and attention and love that all babies crave.

More stringently designed studies have taken place since Spitz's, leading essentially to the same conclusion: babies need contact, affection, and care right from the get-go. A comprehensive review of this field of study—known as attachment research—in a 1998 *New York Times* article shows how detrimental the lack of early affection and contact can be. "The damage caused by early neglect—or even by physically adequate but emotionally indifferent care," wrote Margaret Talbot, "can be deeply intractable, not least because it may have neurological as well as psychological dimensions." Emotional and social development in these children is hampered, as is cognition in areas like language development and visual and sensory processing. Babies need connection. All humans do. This is an essential feature of our lives that we neglect to our detriment.

While an adult human doesn't require the care, feeding, and holding that an infant needs, he still requires connection, a sense of belonging, of being part of a community, and of being understood. Being completely unseen would, for most of us, be a nightmare. Even low levels of being ignored leave us fidgety and worried. How many times do you check your phone to see if someone's responded to your text messages or liked your post on Instagram? How many writers do I know who tie themselves into anxious knots waiting for an editor's reply to a pitch or a draft? Why does being electronically ghosted leave us with such a cold pit in our stomachs?

"We are hardwired to connect with others," wrote sociology researcher Dr. Brené Brown in her book *Daring Greatly*. "It's what gives purpose and meaning to our lives, and without it there is suffering." In her 2010 TEDxHouston talk, one of the most-watched talks in TED history, she said that after being a social worker for ten years, "what you realize is that connection is why we're here." Shame, she says, is a fear of disconnection. It's the conviction that we're fundamentally unlovable.

In one of its more chilling episodes, Netflix's *Twilight Zone*–style TV show *Black Mirror* brings our fear of loneliness and disconnection out into the light. The fourth episode of Season 2, titled "White Christmas," depicts a reality in which people have the ability to block one another in real life, just as we can do on Twitter or Facebook. Pick up your quarter-sized device, scroll your thumb past music and photo options, click once, and the person you're looking at turns into a human-shaped image of static with distorted noises instead of a voice. Like hanging up on someone, except with a more satisfying possibility of permanence. And, like being hung up on, maddening in its ability to make a person feel erased. *Black Mirror* ratchets up the horrifying potential of this technology when one of the main characters in the episode finds himself blocked by every single other person on the planet. He is allowed to be in the world, but never part of it. Never to speak with or touch another human, never to feel the warmth of a smile or a loving hand, never to pass easy conversation with a stranger over morning coffee, never even to argue heatedly about politics with someone. Nothing.

The way we have arranged our infrastructure over the last century gives us a semblance of this reality without our having to take personal responsibility for the choice of blocking others. Far too many of us live in houses severed from our nearest neighbors; we travel to and from work, school, and shops in cars where our only human contact might be in the half-minute at a drive-through window when a server takes our money and hands out an order. This fact of modern life takes on a dark shade when we relate it to the decline of social capital as well as social isolation: "Every ten minutes of commuting," wrote Harvard professor Robert Putnam in his best-selling book *Bowling Alone*, "reduces social capital by ten percent." Maybe the reason we're so prone to the dangerous activities of talking on the phone or texting while driving is because we're so damn lonely, bored by paying attention to traffic and desperate for connection to other people.

When we deny ourselves, or are denied, connection through the simple act of living in places with easy access to normal, everyday interactions—walkable, strollable, rollable communities—we're starving ourselves of the fodder necessary to fulfill a hardwired neurological requirement. Is it possible that our turning toward rage-filled, fear-feeding echo chambers of news and politics, as well as addictive and destructive drugs, is an anemic, desperate attempt to fill this need? We sense that something is wrong in our lives, in our towns and society, and when we *do* manage to turn away from self-destructive despair, it's far too tempting to accept the easiest answers, the ones that humans have turned to throughout history: scapegoats, marginalized people, "others."

LONELINESS IS A concept that's easy to grasp but difficult to quantify, a situation that some researchers are working to change, particularly since, in the UK and the United States, about one-third of people older than sixty-five live alone. Half of those over eighty-five in the United States live alone. Researchers have found that older adults who are socially isolated have suppressed immune systems and higher rates of inflammation, leaving them more vulnerable to viral infections and dementia; other studies in the UK found that chronic loneliness increases a person's risk of stroke or heart disease by 30 percent. The health impacts are so severe, in fact, that the researchers recommended the British government treat loneliness as a public health problem as important as smoking and dietary changes.

On the other end of the age spectrum, professor of psychology Jean Twenge has spent twenty-five years studying generational patterns, and found that the ever-connected, social media–savvy generation she calls iGen (born from 1995 to 2012) are unhappier and more depressed than any other generation she's studied. They're on the verge, she wrote in *The Atlantic*, of a mental health crisis, and it might be because they rarely go out and socialize with their friends in any kind of real-life setting. Instead of getting jobs and drivers licenses, "They are on their phone, in their room, alone and often distressed."

Data from the National Institute on Drug Abuse, which has studied thousands of teenagers every year since 1975, found that, without exception, teens who spent more time on screens were unhappier than teens who spent more time on nonscreen activities. "There's not a single exception," wrote Twenge. "All screen activities are linked to less happiness, and all nonscreen activities are linked to more happiness. . . . Teens who visit social-networking sites every day but see their friends in person less frequently are the most likely to agree with the statements 'A lot of times I feel lonely,' 'I often feel left out of things,' and 'I often wish I had more good friends.' Teens' feelings of loneliness spiked in 2013 and have remained high since."

Social media scholar danah boyd, who specializes in studying how young people use technology (and who spells her name in all lowercase letters), said that adults tend to misunderstand modern teens' tendencies to spend hours on their screens. The young people she interviews, she said, would jump at the chance to hang out with their friends in person. They'd love to go outside, play, meet their friends at impromptu times and impromptu places. Adults she spoke with, with a "kids these days" perspective, would wonder why they didn't get off their screens and go outside. "When I would talk to teenagers," boyd said, "they would look at me and be like, 'I would *love* to have the freedom to just go out and play with all my friends. But I can't." She points to changes in American society over the last thirty years that have kept kids increasingly indoors and dependent on their parents' time and ability to drive them around, from fearmongering about stranger danger to slews of curfew and anti-loitering and anti-trespassing laws, to a changed perception of public spaces like parks being unsafe places for kids to hang out.

Fearmongering and curfew laws contribute to parents' restrictions on kids' mobility, but even more effective are far-flung, unwalkable suburbs separated by miles of impenetrable highway. You can't ride your bike to go play with your friends if your only way of getting to their houses is via a four-lane, sixty-five mile-per-hour freeway that's divided and bordered by concrete barriers. You're dependent on your parents' time and willingness to drive you to a playdate.

Kids are isolated from one another by design, not necessarily because they want to spend all their time interacting with people through screens. When they are able to spend time in person, those screens can become yet another dimension of play and communication—I'm sure I'm not the only parent who's watched her children playing Minecraft in their friends' worlds on separate iPads, leaning so close their heads are almost touching, laughing and building treehouses and farms and fighting off creepers.

John Cacioppo, who had studied the subject for over twenty years before publishing his book *Loneliness*, found that chronic loneliness increases a person's risk of early death by 20 percent, about the same as obesity, with the sobering addition that "obesity does not make you as miserable as loneliness." It weakens a person's immune system and reduces the quality of his sleep. Short-term loneliness, Cacioppo has said, can be beneficial because it reminds us of our evolutionary need for social connection, but chronic, long-term loneliness is detrimental both to our social lives and to our health, a condition that has been studied in soldiers, "one of the most chronically lonely groups of people."

Dealing with loneliness isn't just about being around more people; it is, as Brené Brown has repeatedly pointed out, about feeling connected to them. It's being seen and seeing, being known and knowing. Online connection often fails to serve teens and adults because, online, we curate our lives. We shape "selves" that present only a part of our personalities, our accomplishments, and our failings. We compare our true, imperfect selves to the selves likewise shaped and curated by others and, inevitably, find ourselves wanting.

That does not mean that social media is universally isolating, only that our in-person connections to one another are far more complex and supportive than the Internet has so far been able to emulate. Sometimes social media seems to be forcing us into a false dichotomy in which on the one hand we dwell in thriving physical communities but live as technophobes, or on the other hand we dwell in isolated cities and crumbling suburbs connected only by the World Wide Web. There is no reason why our online lives can't be used as a tool to enrich our restored communities, no reason why we can't recover from the flu with some good friends bringing us soup and others bolstering our spirits through Instagram.

Maria Popova, the creator and curator of the popular website Brain Pickings, wrote in a review of Olivia Laing's *The Lonely City* that, in loneliness, "one's inner scream becomes deafening, deadening, severing any thread of connection to other lives." Laing, recovering from heartbreak in New York, a city foreign to her, wandered by foot throughout the city and intellectually among the painful histories of artists like Andy Warhol. In her explorations, she found that personal loneliness has a complementary relationship with the loneliness brought on by political or social isolation, an idea that is woven obliquely throughout the book, and which she addresses directly at the end: "Loneliness is personal," she wrote, "and it is also political." Every social or political force that seeks to divide us from fellow human beings, to create an "other" to blame for society's ills, is seeking to make people feel isolated, and lonely, and powerless.

Growing up in the Soviet Union, my father was intimately acquainted with this powerlessness. "I remember," he told me as we walked around his small Montana town together one summer, picking chokecherries in the park, "after Stalin started going after 'enemies of the people,' how fast trust was lost, even in families. Wives against husbands, children against parents." Trust was a precious, almost unknown commodity in the Soviet Union. People were persecuted for practicing Russian Orthodoxy, for being of Jewish descent, for being a doctor or a poet, for being in the wrong place at the wrong time, for having a job that someone else wanted. You kept your thoughts and ideas to yourself, or you ended up in the gulag. Denunciations from friends or colleagues or family members came thick, smothering and choking normal human relations like an invasive weed.

My father was raised in this atmosphere, but in a family that valued honesty above all else. He was lucky. He was free in one of the only ways possible in the country of his childhood, able to indulge in freedom of speech and thought in the confines of his family's apartment in Leningrad, and free to roam his city with friends he could trust.

WALKING ISN'T JUST, I wrote in the introduction, about moving from one place to another. It's a manifestation of being as fully present in the world as is possible for each individual. To breathe the air, to walk without fear, to fully inhabit these miraculous bipedal bodies, to feel connected to one another, to remind ourselves that we may be solitary, but that doesn't mean we have to be lonely. Maybe it's time we pause, look back, make that U-turn in the route of our technological progress, shift our feet to rediscover the paths we've forgotten how to walk.

FIVE
QUEST

> In the temples once we were blessed for our "coming in and going forth." The blessing took into account the human as a moving being, a soul with feet, a physical being in the midst of a physical world made to walk in, as Adam and Eve walked in Eden. . . . And that garden was created, you will remember, by a walking God. That image says, there is walking in Paradise; it also says, there is Paradise in walking.
>
> —JAMES HILLMAN

DURING LONG HOURS OF MEDITATION, ZEN BUDDHIST MONKS will rise to their feet, go outside, and walk slowly, extremely slowly, a meditative practice called *kinhin* enacted through their footsteps. Walking meditation is, like all meditation, a practice of being present. Of deliberateness. Of being here, now, where you are and when you are. *Kinhin* adds the extra element of being aware of the body's movement. You're not going anywhere; you're not in a hurry; you don't have a goal or an aim in mind. Your awareness is on the press of each footfall, the slight swing of the arms. As you breathe in, and out, with the lift of the foot, the balance, and the planting down again—walking really is a glorious act—you notice other motions, like the way our shoulders shift and swing with each step forward, a metronomic inheritance of human evolution.

❧

We walk when our hearts burn, when our minds are jumbled, when the pain of loss becomes a raging, inescapable force in our own bodies. Historically, we have walked to find physical healing when nothing else could cure us, and we have walked to confront our deeper internal questions, the chaotic "why?" that is the unceasing, never-answered cry of what it means to be a human being. Why are we here? Why do we suffer? Why do we go to such lengths to inflict suffering on ourselves, and on one another? Why do we hate? Why do we love? Why are we so quick to judge, so slow to forgive? Why do we fail, over and over, at being our best selves?

The technological age has distanced us both from our physical selves and from the physicality of the planet, but it hasn't taken away our need for deeper meaning, felt most acutely in times of grief, heartbreak, or a spiritual crisis. Neither material goods nor a blockbuster Hulu original series nor an engaging Twitter account is enough when we face the reality of our own mortality. We cannot escape the knowledge that we die, that our most beloved relatives and friends die, that relationships end and landscapes we love will inevitably change. We protect ourselves from these realities with the chimes and beeps and pings and harried hurry of our overscheduled lives. But they don't go away, no matter how busy we are.

The deeper we bury our fears under the dings and distractions, the further we distance ourselves from the connection that's defined our evolutionary path to being *Homo sapiens*: that link between ourselves and the delicate ecosystem that makes our existence possible. Walking for spiritual enlightenment or in emotional distress forces us to reengage with the physical world. We have to step in dirt, duck under trees, walk under the sun and through the rain. We have to think about our bodies, how our backs are feeling, whether our feet ache, how hot we are, how cold, how tired. And to marvel at what we are capable of when tested. Walking forces us squarely back into the knowledge that the conveniences of air conditioning, central heating, insulated walls, and chairs have cut us off from the physical reality of life. We have to acknowledge the gravel and tree roots and trash underfoot, smell the apple blossoms and car exhaust, hear the birds and the noise of traffic. We have to remember that we are mammals of the genus *Homo*, and our neglected bodies are capable of more than we can imagine.

The most compelling—and probably least known—pilgrimages face the realities of loss and mortality by directly engaging this physical reality. Most of us are aware of brief annual walks in support of breast cancer or diabetes or multiple sclerosis research—Stop Diabetes, say, or Making Strides Against Breast Cancer—and many of us know of popular religious pilgrimages like the Camino de Santiago in Spain and France, or France's healing grotto at Lourdes. But very few know about events like the annual two-hundred-mile Sand Creek Massacre Spiritual Healing Run/Walk that begins at the Sand Creek Massacre National Historic Site near Eads, Colorado, and ends in Denver. The run/walk was first organized by the Cheyenne and Arapaho nations in Montana, Wyoming, and Oklahoma to keep alive the memory of the Sand Creek Massacre: on November 29, 1864, nearly two hundred Arapaho and Cheyenne people were murdered in an unprovoked attack by the US Calvary under the command of Colonel John Chivington. The Healing Run/Walk takes place on this same territory, the stretched-out plains of Colorado that once rolled under native grasses and the thunder of buffalo herds, now throttled with highways and tumbleweed caught in barbed-wire fences.

While for many Americans Sand Creek is a barely remembered paragraph in high school history textbooks, the century-and-a-half-old atrocity is very much alive for people of the Cheyenne and Arapaho nations. "Sand Creek is a place history has tried to forget," tribal leaders said in *Sand Creek Massacre Spiritual Healing Run/Walk*, a documentary created about the run; it's been subsumed under the stories of hardy white settlers venturing into the West in search of land and gold.

To keep it from being erased from history, and to heal the intergenerational wounds left by the massacre, every November members of the Cheyenne and Arapaho tribes gather to walk or run through the memories and pain of Sand Creek, moving through snow and freezing rains, the strong plains winds whipping around them, carrying an eagle staff as they go. "The purpose is healing—spiritual, emotional healing," tribal elder Otto Braided Hair said of the walk. The documentary describes the Healing Run/Walk not as a race but as a commemoration for the victims and survivors of the massacre, and for healing of the homeland. It is, in the words of those who participate in it, a prayer.

In western Montana, the Confederated Salish and Kootenai Tribes have followed in the Cheyenne and Arapaho's footsteps, so to speak. Honoring the memory not of a massacre but of loss nearly as raw, in 2016 they walked fifty-one miles from the current tribal reservation in the mountain-ringed Flathead Valley, over the hilly borders of the National Bison Range, to their ancestral homeland in the Bitterroot Valley.

The walk took place on the hundred and twenty-fifth anniversary of the tribe's expulsion from the Bitterroot. In a story of betrayal and injustice that is all too familiar, the Bitterroot Salish, Pend d'Oreille, and Kootenai tribes had signed the poorly translated Hellgate Treaty of 1855 without realizing that it would require them to leave their homeland; they agreed to relocate only after they had been nearly starved out and a railroad had been built through their territory without their permission and with no compensation.

The federal government promised to allocate funds for the move in 1887, but the money never appeared—two years later tribal members had to sell most of their possessions to buy even basic supplies for the journey and for lives now severed from the lands of their ancestors.

According to stories passed down by tribal elders, people were threatened during the removal walk if they stopped to relieve themselves, and shot if they tried to run away.

Pilgrimages like the Confederated Salish and Kootenai tribe's 2016 walk take place not in search of joy, but, like the Sand Creek Massacre Spiritual Healing Run/Walk, to help close very old wounds. "It was not a celebration," Chaney Bell, a Salish–Pend d'Oreille Culture Committee member, told the local newspaper. "It was not a protest. It was a time for our people to remember." Tribal member Myrna Adams Dumontier said that she wanted her children and grandchildren to experience what their ancestors had gone through by "walking the distance" and called the walk emotional. "It's all in our hearts—to find healing," she said.

To walk the hills that their people had lived in for tens of thousands of years, to speak with the rocks and soil and wind that their ancestors remained part of, has a power that those of us with weaker connections to the land have rarely understood. But we can begin to learn from the earthbound intention of these walks. Our faith can deepen, our mourning and yearnings take meaning. We can repair the ruptures of our hearts, and at the same time repair the breach between ourselves and our environments, to expose as false the belief that what takes place within the confines of our own skin has nothing to do with the world outside us.

KATHERINE DAVIES, A fifty-two-year-old mother of two and a former journalist, sat in a London café one sunny winter day in 2015, reading a harshly critical *New York Times* opinion piece about the recalcitrant, ongoing Syrian peace process taking place under the auspices of the UN in Geneva.

By that time the Syrian war had been raging for five years, and while peace remained elusive, the fates of those driven out of their homes by bombing and chemical attacks were becoming ever more dire. People who had a short time ago been going to work and making dinner and kissing their children goodnight found themselves running from those homes, those jobs, those dinner tables, carrying their children but almost no possessions. They had become homeless and borderless; the only international law that mattered was how far their feet could carry them. They had become refugees.

"I wanted to walk right out of that café, out of that life," Davies told me, her Australian accent still strong after half a lifetime in England.

At the time the impulse to walk out of the café hit her, Davies was running a nonprofit called iguacu, which she'd launched two years previously. Iguacu took her particular background and expertise as an Australian parliamentary researcher and newspaper journalist to help donors focus their efforts during humanitarian crises.

Iguacu had already been active on several fronts in Syria to raise international awareness about the growing refugee crisis. "It's so severe," the organization's Syria-based contacts said, that what was most important was to keep putting Syria "in front of people." But the humanitarian devastation in the war-torn country had been going on for so long and with such tragic consequences—the refugee crisis has been called the largest since World War II, with millions of people displaced—that Davies suddenly felt compelled to do more.

Most of us know this compulsion. We're watching the news or reading an article about war or an environmental disaster, and the urge to *do* something grabs us. We want to drive or fly to the flooded city, the tornado-torn county, the village buried under a mudslide, the border camp of hungry, war-shattered refugees. We want to help, yet expressions of sympathy and monetary donations sent via text message are unsatisfying. It's as if embedded in our DNA is a conviction that our bodies can be a vehicle for changing the world. On first impulse we stand up, walk, pace. And then, most likely, we sit down again and Google something.

That day, her extensive nonprofit work wasn't enough for Katherine Davies. Her body called on her to walk. "I had this nice life in a nice part of London," she said, "and I was in this nice café, and literally, I wanted to walk right out of there, away from it all."

Instead, she took an idea to her colleagues at iguacu: what if she walked from London to Geneva (where Staffan De Mistura, the UN special envoy to Syria, was based) to raise awareness about the humanitarian crisis of Syrian refugees? She didn't want the journey to become about her, or to turn into a mass walk, so one of her colleagues suggested collecting messages for peace in Syria along the way. After that, they began planning and building a website.

As a mother of two and the leader of a nonprofit organization, Davies knew she couldn't just step onto the road. Besides, walking twenty miles a day wasn't something she could launch into without physical training. "I wasn't particularly fit," she said. So even before she sat down with her colleagues, she turned to Google, curious about the logistics of the type of walk she was contemplating. The Internet, as it tends to do, came through with a wealth of information. "You ask a search engine what it would take to walk daily for six hundred miles, and detailed plans and advice pop up, down to what kind of socks to wear."

Two months later, she had launched a website where people worldwide could send in messages supporting peace, honed her ideas and aims so her mission was clear to the world, and trained her body as best she could. She was ready to go.

Then, a week before she was scheduled to leave, Davies was hit by a cyclist while walking through London's Battersea Park.

THE ORIGINAL PEACE Pilgrim was a woman named Mildred Lisette Norman. Born in 1908, she walked the United States for twenty-eight years, vowing to "remain a wanderer until mankind has learned the way of peace." In her nearly three-decade-long pilgrimage, Peace Pilgrim walked over twenty-five thousand miles, eventually stopping her journey in order to begin giving talks and presentations about her mission to accomplish world peace through walking. She died in 1981 in a car crash while being driven to a speaking engagement, the worst kind of ironic tragedy.

John Francis, nicknamed "Planetwalker," gave up all forms of motorized transportation in 1972 after struggling to save birds soaked in the half a million gallons of oil spilled when two tankers collided beneath San Francisco's Golden Gate Bridge. He took a vow of silence and crisscrossed the United States on foot for seventeen years. When he eventually began talking and teaching again, he said that his experience walking the country as an African American man led him to view environmental destruction—how we treat the planet—as being intimately connected to how we treat one another.

In 2010, a young man named Jonathon Stalls began his own walks across the expanses of the United States, searching for an answer to the question of what would happen to human connections and our mutual existence if we tried living at a walking pace of three miles per hour. He calls the experience of walking across the country transformative. In his 2013 TEDx talk he said, of the changes walking had wrought in his life, "It was as if something had awoken from a long sleep."

Sharon Day, a member of the Ojibwe tribe, is the leader of an organization called Mississippi River Water Walk, which in 2013 walked from the headwaters of the Mississippi to the Gulf of Mexico to raise awareness about water pollution and the necessity of clean water. In a traditional Ojibwe water ceremony, the walkers collected a copper pail of river water from the Mississippi's headwaters and carried it over seventeen hundred miles, passing the precious weight among the group's members as they walked. Sixty-four days later they poured the clear water into the heavily polluted Gulf of Mexico.

Sharon Day had walked once before, around Lake Superior, to advance the cause of clean water; she believes that it's necessary to do something every day to honor the water that gives us life, to create a relationship with it. "We want the walk to be a prayer," Day told the *Minnesota Women's Press* before embarking on the Mississippi walk. "Every step we take we will be praying for and thinking of the water."

There was no sponsorship for this walk, or for most other pilgrimages for peace and justice. No shiny T-shirts or finish-line banner with the logos of companies lending their names and a bit of money to the event, no support stands handing out bottles of water, no cheering families by the sides of the roads. But that's not the point of these walks. To raise awareness, to walk for peace, these require deeper commitments, something from the very center of ourselves. Something that says this one person is giving his or her life to this one cause, his or her whole self, even if temporarily. Through that act of faith, they are changed. And through their act, we are all changed.

"Prayers have to be walked, not just talked," Regina Lopez-Whiteskunk, a member of the Ute Mountain Ute tribe and former co-chair for the Bears Ears Inter-Tribal Coalition, once told writer Terry Tempest Williams. "The walk is a prayer," said Sharon Day. This truth echoes through almost every story of spiritual or healing pilgrimage, and with good reason: walking with this kind of deliberation resembles nothing so much as prayer. Deep, soul-searching, heartrending prayer, the kind of prayer that leaks tears and breathes in sobs.

All pilgrimage, for whatever reason, follows in an ancient tradition that has its foundations in religious observance. "Returning to the centre of one's religion or to sites associated with its holy figures," Ian Reader, a professor of religious studies at Lancaster University, wrote in his book *Pilgrimage*, "provides an intensification, reaffirmation, and invigoration of faith." Some of the best-known pilgrimage journeys are hundreds of years old, like the Camino de Santiago, a network of paths that winds hundreds of miles through France and Spain to end at the shrine of St. James the Great. Known as the Way of St. James in English, the Camino de Santiago began in the Middle Ages over an ancient Roman trade route and is imprinted with the footsteps of hundreds of generations of pilgrims.

The annual Islamic pilgrimage to Mecca, called the Hajj, is a required journey for most adult Muslims. The word "hajj" itself is reflective of the pilgrimage tradition. It means "to intend a journey," which encompasses the actual journey itself and a pilgrim's internal commitment. While most people associate the Hajj with the Prophet Muhammad's journey in the seventh century, pilgrimages to Mecca supposedly go back thousands of years, to the time of Abraham in around 2000 BCE. The Hajj is an intricate, several-day pilgrimage, which includes walking seven times, counterclockwise, around the Kaaba (a building at the center of Islam's most sacred mosque, Al-Masjid al-Haram), running back and forth between the hills of Al-Safa and Al-Marwah, and symbolically stoning the devil.

For Buddhists, Hindus, Jains, and Bön, walking to and circling Mount Kailash in Tibet is one of the most physically demanding and spiritually fulfilling pilgrimages imaginable. The mountain has been described as a temple, one of the holiest spots on Earth. It is so revered that it has, according to all known accounts, never been climbed. One circuit around Kailash is said to remove all the bad karma from a pilgrim's current lifetime.

The formal Kailash pilgrimage is called the *kora*, a walk circling the sacred mountain. The *kora* is thirty-two miles long, starting at an elevation of fifteen thousand feet and rising up at one point to over eighteen thousand feet, a path speckled with prayer wheels and heaped with prayer flags and ceremonial scarves. Getting to the starting point involves a two-hundred-mile overland trek from Lhasa across the Tibetan plateau. Most pilgrims take three days to circle the mountain itself, but some Tibetans will commit to walking the entire *kora* in one long fourteen-hour day, and there are many who have made the arduous journey more than once. On the other end of the spectrum, some of the most devout pilgrims stop at each of the four prostration points along the Buddhist route, where a pilgrim will place her palms together in prayer, bring them to her chest, lift them to her forehead, and then bow down to touch her hands and forehead on the pilgrimage path. Some pilgrims prostrate themselves every step of the entire *kora*, a practice that can lengthen the circumambulation to two weeks or more.

Most accounts of the Mount Kailash *kora* speak to the dual nature of pilgrimage: its power to influence us internally as we reconnect to the external and spiritual worlds. "It is an inner journey, not an outer journey," said Samut, a pilgrim from India, in *Nine-Story Mountain*, a documentary film about Mount Kailash. Artist Carol Brighton wrote of her walk that she "wanted the influence to change me, to nick bone deep . . . marking a place in me that is beyond time. Maybe one person's intent on pilgrimage could be of benefit to everyone—to our collective consciousness."

Pilgrimages like Mount Kailash and the Camino de Santiago require a commitment of time and physical energy. But there are others, like the Zen Buddhist *kinhin*, that make up in quiet focus what they lack in days or weeks of walking. Walking meditation and walking a labyrinth—the latter being a largely Christian tradition with ancient roots—both have this intensity of time-short but distilled dedication.

Labyrinths are pilgrimages in miniature. The labyrinth at Chartres Cathedral in France, with its broad, smooth lines tightly wound around in four quadrants, is one of the most-walked and oldest labyrinths in the world. Pilgrims have been walking the forty-two-foot-wide path for at least a thousand years, sometimes on their knees, in hopes of becoming closer to God.

"When you step into the labyrinth," said Episcopal priest the Reverend Lauren Artress, "psyche and spirit come together. It's a place where the boundaries between mind, body, and spirit drop away." Artress's first experience of a labyrinth, at Chartres, was life-changing, leading her to build a replica of the Chartres labyrinth at Grace Cathedral in San Francisco, and to found Veriditas, a worldwide labyrinth advocacy nonprofit. Walking a labyrinth, she wrote in her book *Walking a Sacred Path*, brings people to "realize that they are not human beings on a spiritual path but spiritual beings on a human path."

MODERN ITERATIONS OF what might be called pop-culture pilgrimage seem humdrum when compared to the Mount Kailash circuit or walking the Camino de Santiago, but there remains something in them that connects us to those more ancient and spiritual journeys. A trip to Liverpool to see the homes and early venues of the Beatles. A journey to Elvis's Graceland. The homes of innumerable authors beloved as long as literature has existed. I myself have traveled to Bath in England just to walk the streets of the city that Jane Austen reportedly hated, but that formed the background of some of the most famous scenes in her novels: Anne Elliot's final stroll with Captain Wentworth after the lovers spent eight years nursing misunderstood broken hearts, Catherine Morland's walk out to the countryside to learn an appreciation for both reading and the picturesque in the company of Henry Tilney and his sister Eleanor. I've paced the Spanish Steps in Rome, near where John Keats rattled his last breaths, and wandered the gardens of Newstead Abbey, Lord Byron's ancestral home. I've trodden the beaten, scraggly paths of Peredelkino, the artist's colony outside Moscow where Boris Pasternak walked and talked and contemplated, so many times that it almost feels like a second home. And I've spent much of my life roaming the lanes and bridges of St. Petersburg that fed Fyodor Dostoevsky's ample imagination, seeking something of that Russian fatalism and yearning for truth that come through so clearly in his novels.

THE CAMINO DE Santiago, Mecca, Mount Kailash, Shikoku in Japan, Nidaros Cathedral in Norway, the shrine of Shri Mata Vaishno Devi in India, Nhlangakazi mountain in South Africa, Croagh Patrick in Ireland, England's Canterbury Cathedral—throughout the world, there are more opportunities for pilgrimage than any one person can comprehend, and they all carry psychological weight for those who seek them out and follow them on foot. These spiritual lodestars have called to millions of pilgrims over thousands of years. In kind and longevity, they seem to have little in common with more recent journeys to the former homes of writers, artists, or pop stars, but they all tap into basic emotions that we humans long to express: to honor and to mourn. We honor our gods and our faiths and the artists, writers, leaders, and dissidents who have in some way influenced our lives or worldviews. We mourn the losses of loved ones, our marriages, the ever-present sorrow of the human condition, the saints and spiritual leaders who guide our paths. The ground of pilgrimage trails is hallowed by the feet of those who have gone before.

Walking is what we turn to when we wish to show our devotion to our gods, and how we move when the precariousness of our precious human existence is laid bare. It reopens our relationships with our values, our fears, our purpose. It shows us the path to our own private souls. "The longest journey is the journey inwards," wrote former secretary-general of the United Nations Dag Hammarskjöld in his spiritual diary *Markings*, "of him who has chosen his destiny." We walk to find our prophets, our guides, our ancestors, but ourselves most of all, and through ourselves, we find one another.

IN THE ESSENTIALS, the pilgrimages of ancient peoples were probably little different from the pilgrimages of today. We might fly or drive to a starting point—Pamplona in Spain for the Camino de Santiago; Lhasa or Darchen for the *kora*—but all pilgrimage still begins the same way it did thousands of years ago: with the step of a foot, and then another, and then hundreds, thousands more, on a path that generations have walked before us. Even in our hurried, over-committed, technology-driven modern times, these paths are charged with meaning, and the act of walking them has a power that eludes our understanding.

Take the Nazca Lines in Peru, estimated to be between fifteen hundred and two thousand years old. They wind around one another, creating intricate shapes whose purpose has been a mystery to travelers and anthropologists for over four hundred years. Were these massive tracks in the dust some kind of ancient road? If so, where did it go? Was it related to ritual? To travel? To both? To daily treks to water sources? These are questions that only the lines' long-dead creators could have definitively answered. All we're left with is the mystery.

Many of the Nazca Lines run straight, meeting as if at the point of a triangle. Others are in the shapes of animals and other creatures. A monkey with a curled tail. A spider, a man, a hummingbird. The largest actual figure—of which there are seventy, although there are hundreds more plain straight lines—is over twelve hundred feet across. First mentioned in print by a Spanish conquistador in 1553, the lines weren't seriously studied until the 1940s. And it wasn't until 2015 that archaeologists in Japan concluded that the lines' first purpose was most likely as pilgrimage routes to a pre-Incan temple complex known as Cahuachi.

It's the kind of image that, if you dwell on it long enough, sends shivers up your spine. Picture them: people, for all intents and purposes people just like you and me, *Homo sapiens* with different clothing but the same forward stride and swinging arms, walking a well-known route used for obeisance, worship, ritual, prayer. The import of each footfall far more than a simple step forward. As the ball of the foot presses down and rocks forward from the heel, the pendulum of the hip and knee shift weight to keep the body upright, laden with meaning, not just with movement. The body and mind together directed to a ritual act, walking the paths that honored the spiritual practices of the day, honored the gods.

I TOOK UP walking years ago as an intentional goal when I was stuck in my completely unwalkable upstate New York community and struggling with debilitating chronic pain. At that time, when my children were small and intense and the days felt impossibly long and emotionally charged, I began walking out of the dual desperation of early motherhood and chronic back pain. We walked and looked at red-winged blackbirds swaying on cattails, euphorbia hiding pale green among the field grasses, the goose poop along the driveway. I shifted my feet while watching my toddlers throw pebbles into the tiny stream running through our front field. We couldn't walk far because our semirural road was busy and had no sidewalk, but even that little bit down the driveway and into the field made a difference. We went back in for lunch or naptime or some silly craft project calmer, gentler, quieter.

Slowly, without realizing it, I was developing a habit of walking meditation. Forced to walk at a toddler's pace, and before that with the back-bent waddle imposed by a well-fed infant in an Ergobaby carrier, I got very bored walking. The first iPhone was released the year my first child was born, but I wouldn't own one for several years after that, so I couldn't escape by listening to a podcast or talking on the phone as I walked. There was truly nothing to do but either let my attention wander off to nowhere or land like a moth on the swamp grasses, the cattails, the strong, hairy vines of the ubiquitous poison ivy that seemed to sucker onto every tree in every forest where we lived. I was bored, I was walking, I was bored, I was walking.

I remember the feel of the air during those now long-ago walks and the sound of the wind through tree branches far better than I remember the feel or sound of more recent walks, when I was listening to an audiobook or had just paused to check a text message or was looking for photo opportunities for Instagram. I don't, though, remember what I was thinking about. Which is the point. Meditation is partly about letting go of your thoughts, or letting go of your attachment to them. Inside, with my first infant, and then a toddler and another newborn, my thoughts sometimes drove me wild. I couldn't meditate inside, and with my back pain ever-present, I hated to meditate sitting down at all. But at those inching little paces, my mind finally learned to rest.

MEDITATION IS OFTEN advised, or even prescribed, as a way for us to reduce stress, to stop feeling overwhelmed in our lives, to build more patience and mindfulness into our parenting, to improve health, to help us form good eating habits and strong relationships. Whether it's a cure-all or not, meditation has been shown to be beneficial for many aspects of human life.

But most meditation is performed while sitting. And *sitting* itself is harmful. Not sitting for a few minutes or sitting for the duration of a meal. No, the kind of sitting that damages our health is the kind far too many of us accept as an immutable aspect of our lives. Sitting in a car, often stuck in traffic, to drive to work for an hour, maybe more. And then sitting for hours at a desk, our spines slumped far from the stance of *Homo erectus* as we answer emails, write reports, talk on the phone. Eight hours a day find many of us in this position, maybe more depending on how long your commute is and whether or not you can get yourself to take that lunchtime walk.

The research on sitting's damage is extensive. Dr. James Levine, who was the first to say that "sitting is the new smoking," wrote in *Get Up!* that "for every hour we sit, two hours of our lives walk away." His conclusions, and his book, are based on over three decades of researching sitting's detrimental effects on our health, including circulation, blood pressure, obesity, creativity, clinical depression, stress, and cholesterol levels.

One of Levine's most thought-provoking findings revolves around an uncomplicated emotion we can all relate to: sadness. Sitting too much, Levine wrote, forces the brain to adapt to lack of movement. It—the brain, or the mind, or simply "you"—becomes sluggish and sad, a fascinating and sobering finding when thinking, also, about the necessity of walking and other vestibular movement to stimulate the brains of infants, toddlers, and older children. Because sadness, and its companion depression, leads to anhedonia (a lack of desire to do anything, particularly move or exercise), the brain then adapts to sit more the sadder we get. "The chair," he wrote, "is the inevitable home of the sad. . . . The chair becomes the depressive's sanctuary." A finding echoed (unconsciously, perhaps) in Geoff Nicholson's tongue-in-cheek book *The Lost Art of Walking*. A pervading theme in his book, which covers literature, music, art, and walking's relationship to our human selves, is his own discovery of simple walks around Los Angeles as effective treatment for his depression.

The research speaks volumes: A study in Japan found that the less you walk, the higher your cholesterol levels; another in Sweden found that increased sitting leads to greater risk of heart attacks. Dutch scientists found that sitting too much stiffens arteries, and German researchers concluded that too much sitting softens the human skeleton. Sitting, found one Australian study, "accounted for seven percent of all premature deaths." Even going to the gym regularly can't reverse the detrimental impacts of excessive sitting. Doing thirty, or even sixty, minutes of exercise a day doesn't do enough to counter the other twenty-three or twenty-three and a half hours we spend mostly sitting.

From childhood to adolescence through adulthood and old age, wrote Levine, "movement is not only the essence of life; it is the rhythm that defines our stage of living." Not just our bodies, but our minds, too, evolved to move. We think with our feet; we solve problems through wandering; we walk to come to terms with our depression and our prayers. We walk to remind ourselves that we are free.

SO HERE WAS a question I presented to researcher after researcher: If sitting is so damaging for our bodies, how beneficial is it for your average commuting office worker to come home after a long day and sit for another ten to thirty minutes to clear his mind? Consider Dr. Levine's findings that "the average American sits thirteen hours per day; eighty-six percent of Americans sit all day at work and sixty-eight percent hate it"—and more from Public Health England, which found that sedentary behavior accounts for around 60 percent of British workers' total waking hours, and 70 percent for those at high risk of chronic disease. How does sitting meditation stack up, mental health–wise, against a walk through a park, or along a tree-lined street, or simply downtown or down the road? Assuming said office worker has access to a walkable space for thirty minutes to an hour, wouldn't getting off of his butt for that period of time (leaving the cell phone behind, preferably) and taking a mindful, meditative walk be even more beneficial?

It was strange to discover that nobody, that I could find, has done extensive research on this question.* Walking is beneficial to us. Exercise is beneficial to us. Meditation is beneficial to us. Sitting is bad for us. But the specific question of "Is mindful walking better for someone who sits all day than sitting meditation?" is one that has so far been answered with "That's an interesting question."

It is an interesting question. It seems obvious that sitting meditation would be far better for us than sitting answering mind-numbing emails or making twenty annoying phone calls, but considering the health benefits of bringing walking more fully into our lives, a walking practice like *kinhin* or a medicine walk akin to those practiced in some Native American cultures might heal and enrich our lives in ways that we can't predict.

Could every walk, every pilgrimage, every mindless turning of the foot in response to grief be a kind of walking meditation? Was that not where the Salish and Kootenai tribes ended up when they walked

*The closest I got was cornering Dr. Clifford Saron, a neuroscientist based at the University of California at Davis's Center for Mind and Brain, after a talk he gave called "Minding Mindfulness." He introduced me to the phrase "tuches effect"—physiological changes that come from the practice of sitting meditation. In 2017 *Teen Vogue* published a good overview of a more extreme problem: Dead Butt Syndrome, in which the gluteal muscles simply stop working, usually caused by too much sitting, although even some athletes can suffer from it.

back to the land their ancestors were forced off of? Or Peace Pilgrim as she walked the world yearning for peace? If we walk every day with intention and presence, even for thirty minutes, or ten, are we not, in this kind of walking, treading the paths of our hearts and our souls, all the while healing our minds and bodies?

KATHERINE DAVIES DID not let her bicycle-caused injury delay her walk for peace. But the first part of her journey was difficult. Twenty miles on foot is a grueling regimen. At a normal walking pace of three miles an hour, it's an average of six to ten hours of putting one foot in front of the other. Beyond that, she was in pain from her bicycle crash injury and still taking strong painkillers, dangerous when undertaking a long, physically demanding journey. She lost a toenail. She was frequently on the phone with iguacu staff dealing with work issues. She had to be at Canterbury Cathedral on time for a meeting. Only once the meeting was over and the phone calls had petered out could she let her mind and body more fully drift into the task at hand.

The way she described that first week to me sounded like a river in flood season, scooping away banked earth, washing rocks, leaving a lot of detritus behind. After her meeting at Canterbury Cathedral, Davies's mind began to carve out its own channels. She walked those narrow English lanes with their high field hedges, listening to music, or to an audiobook she'd downloaded about Peace Pilgrim's life, or sometimes just to the silence of the air, processing many things, including the recent deaths of her parents. "Getting to the edge of England, thinking about them, that grieving was a big piece I had to move." The space she was given to truly grieve for her parents was, she said, "magnificent."

These days, to be given time to mourn a loved one, a friend, a parent, a child, a teacher, is almost unheard of. Space for mourning has become a luxury rarer than a day of paid sick leave. How many of us even have the time to attend a funeral, or to sit with a dying loved one? Yet that grief lodges within us and refuses to leave if we don't make the time to look it in the face. To walk through grief undisturbed by a job or a family member's needs or phone calls or the thousand other daily demands for our attention seems like the greatest gift a mourner can receive.

Pilgrimage and walking out personal pain are parallel quests: searching for ourselves, or for spiritual guidance, and our connections to the wider, deeper meanings of human existence. In this way, walking as a spiritual practice reflects its physical place in our evolution. When we walk, we don't just use balance and muscle control to stay upright; we also have to unconsciously account for the fact that we are in motion on a planet that is spinning at a rate of a thousand miles per hour, orbiting the sun. We have to respond to the planet's movement and its considerable gravitational pull on our bodies.

Walking through grief can almost be a metaphor for this motion, although its effects on our psyches are anything but metaphorical. The changes chronicled within themselves by pilgrims over the centuries are both real and profound. Walking for long periods settles the mind, redirects ideas, loosens solidified thought patterns, keeps us from brooding in dark places. We are rebalanced, emerging in a new relationship with gravity and the planet and the whirling intricacies of existence.

These shifts are especially noticeable when we walk in nature. It seems absurd to turn this most human of acts—walking through green spaces like parks or forests, basically what we've been doing for most of our evolution, starting with the forests and savannahs in Africa—into the bland, Byzantine language of a medical study, but it's been done more than once, and the results reinforce what many of us know by instinct. Walking, particularly in nature, decreases rates of depression and anxiety and reduces a tendency to ruminate and obsess over thoughts. Considering these effects, walking's attraction for those in mourning or those simply struggling with mental balance becomes obvious.

The landmark study on nature's effects on our overall health took place in 1984. Using the medical records of people recovering from gallbladder surgery at a Pennsylvania hospital, Roger Ulrich, an environmental psychologist, and a team of colleagues found that patients who were able to see leafy trees through their bedroom windows healed a day faster on average, had fewer complications after surgery, and needed less pain medication than patients who had only a brick wall to look at. Ulrich followed this study with another nine years later, when he found that even pictures of nature scenes reduced stress and the need for painkillers. His work has led to movements in hospitals to design gardens that patients can walk or roll wheelchairs in, with a high proportion of trees and a minimal amount of asphalt and concrete.

More recent studies have found that natural environments improve attention and focus, have measurable cognitive benefits, and have positive impacts on depression, anxiety, dementia, and Alzheimer's. Psychologists at the University of Michigan found that being in nature grabs our attention in a modest, gentle, bottom-up fashion, allowing our brains to relax and replenish themselves.

Walking itself, especially in green spaces, significantly heightens these benefits. Dr. Robert Zarr, the Washington, D.C., pediatrician who launched Parks Rx, came up with his initiative in part in response to startling statistics, like that a short twenty-minute walk in nature helps children with ADD and ADHD concentrate more easily, and that being in nature reduces children's stress levels by 28 percent. Not only that, but a study of over twelve hundred teenagers in Los Angeles found that those who live in areas surrounded by green space were less aggressive than those who live in areas defined by concrete and asphalt, even accounting for socioeconomic factors.

A study out of Scotland backs these findings. Using head-mounted lightweight brain-scanning devices, a combined team of environmental psychologists, health studies researchers, and urban design professionals sent twelve people out to stroll through the streets and hills of

Edinburgh. The busy urban areas, they found, provoked irritation and frustration in the walkers' mental states, while the woods and parks led to brain states that were "calmer and more meditative."

Dr. David Sabgir, a cardiologist in Columbus, Ohio, started inviting patients to go for walks with him in a local park because he was frustrated by an "inability to effect behavior change in a clinical setting." He's now run the Walk with a Doc program since 2005 and has extended it to hundreds of chapters all over the United States. And Scotland's Forestry Commission has been running a program called Branching Out since 2007, which teams up with health care professionals in Glasgow to teach adults with long-term mental health problems bushcraft skills in the woods. At fifty pounds (about sixty-five dollars) per person per day, the program is inexpensive and impressively effective: in the first year 70 percent of those who completed the course reported improvements in both physical and mental health.

Walking and nature, these and many other initiatives and scientific studies now affirm, slide themselves into our minds, easing tension and stress, providing constant but undemanding stimulation, and quietly building the millions of synapses we rely on to keep our brains sharp and alert throughout our lives.

ALL OF THIS, our mental health, our moods, our attention levels, and even our spirituality, also plays a role in one of the least understood and most revered human qualities: creativity.

The wealth of walking literature that rests on my bookshelves revolves largely around the history of walking as a creative practice. From Rebecca Solnit's now-classic *Wanderlust: A History of Walking* to the more recent *A Philosophy of Walking* (Frédéric Gros), *The Lost Art of Walking* (Geoff Nicholson), *Flâneuse: Women Walk the City* (Lauren Elkin), and many more, writers entranced with the subject of walking have brought forth, again and again, the stories of Wordsworth,

Thoreau, Darwin, Goethe, Einstein, Woolf, George Sand, Kant, and so many others—famously creative, often revolutionary, minds, all of whom sought inspiration, solace, ideas, and solutions in daily walks. "All truly great thoughts are conceived by walking," said Friedrich Nietzsche. Philosopher and composer Jean-Jacques Rousseau wrote, "I have never thought so much, existed so much, lived so much . . . as in the journeys which I have made alone and on foot"; he claimed that he couldn't even think properly except when walking. Pyotr Ilyich Tchaikovsky took a forty-five-minute walk every morning before sitting down to work, followed by another after lunch, stopping frequently to write down ideas. Ludwig van Beethoven depended on his long walks through the Vienna woods after lunch to keep his creativity loose-limbed.

This dependence on walking to stimulate creativity is alive and well today: Travel writer and essayist Pico Iyer takes two long walks every day around his neighborhood in Kyoto, Japan, and it is during those walks, he says, not during the preceding hours at his desk, that he does his true work. "To reorder the whole tapestry, and see through to the heart of the larger picture," he told me, "I have to be in motion." The novelist and rhetorician Anita August, author of *Gut Bucket Blues*, itches if she doesn't walk often enough. "Walking exfoliates my mind," she says. And the effect applies to all creative thinking, not just the arts. Steve Jobs, CEO of Apple until his death in 2011, was famous for insisting on walking meetings to stimulate ideas and conversation, a practice that Mark Zuckerberg of Facebook also uses. For creative minds throughout history, walking has been a practice closely allied to art and innovation.

Walking reinforces every aspect of the creative process, so why should walking's benefits be confined to our most revered artists, scientists, and thinkers? Both creativity and walking are all of our birthrights—to muse, wander, grieve, be inspired, gain insight, solve problems, lose ourselves. It's not such a stretch to see that feeding and strengthening our creativity can also make our depression and stress more manageable, and vice versa, and that all of these practices build a brain strong enough, one hopes, to sustain itself for the long haul of a long life.

THE INCREASING NUMBER of studies linking walking and mental virility reminds me of the topographical maps that my mother had when I was a child. They were huge and stiff, around two or three feet on each side and made of some kind of semiflexible plastic. When rolled out they revealed the ranges, valleys, rivers, bluffs, lakes, buttes, and plains of Montana in such detail that I could run my fingers over the bumps of mountains and hills, the dips of rivers and lakes, and feel their rises and grooves in my calves. I traced the ridgelines and streams I knew by heart and others in nearly inaccessible wilderness. Those maps brought into relief a complexity of landscape that continues to fascinate me.

The connections between walking and our minds are like that. Walking reduces anxiety, staves off Alzheimer's. It alleviates depression and worry, energizes creative thinking. Wandering a landscape with only our feet, our eyes, and a paper map as guides—as opposed to GPS—has even been shown to increase volume in the hippocampus, an area of the brain whose health is strongly linked to the risk of dementia.

All of these studies tumble over and around one another, over ranges and hillocks of the human experience. Katherine Davies with her "big piece to move," working through the grief of her parents' deaths as she walked in pursuit of peace; the Cheyenne and Arapaho nations and their walks of healing and commemoration; Peace Pilgrim, Jonathon Stalls, the Ojibwe women of the Mississippi River Water Walk, the countless pilgrims making their journeys to Mount Kailash and Mecca and along the Camino de Santiago: they are the rises and falls, the crevasses and tectonic uplifts of our humanity, of our questions, of the power of the human mind to seek and query, answer and create.

"Blood is thicker than water, my mother had always said when I was growing up," wrote Cheryl Strayed in her memoir *Wild: From Lost to Found on the Pacific Crest Trail*. "But it turned out that it didn't matter whether she was right or wrong. They both flowed out of my cupped hands." Strayed walked out into the mountains grieving her mother, but also herself. After ninety-four days and over a thousand miles of walking the Pacific Crest Trail through California and Oregon, she found what so many others have when employing their feet in service of grief: "I'd finally come to understand what it had been: a yearning for a way out, when actually what I had wanted was to find a way in."

Perhaps the relationship between walking in nature and depression or anxiety relates to those personal pilgrimages we sometimes find ourselves embarking on after divorce or the death of a loved one. We seek, in these times, some kind of answer, while knowing that there is none, and in this seeking we begin to act on instinct, shifting and turning and moving our bodies in response to psychic and emotional pain. Words fail us. Our most ancient relationship, that with our bodies, our physical selves, steps in. "*This*," it seems to say. "To move, to do. *This*." Not as sympathy or as a balm, but as a simple act of living.

WHEN KATHERINE DAVIES left England and stepped onto French soil, she wasn't sure what to expect. She'd heard a great deal in the news about rising tensions over refugees in Europe. The resentments, the fear of terrorism, the nationalist backlash. How would people receive her? How many would sympathize with her quest? How many would respond with anger?

As she walked the roads and paths of France, Davies found something she didn't expect. "When I explained to people what I was doing, the moment I mentioned Syria, their faces would change." Not to anger or dismissal, but to sadness, pity, a longing to *do* something, an urge not all that different, perhaps, from the one that had led her to walk out of London in the first place.

All but one person, whom Davies says was more indifferent than anything else, said yes, of course, I'll write a message for you to deliver to Geneva; yes, of course, it's an awful, tragic situation. There was none of the heated immigrant hating that gets hyped up in the news. What greeted Davies as she walked through France was communal sorrow for the suffering of our fellow humans.

"I felt," she said, "as if I was witnessing the collective human heart."

This walk of Davies's, of Peace Pilgrim's, of so many others, reads like a bird's-eye view of creeks and streams running into a river. Our communities, our societies, our neighborhoods—they're all built of these small, unnoticed, everyday connections. To look another human in the eye, to hear her voice, to touch her hand, to know her story, these are the things that make possible our ability to live together. When we shut off these connections, it's like damming up all the mountain streams that feed our great lakes, our rushing rivers: they go dry.

We go dry. We forget that our internal richness is fed by our connections to one another and seasoned by the way we move through the world.

At the foundation of every pilgrimage might be a submerged, unuttered question: What is the best, and most, that a human being is truly capable of? What is the best, and most, that humanity is truly capable of?

Katherine Davies learned something on her journey about the capacity of humans for fellow-feeling and generosity in the face of suffering. Individually, people tend to believe firmly in their own powerlessness, yet she saw clearly that the collective power we all have to change the world for the better is immense. The collective human heart would show plenty of greed and anger and selfishness, but the potential we have to be so much more than that, so much better, is incalculable.

"WHY?" IS THE repetitive mantra of a child just out of toddlerhood, the bane and delight of every exhausted parent. But it's a habit that never ends; as we reach adulthood the questions only deepen and broaden out into the wide galaxies of the unanswerable. We address these questions in prayer and meditation, in contemplation and conversation, and in walking. A tense family holiday dinner that erupts with old grudges: "I'm going for a walk." The melting, not-quite-molten mortification of a broken heart: "I'm going for a walk." The grief of a child for a parent she wished she could have walked and talked with for years to come. Just a step or two, she tells herself, tells her friends, tells her relatives. Open the door. Go outside. Feel the press of your foot against the earth. Feel the air move around your body. Feel the unbearable "yes" of life with every step forward, even as your mind and your heart scream "no." In our darkest moments, the smallest steps can force us to live.

"Pilgrimage" should be an evocative word, rich and full in the mouth, like "chocolate" or "silk" or "pray." The truth of the word, ignored at first utterance, becomes more clear in the practice of it. Pilgrimage doesn't necessarily have to be religious; it is, though, a powerful act that, like walking meditation or walking off grief or anger or depression, is contained within the individual. One individual's soul, one individual's heartrending loss, one individual's struggle for sanity and equilibrium, one individual's bright, unvanquished spirit.

SIX
STRIDE

> We believe that women walking and talking together to solve their problems is a global solution.
>
> —VANESSA GARRISON, cofounder of GirlTrek, TED 2017

JANE JACOBS WASN'T VERY OPTIMISTIC ABOUT THE FUTURE OF North American cities. "While people possess a community," she wrote in *Dark Age Ahead*, "they usually understand that they can't afford to lose it; but after it is lost, gradually even the memory of what was lost is lost." The responsibilities of modern life, from raising children to taking care of aging parents to keeping a marriage together to learning to live with and among millions of people of diverse backgrounds, had become impossible for normal, everyday people, Jacobs believed, but not because we've lost our moral compass or the reliable trajectory of job-for-a-lifetime followed by a secure retirement. "Only membership in a functioning community makes handling these responsibilities feasible," she wrote, and communities had been destroyed both by the highways that were meant to serve neighborhoods and by the cars that were meant to serve us.

There are movements and shifts all over the country, continent, and world, though, that belie Jacobs's pessimism; we might not remember how we got here, but we do have some sense of what we've lost—and it's not something we've abandoned, not completely. Humans do, increasingly, want walkable lives, and a significant part of that shift isn't just a desire for better health and the ability to go places without a car; it's also that we want to remember what it feels like to be part of a community again—varied, heterogeneous, sometimes contentious, but a necessary and integral human support system, tributaries to and from our individual lives.

Most towns in the United States don't necessarily have either the long-term holistic attitude or healthy tax base that together make walkability possible. Very few American municipalities require developers to include "whole street" planning that allows for ample sidewalks and bike lanes. Walking, whether for leisure or a purpose, becomes in many places a proposition at best laughable and at worst lethal; as commuters move farther out into rural areas hoping for more space and cleaner air, roads that were once safe for kids on bike or foot become hostile to anyone outside of an automobile. But the desire for walkability is swelling up from the ground rather than being imposed from above for a reason. Instinctively, people understand that the consequences of continuing our current ways of living are dismal. How we build walking into or out of our lives says everything about the kind of humans we imagine we will become.

In March 2015, Paris, France, temporarily became the most polluted city on Earth. Partly in response to its significant, largely traffic-related pollution, the City of Light that has inspired so many famous artists has since then moved forward in reclaiming both its spaces and its air quality: Paris's car-free days, first tested in September 2016, have become internationally famous, especially when researchers were able to track the drastic drop in air pollution to lack of traffic. Less known but no less relevant is Boise, Idaho's, shift toward walkability, encouraged by local organization Idaho Smart Growth. *The Guardian*, CNN, and other major news outlets run plenty of articles about London mayor Sadiq Khan's car ban proposals and walking initiatives—London, like Paris, suffers from some of the dirtiest air in Europe, leading to the early deaths of nearly ten thousand residents annually—but only *The American Conservative* among general-interest news outlets has devoted an extensive article to Buffalo, New York's, reclaiming of its public spaces and neighborhoods. In a surprising move, Los Angeles is engaged in a long-term effort to reverse its image as a car-centric dystopia and consider both the safety and mobility of pedestrians through adoption of its Mobility 2035 plan; but it is in Denver, Colorado, that the creaky machinery of city governance is truly shifting its foundations to begin viewing the city from the point of view of people, not cars. Denver's refocus on pedestrian needs is part of a revitalization spearheaded in large part by Mayor Michael Hancock, who championed a European-style train between downtown and the airport, with stops in between, and a revamping of downtown's Union Station, which he described at the 2017 Rail~Volution conference as a former "craphole." Seven years after emerging from recession, the area around the rebuilt station is seeing a six-to-one return on what Hancock said was a "scraped-together" investment in revitalization with a focus on walking and biking.

Denver is taking its people-centered future seriously. Paul Kashmann, a Denver city councilor who had almost inadvertently become walking's representative at City Hall, told me when we met at his office that through the mayor's sidewalk working group and collaboration with organizations like WalkDenver, Denver is "envisioning an entirely new way of getting around." Kashmann and I spent a whirlwind hour talking through sidewalk funding, pavement repair, bond issues, and his own introduction to the subject: the mother who demonstrated the lack of walking access to the school in his district. If you could really walk comfortably around the whole city, he said, it would completely change the way Denver's residents move.

It's not, though, an entirely new way of getting around. It's an old one; thinking of it as new is to forget our own history, the very practice Jane Jacobs warned against in *Dark Age Ahead*. As Jill Locantore of WalkDenver had told me the day before, "I don't know that Americans *ever* wanted a car-oriented society."

I'VE WALKED FOR days, even months and years, in Boston, New York City, London, Paris, Moscow, Vienna, Rome, Sydney—all beautiful, unique cities with varying grades of walkability. I went to Denver partly because all the books I'd read about walking tended to orbit around either these world-renowned cities or hiking and mountain climbing. "What about New York?" people invariably asked me when I talked about the lack of walkability in the United States. Sometimes they'd bring up Chicago, every now and then Boston. It's so easy to turn to New York City and its fellow high-profile cities and ignore the rest of the country, the rest of the world. Yet all over the United States, towns and cities are quietly regaining their right to walk. From health initiatives like the Walk with a Doc program to the surprising removals of Futurama-inspired freeways in cities like Dallas, Texas, and Rochester, New York, to Atlanta's one-*billion*-dollar commitment to walking and biking infrastructure over twenty-five years, walking is making a comeback. A slow, step-by-step comeback, as might be expected of such an endeavor, but with the strength one would also expect of a movement seeking to reclaim our free-striding bodies' rights to our public spaces. I went to Denver to find how at least one lesser-discussed city was reshaping itself around the pedestrian.

On a Tuesday morning, after walking about an hour from my hotel in search of hot coffee and something to eat, I set out to tramp six miles from Aurora to downtown Denver, where I was meeting with Paul Kashmann, the city councilman who chaired the mayor's sidewalks working group aimed at identifying the problems and roadblocks that prevented Denver from being a completely walking-friendly city.

Depending on your pace, it takes nearly three hours to walk from where I was in Aurora to the City and County Building in downtown Denver. The route that Google Maps gave me was a mostly straight shot down East 13th Avenue through the full spectrum of Denver's sidewalks, pseudo-sidewalks, and utter lack of sidewalks. There were long stretches where even desire lines (natural paths created by erosion from foot traffic) were absent and I was shoved onto the busy road, wondering how a person with even moderately impaired mobility, or vision or hearing, could safely get from here to there on foot. Forget a wheelchair or walker; that was impossible.

Sidewalk maintenance and repair are only two of the challenges faced by a community interested in promoting walkability. Problems plaguing either very old or very new neighborhoods, like heaving sidewalks and signs placed right in the middle of a wheelchair or stroller route, are easier to fix than some of the odder infrastructure embedded in Denver's midcentury neighborhoods. Built up during the 1950s and 1960s, these areas are characterized by a feature I'd never seen before: those "Hollywood sidewalks" mentioned in Chapter 4. The Hollywood sidewalk, or Hollywood curb as it's also called, combines the gutter, sidewalk, and curb into one unit, but because the sidewalk portion is only about thirty-two inches wide (less than three feet), its uselessness as a functional sidewalk is obvious to anyone who wants to walk safely from one place to another.

I'd first run into these sidewalks near my hotel, which was plopped out in a cobbled-together area of the city where swathes of big-box stores sat plumply next to a fast, dangerous four-lane boulevard. Walking along this road toward the train station, I came across slim sidewalks rolling straight up from the street. They presented no barrier between pedestrians and traffic, and not even close to enough room for two people to walk side by side, much less for anyone who needed a mobility aid. The thought of walking a small child down those sidewalks made my skin crawl, but if a parent were getting around the city by bus, there were no other options, as the bus stops were right on the edges of these strips of pavement.

Why, I wondered, would anyone build such a thing? But the answer is obvious: To save money, especially during the decades when it was assumed that most people would be getting around by driving.

Most of these weird constructions were, in Denver, wrapped around neighborhoods that seemed to be on the lower end of the socioeconomic scale. Smaller houses in greater disrepair, set close together, and very few trees. Unshaded, exposed, unsafe walking. What it shows is not that those neighborhoods are bad places to live, but that, as is too often the case, people with less political and financial power get fewer amenities and greater barriers to health and mobility.

THIS ACCESS INCLUDES the presence of trees, with their attendant shade and pollution-filtering, stress-lowering benefits. Trees get barely a nod in conversations about walking, but, as shown by detailed studies about the value of walking in nature, they are integral both to understanding walking's complex benefits for our minds and bodies, and to realizing cities that are once again truly walkable.

Throughout the eons since we first slipped out of their branches and onto the ground, trees have been silent witnesses to the evolution of our walking, its loss, and now, perhaps, its reclamation. Trees have nurtured our steps, our imaginations, and our health. We've spent hundreds, if not thousands, of years ignoring the ways trees—like many aspects of our ecosystems—shelter and shape our lives.

Their impact is, in tandem with the gifts of walking itself, finally filtering up to active consciousness; in Japan, the practice of *shinrin-yoku*, or "forest bathing," has become so popular that researchers began studying it to find if, indeed, hanging out among trees had any actual health advantages, or if the decreases in stress, among other reported benefits, are imaginary. The Japanese government spent eight years and over four million dollars to find that the practice—which in essence consists of spending quiet time among trees—does in fact significantly boost the human immune system, lower blood pressure and cortisol levels (which are linked to stress), and even lower tendencies toward depression and aggression. The effects are attributed to phytoncide, a compound produced by trees to protect themselves from insects and infection. Inhaling it appears to be beneficial to human beings. One weekend in the woods can lift physical health for up to a month, and even thirty minutes hanging out or strolling among trees can measurably reduce stress and blood pressure for a whole day. Forest bathing isn't just an eco-idealist's cloud-nine fantasy of what's good for humans' minds and bodies; it's so effective at improving health that governments from Japan to Scotland are making active use of walkable forests to supplement a variety of treatments for mental and physical wellness.

It's no wonder that when June arrives and nights finally hover above freezing, I start mentally packing for our family camping trips into the abundance of national and state forest lands I'm lucky enough to live among. If there's one thing Montana can lay claim to besides its fabled big sky, it's trees dripping with phytoncide.

Journalist Florence Williams, a contributing editor to *Outside* magazine, spent a lot of time detailing the Japanese research on *shinrin-yoku* in her 2017 book *The Nature Fix: Why Nature Makes Us Happier, Healthier, and More Creative*. She also covered the importance of extensive vigorous outdoor playtime for everyone from kids with ADHD to Iraq War vets with post-traumatic stress disorder (PTSD), from adults suffering from depression, anxiety, obesity, or myopia to children with rickets—a childhood disease caused by vitamin D deficiency, or lack of sunlight, that was all but a footnote of history until we started spending so much time indoors and in cars.

Williams went into the woods and wilderness with researchers in Japan and scientists in the American West, studying the effects that being in nature—usually but not always unplugged from smartphones, iPads, and the like—has on our mental and physical health. Trees are a constant theme in her book, trees in city parks, trees in Japan's *shinrin-yoku* destinations, trees in the mountains of Boulder, Colorado, the home she has to leave to move to Washington, D.C., for her husband's job. The trails near her Colorado home, she wrote, are "ribbons of delight" and it tears her apart to leave them.

Lack of trees, and green space in general, affects our health in seemingly unrelated and often unconscious ways. A study conducted at the Max Planck Institute for Human Development using participants in the long-term Berlin Aging Study (involving twenty-two hundred residents) and published in 2017, found that city-dwellers who live near forests are healthier and happier than those who don't, including those who live near non-forest green spaces. A different study found that people who live in urban rather than rural areas are at higher risk for mood and anxiety disorders and schizophrenia, but access to nature, particularly trees, seems to alleviate some of that risk. Pointing to studies on *shinrin-yoku*, the Max Planck researchers said in their conclusion: "Walking in a forest as well as sitting in a forest and watching lead to a reduction of prefrontal haemoglobin concentration, an observation that has been interpreted as a sign of relaxation."

I'd never heard of phytoncide until I attended a one-hour forest-bathing class in Canada in 2016, but the scent of pine trees has always been, for me, the scent of home. Growing up in Montana, I'd been raised to view the forests and rivers of the Rocky Mountains as my family's escape, vacation destination, solace, playground, backyard, and food source. Attending a forest-bathing class felt a bit silly only because it imitated the woods-walking I've done regularly most of my life without thinking much about it. I tried, while I was learning about *shinrin-yoku*, to remember what it was like during the twenty years I lived mostly in cities, when culture was everywhere but so were pavement and traffic and noise, and trees were few and far between.

When suburbs were first built, trees were considered normal accessories to an idyllic white middle-class life. Later, as commuting became the defining experience of that same middle-class life, trees posed a crash hazard for the inevitable times when a driver, drunk or distracted or going too fast, allowed his car to leave the roadway and jump the curb. Those trees promised shade and pleasure for walkers, as well as a protective barrier from the road, but their existence was considered only in light of the danger to drivers.

As cities across the United States and elsewhere restructure themselves around walking as a way of regaining health and reconnecting communities, it is the trees that I look for. My experience has been that how far and how often most of us are willing to walk is directly proportional to how exposed our route is to unfiltered sunlight, especially in the summer. And I'm not alone. In Dallas, a team at the University of Texas at Arlington's Institute of Urban Studies began painstakingly tracking the famously unwalkable city's shade and tree cover. They're doing it because residents and business owners want walkability, a concept that includes the trees that provide cool shade and psychological solace to pedestrians.

Whether the trees that lend companionship to our strolling are towering, leafy reminders of a different generational legacy, or are newly planted, spindly along lonely concrete, they are a promise of a different kind of future.

DENVER, ON THIS journey, was scorching hot; at least it felt that way to my pale, easily burned self. I kept careful track of where reliable shade would make walking a pleasure, where the fluttering of leaves and the smell of green growing things would make me smile and lighten my steps, and where the glare of concrete and sky and traffic would make my body feel burdened and wearisome. Walking ten to fifteen miles a day over the course of five days, my internal mapping system started to orient itself to the layout of the city, to its districts and neighborhoods, highways and side streets, gentrification and decline, the existence or lack of trees, and to its sidewalks.

Denver's sidewalk system, comprising around 2,700 miles of pavement, feels like a code to the city's history of development. Very old (by American standards) neighborhoods have the standard-width sidewalk, about five feet, buffered by a grassy verge between pedestrians and the roadway. The city's pedestrian master plan, with straightforward practicality, calls these verges "street lawns" and the trees, when present, "street trees." Together the lawns and trees make up a network of "tree lawns," which add to the feeling that Denver—or at least parts of it—is a set of widespread and walkable urban developments that connect a network of open, rolling, mostly shaded parks.

The city is fortunate. In 1878 its civic leaders envisioned a city of parks connected by wide boulevards lined with trees. This vision was enacted in the early 1900s, and, although Denver suffered from the same car-centric infrastructure craze that hit the rest of the country in midcentury, its efforts to chip its way back to a pedestrian-friendly design are made easier by the patterns and groundwork laid out by its earlier residents and leaders.

No matter how determined Denverites are to make their city walkable, though, doing so won't be easy. Although older neighborhoods are accessible for children, many elderly walkers, and cyclists, disrepair is an enormous problem for anyone who might be less sure-footed or using a wheelchair or walker. And sidewalk repair is a fraught, complex issue. As in most towns and cities across the United States, Denver's landowners (homes or businesses) are responsible for the sidewalks directly in front of their buildings. While sidewalks are technically public spaces, users must rely on private homeowners to shovel, de-ice, repair broken concrete, and deal with bulges caused by frost heaves or those beautiful shade trees' roots. Sidewalk maintenance is expensive, and many homeowners aren't even aware that they are legally required to clear snow and repair broken concrete.

Does Denver take over responsibility for the thousands of miles of sidewalk maintenance itself? Should it subsidize homeowners' obligations? If a disabled person can't use a sidewalk, who bears the responsibility to make the walkway accessible? Because Denver is taking walking seriously, it's already begun to address some of these issues, passing a bond of forty-seven million dollars in 2017 for sidewalks, and allocating over four million dollars of a revolving fund to help low-income homeowners make sidewalk repairs.

Reclaiming our walkable world is a process we can't afford to abandon, but it's full of these exhausting, detailed questions, the realm of policy wonks and budget hawks. Where do we place our priorities? What does the law say in the first place? What about the potentially sticky issue of legal liability, which eviscerated Los Angeles's budget after it took control of its sidewalks?

This level of detail is where many passionate walkers lose focus, get bored, wander off to talk about Thoreau, Beethoven, Wordsworth, and Solnit. Attention to these details, though, is the only concrete action that will bring everyday, accessible walking back into our lives. Denver is a wonderfully walkable city, but disparities are stark: consistently, Denver's lower-income areas tend to have the worst sidewalks; the areas with the highest rates of childhood obesity also lack walking accessibility. Only 5 percent of Denver's nearly three thousand miles of sidewalk meet its own design standards—where, that is, the sidewalks exist.

DESPITE THEIR LIMITATIONS and drawbacks, Hollywood curbs are a step up from the neighborhoods I walked through on that Tuesday morning, where any pretense at sidewalks disappeared completely. It's reflective of how reviled walking became over the past fifty-plus years that these areas tended to look like they housed the slightly better-off. Larger yards, more expensive landscaping, shinier, newer cars in the driveways. In cities all over the country, these are often the neighborhoods where the reintroduction of sidewalks is fought most fiercely. Anecdotally, young families moving onto these streets tend to be the ones pushing for sidewalk infrastructure, while longer-term residents push back with resentment and something akin to horror. Nobody wants sidewalks, some will say. It's just a way for concrete companies to make money, others claim.

Sidewalk resistance came as a surprise to me when I first started researching walkability, but its seeds are simpler to pick out than local debates make them sound. It usually comes down to fear: sidewalks bring other people near one's home. "People get this fear that 'undesirables' will be walking through their neighborhoods," Kate Kraft, the national coalition director for America Walks, an advocacy organization, once told me when I asked her about resistance to building sidewalks.

I'd theorize that our distrust of the unprotected pedestrian—the No Trespassing signs, the gated communities, those neighborhoods with no sidewalks—goes further back, tapping into instincts developed long before suburbs and motorways, before human record. Our bipedal ancestors evolved in a paradigm of leaving shelter, which meant protection, to search for food at enormous physical risk. Those early humans nipped off the trees all those hundreds of thousands or millions of years ago for one reason or another, but when a carnivore showed up they had no hard-sided SUV to retreat into.

Walking opens us up to the menace of a world outside the built environments that we control. Driving, despite the high risk of crashes, injury, and death, masks itself as safety: we're not watching our backs. And once we've become unaccustomed to the sight of other people, they can startle. People who move differently and think differently than we do become, from the safety of our fortress-homes and echo-chamber media and car-conduits that feed it all, threats to our way of life. And so we design towns and suburbs, neighborhoods and cities to be unfriendly to the walker, to those who break out of the paradigms we've deemed safe.

As I walked down miles of Denver's East 13th Avenue, Kraft's statement about our fear of those who walk came back to me, particularly when street design shifted abruptly from Hollywood sidewalks to no sidewalks at all, just lawns and landscaping rolling out to the busy road. I tried walking on the lawns, but eventually even the desire lines and goat paths petered out, deterred no doubt by formidable bushes and strategically planted boulders. So I stepped onto the road and pondered how unwanted my footsteps were in that neighborhood, how obviously pedestrians are driven away, not through overt violence or rules, but simply through design.

America Walks, the advocacy organization Kraft works for, is one of several around the United States aiming to change our relationship with walking. America Walks trains community outreach advocates through its Walking College program, which saw eighty applicants for twenty positions in 2015, its first year of operation, and promotes urban design focused on pedestrian safety and transportation planning.

America Walks also hosts a National Walking Summit every other year, which brings together transportation and transit engineers, city planners, leaders of walking groups, disability advocates, experts in the relationship between racism and urban planning, police officers, former employees of the Environmental Protection Agency, walkability advocates, and many, many health professionals. Doctors, after all, know what we need to regain our individual vitality, but they can't give it to us without the infrastructure that makes it possible.

"Health disparities don't just happen by accident," Dr. Robert Bullard, founder of the environmental justice movement and former dean of the School of Public Affairs at Texas Southern University, said during his keynote speech at the 2015 National Walking Summit. "Tell me your zip code and I can tell you how healthy you are. That should not be. . . . All communities should have a right to a safe, sustainable, healthy, just, walkable community," and the fact that they don't is due less to individual choices than to divisions and shifts that reach deeply into our past and continue to eat at communities from the inside today. Much of the zip code–based health discrepancy stems from preventable factors like obesity and high blood pressure—in other words, while access to health insurance and health care play a role, so does access to high-quality food, clean air and water, and simple, everyday activities like walking. And according to the research and consulting organization Active Living Research, African American neighborhoods are thirty-eight times more likely to have low-quality sidewalks; 70 percent of African American neighborhoods and 81 percent of Hispanic neighborhoods lack recreational facilities, and children living below the poverty line are 159 percent more likely to be deprived of recess. Across the board, lower-income areas, often historically segregated by race, have control over their individual health cut off at the knees.

At the 2017 Walking Summit, Tyler Norris, a former vice president of health insurance conglomerate Kaiser Permanente and current CEO of the Well Being Trust, pinpointed the central goal of almost everyone in attendance: "The basic building block of public health is to make the right thing easy to do," he said in an opening speech. "Walking is stunningly important" for health, which means not designing streets and residential areas that actively force people to drive. Glenn Harris, the president of Race Forward, an advocacy and solutions-oriented organization focused on racial equity, stressed similar points: "If we fix what is most harmful to those in the community who are the most vulnerable," he said at the summit, "then we will fix our communities for the benefit of everyone."

OVER TWO HUNDRED miles of Denver's streets have no sidewalks. On East 13th, I walked for nearly an hour before meeting up with one again. This time it was a luxurious five-foot-wide sidewalk, abutting ample lawns with large, historic houses on one side and an enormous tree-covered verge on the other, with another tree-lined median separating two sides of the four-lane boulevard. In less than two hours, it had become obvious who got to walk in Denver, and who didn't.

But Denver is, after all, working to change its lack of walkability. And it's doing so not just with an active city council working group, but through the concerted efforts of truly grassroots organizations run by people who walk the streets of Denver every day, stretching their legs, cataloguing the blocks that leave children or disabled users in the lurch, becoming intimate with their communities, and reclaiming, with every step, their right to walk in the world they inhabit.

Rewiring our broken connections to one another is the bedrock aim of one group, Walk2Connect, which was founded by Jonathon Stalls, the man who walked across the United States in search of a different kind of value system than the hyper-competitive one we're taught is the norm. What he found on his eight-and-a-half-month walk across the country is something similar to what Katherine Davies found in her pilgrimage for peace in Syria: that people, no matter what their class, ethnicity, religion, gender, or political bent, are, for the most part, kind. People are, for the most part, welcoming. Most long for connection; most are eager to show hospitality and to hear the stories of a stranger.

THE REALITIES OF these stories run counter to the world we've designed to accommodate cars and the narratives we tell ourselves to justify perpetuating those choices. The century of highway building and suburbia was quintessentially a century of maniacal boundaries. This is the predictable world of the TV show *Mad Men*, where everyone knew their place and cars were never stuck in traffic but instead were a passport to the freedom of the open road.

Walking is the opposite of these clearly defined expectations. It's the wandering, meandering, strolling, roaming side of human life. It's like a nautilus shell, fine, delicate chambers of structure and meaning circling out from and into who we are as human beings. As Jonathon Stalls told me, there are innumerable mental, spiritual, and emotional factors that "spiral out of our most sacred form of movement."

When Stalls returned to Denver from his walk across the country, he devoted his life to continuing the lessons he'd learned on his journey. Starting with an invitation for accompanied walks, posted in coffee shops, he then founded Walk2Connect, which now has several member-owners, and its trained leaders run between fifty and seventy guided walks in and around Denver every week.

One of Stalls's favorite regular walks is with a group of Iraqi refugees, women who had lost sons and husbands who'd fought alongside US troops in Iraq. Refugee communities, he's found, have a great deal to teach us about connection that we've forgotten. "We're in a relationship with people we don't understand," Stalls said when we talked about politics and widening divisions. We have to walk with one another, learn from one another, connect with one another, and then take the time to process and transmute our experiences, in order to begin dissolving those barriers.

ONE OF WALK2CONNECT'S most active group leaders is Pam Jiner. She was one of the main reasons I'd left northwest Montana, with its cool lakes and sanctuaries of pine forests, during a scorching August to fly down to hot Denver with its hundreds of thousands of people and little escape into water. Jiner is a grandmother with about five times as much energy as I can muster on any given afternoon, and in addition to being a Walk2Connect walk leader is also a community leader with GirlTrek, one of the most vibrant and powerful walking movements in America.

When the founders of GirlTrek, T. Morgan Dixon and Vanessa Garrison, were invited to the high-profile TED stage in Vancouver, British Columbia, in 2017, Dixon asked the audience to imagine a plane filled with Black women crashing to the ground every day, because that is the seriousness of the health crisis that African American women face. "Every single day in America," Dixon said, her voice choking up, "one hundred and thirty-seven Black women die of a preventable disease, heart disease. That's every eleven minutes." That number is more than the deaths caused by gun violence, cigarette smoking, and HIV combined.

Dixon and Garrison founded GirlTrek in 2010 in response to their own growing awareness of these dire mortality statistics. African American women die at a faster and higher rate from preventable, obesity-related diseases than any other group of people in America. These aren't just statistics that GirlTrek can rattle off, Garrison and Dixon pointed out in their talk. These are statistics they live. When Garrison calculated the life expectancy of the women in her own family, those who were left after her grandmother and aunts died in their sixties, she found that most of them would be lucky to live past the age of sixty-five. Eighty-two percent of African American women are over a healthy weight; 53 percent are obese.

Dixon used to be a history teacher. One day, she looked out at her classroom after reading that half of all young African American women could expect to be diagnosed with Type II diabetes unless diets and lifestyles changed, and found she couldn't teach anymore. Instead, she started a hiking club for girls, which was where the name GirlTrek came from.

Why, these two women asked themselves, don't existing strategies improve the health of Black women? From weight-loss regimens to government interventions, nothing was shifting the needle of this community's health, and the reason, Garrison said, is that those strategies refuse to acknowledge the weight of existing racism and its history, the weight of trauma and sorrow that most African American women carry in their bodies, passed down from their ancestors. Without acknowledging systemic racism—from overt racism experienced every day at work and in schools and in our public spaces to practices like redlining and the smashing of African American communities to build highways serving white suburbs in the mid-1900s—none of these weight-loss strategies will have any effect because they're not addressing the underlying problems. "For Black women whose bodies are buckling under the weight of systems never designed to support them," said Garrison, "GirlTrek is a lifeline."

The very real physical consequences of living with racism, both active and historic, is illuminated by research that now goes back decades. Bessel van der Kolk, a psychiatry professor at Boston University Medical School and former medical director of Boston's Trauma Center, has spent his career becoming one of the best-known experts on trauma, post-traumatic stress disorder, and their effects on our bodies. Stress hormones, he said during an interview with Krista Tippett on her podcast *On Being*, are actually good for us. They give us energy in extreme situations. Our problems come when we're kept from *using* them. Stress works by getting us to move and use our bodies—which is why in the aftermath of disasters like hurricanes, people tend to get very physically active—and if we're forced to be stationary, the hormones build up because they can't be released through action. As long as you can move in a stressful situation, you'll likely be okay, but if not, "the stress hormones really start wreaking havoc with your own internal system."

Van der Kolk's profession, he told Tippett, has a confusing insistence on seeing people as "individual organisms who are independent of the social environment," rather than the socially interconnected beings that we actually are. If you have trouble with memory, decision-making, and emotional control, it's important to know what your home life looks like; if you're a child with asthma, it's crucial to know whether you attend school near a heavily polluted freeway. If you're prone to stress-induced headaches and high blood pressure, it probably helps to know whether you habitually make yourself small and tense during neighborhood walks because of your gender or sexuality, or because you've had experience with the color of your skin provoking fear or violence. Or maybe you don't walk at all for the same reasons. "The social context in which we live," said van der Kolk, "has a very profound effect on how we feel and how we see ourselves."

The work of Rachel Yehuda, a professor of psychiatry and neuroscience at Mount Sinai's School of Medicine, intersects with van der Kolk's in her studies of intergenerational trauma, specifically in Holocaust survivors. The science behind her research is detailed and finicky—people don't just inherit PTSD. But what she found in her early research was that the children of Holocaust survivors were three times more likely to develop PTSD if exposed to a traumatic event than were demographically similar Jewish people whose parents were not Holocaust survivors. This is not, to be clear, a change in a person's genetics; it's a change in how a person's genes will respond to their own particular environment.

Yehuda found similar results in the children of women who were pregnant and present at the September 11, 2001, terrorist attacks on New York City's World Trade Center. "For somebody to be pregnant and in the World Trade Center while those buildings are coming down," she said in an interview, "that's your own personal holocaust."

The field of epigenetics and the effects of intergenerational trauma are still very new areas of study, and its researchers, like most scientists, are cautious of overstating their conclusions. That said, the implications for many communities are profound. From America's legacy of slavery and its aftermath, to the historical trauma inhabiting the lives of Native American people (according to theories proposed by psychiatrist Maria Yellow Horse Brave Heart on the Pine Ridge Reservation in South Dakota), to veterans from the many wars the United States has engaged in since World War II, it seems that we carry these "soul wounds" with us and pass them on to our children, unable to reclaim our own health unless we can face and process the underlying trauma. Epigenetics is unlikely to ever determine that one type of trauma is carried forward in an easily predictable way, but it can, as Yehuda says, not only teach us a new way of thinking about the damage we carry, but also give us a modicum of control over what we pass on to our offspring.

Nobody can go back in time and change the reality of American slavery, or the genocide and forced removals of Native American and First Nations and Aboriginal peoples, or the serfdom of peasants practiced by the Russian nobility, or the expulsion of Scottish residents from their homes by absentee English landlords. Justice cannot work backward through time. The smallest steps, though, not only discharge stress through action but also allow a person of any demographic to restake her claim to a place in the world.

GARRISON AND DIXON both found their own personal healing through walking, but they didn't stop there. They took their intimacy with walking's power and their knowledge of the dire health statistics facing African American women, and they decided to do something about it. GirlTrek held its first annual Stress Protest, "a rebellion against stress, disease, and pain," by engaging in the "revolutionary act of self-care" at Rocky Mountain National Park near Denver in 2017. By the end of that same year they had well over 100,000 African American women committed to walking at least thirty minutes every day, drastically reducing their risk of dying from heart disease and stroke.

GirlTrek's mission spans the space between individual health and community vitality. Once a member starts reclaiming her health, she often starts getting her family walking, and then people in her neighborhood. Once women start walking together, they start noticing where walking is difficult or impossible, where infrastructure is crumbling, where their neighborhoods have enough concrete to serve thousands of cars but not a single tree. And they start doing something about it. They fix abandoned buildings, they chivy city councilors to repair sidewalks, they log the dangerous intersections that pose a threat to crossing pedestrians. And then they turn around and take more women by the hand, guiding their footsteps out the door.

GIRLTREK ISN'T THE only group championing walking as a way to reclaim health and community. In Valley Hi, a community in Sacramento, California, an organization called the Health Education Council has worked with a similar ethos, using walking both as a means of improving residents' health, and as a way to reduce the community's high rates of violence.

A region with high numbers of fast-food outlets and attendant high obesity rates—36 percent of adults in Valley Hi are classified as obese—Valley Hi also has an extremely high rate of violent crime. According to the Health Education Council and the California Department of Justice, Sacramento as a whole has the second-highest rate of crime per capita in California, much of it due to "violence along Valley Hi's main corridor," Mack Road.

Partnering with local law enforcement and churches, the Health Education Council focused on cleaning up and improving facilities at a local park, including identifying risky pedestrian routes to the park and installing crosswalks at a particularly dangerous intersection. Their flagship project was forming a local walking group called Walk with Friends, which not only initiated regular neighborhood walks but connected with local doctors and health screeners, as well as the Sacramento Food Bank, which worked through a local church to deliver fresh produce for those participating in the walks.

Valley Hi saw an increase of nearly 300 percent in usage of the park, and just as crucially saw a drastic decrease in firearms assaults. The council noted that Walk with Friends participants also became "civically engaged," and the program has expanded to three other parks around Sacramento. Through walking together, residents became involved in improving access to healthy food, enhancing pedestrian and other forms of safety (like reducing violent crime), and promoting involvement in civic life. Walk with Friends, like GirlTrek, uses our most natural and ancient form of motion to bring back sorely needed community strength and involvement, while at the same time giving participants long-lost control over their own physical and mental health.

"I believe that walking can transform our communities," said T. Morgan Dixon during her TED talk with Garrison, "because it's already starting to."

Like the Sand Creek Massacre Spiritual Healing Run/Walk, and groups like Walk2Connect, GirlTrek is also about rebuilding connection through reclaiming, and in some cases cracking open and finding deeper truths of, the stories and accepted histories that define all of our lives.

Pam Jiner is an embodiment of that spirit. Montbello, an area of Denver where she leads Tuesday evening walks at the brisk GirlTrek pace of a little over three miles per hour, is an archetype of the city's strengths and weaknesses around walkability, and Jiner is intimately acquainted with the neighborhood's problems as well as its friendly, cohesive neighborliness.

I met her and a few other GirlTrekkers, plus another leader from Walk2Connect, at the corner of a local park. Before we set out, Jiner invited us to talk about what walking has done for us, why we believe in its capacity to change individuals and communities. The women, dressed in the distinctive electric-blue GirlTrek T-shirts, talked about high cholesterol levels and other health scares, about children and education and nutrition, about seeing people in the community and saying hello. While we were chatting, Jiner got a text from a woman who was struggling with depression. She wanted to get out tonight, she said, but she just couldn't. Jiner considered going over to the woman's house later, bringing the connection to her if she couldn't make that first heavy-hearted step out of her door.

This is the heart of Jiner's work, and the work of GirlTrek. Jiner often reaches out to women struggling with depression and loneliness. She was an enthusiastic participant in GirlTrek's Stress Protest. And she regularly works with Walk2Connect and Jonathon Stalls to lead city and neighborhood councilors, as well as representatives from the Colorado Department of Transportation, on walks around some of Denver's most underserved pedestrian areas.

Due in large part to the dedicated advocacy of people like Jiner and Stalls, and other organizations like WalkDenver, the mayor's office finally began taking pedestrian safety and walkability seriously. "Good sidewalks are particularly important for the one-third of the population that doesn't drive due to age, disability, or income," WalkDenver noted as it launched its Denver Deserves Sidewalks campaign in 2015. In October 2017, the mayor released a Vision Zero (a program originally from Sweden) action plan with the goal of zero traffic-related deaths or serious injuries in the city by 2030.

IT IS THROUGH this kind of clear thinking that we can avoid the amnesia that worried Jane Jacobs. We don't have to agree on the answers to all our societal ills, but every community, from cities like Denver to small towns like the one I live in, must face these questions openly if we are to avoid making the same mistakes we've made in the past: How do we build our cities? How do we keep our communities alive? Whom do our roads serve, and whom do they harm? Who gets to live in which neighborhoods? What do we actually mean by "safety"? Who gets access to healthy food and stress-reducing trees? Who gets to walk without fear? Who gets to walk with pleasure and ease? How do we live together in all the diversity of our selves and our shared spaces?

All over the United States, all over the world in fact, people are taking these steps. Unless their walks launch a powerful movement like GirlTrek, their stories rarely make it into the tops of our newsfeeds, but they change lives and repair connections just the same. Like eighteen-year-old Jourdan Duncan, whose two-hour-plus walks to and from work each day through an industrial region of California brought him to the attention of local police officer Kirk Keffer, who pooled resources in the local community to buy the hard-working teenager a bicycle. Or Walter Carr, a twenty-year-old Alabama college student and Marine hopeful who walked twenty miles his first day to a new job because his car broke down, prompting police worried for his safety to give him rides, and inspiring his new boss so much that he gifted Carr his own car. Or John Clarence Kawapit, who walked eight hundred kilometers in a desperate attempt to escape his alcohol addiction, eventually finding new bonds and support in Inuit villages in the far north of Canada, helping to heal centuries of conflict between the Inuit and his own Cree nation. "It's not right to live," he concluded, as so many walkers of the world have done, "as though we're ignoring each other."

THE MUNICIPAL PARK Pam Jiner walked me through for the hour of brisk steps and vibrant conversation was full of trees, gorgeous old things, oaks, maple, ash. Denver itself has over two million trees, and the full Metro Denver area has nearly eleven million, providing thirteen billion dollars in economic value due to their ability to absorb air pollution, provide cooling in that relentless heat, and increase property values.

But their other benefits—the drops in stress and lifts in mood, the lowered blood pressure and encouragement to walk that much farther—haven't been quantified in Denver. And beyond that are the most important things Jiner demonstrated as I strove to keep up with her and the other women's quick steps around Montbello: under the park's pleasant tree canopies, she greeted other area residents we came across, also out taking an evening stroll, or walking their kids to a place where they could bike freely, or walking home from work. Some people she'd seen repeatedly; some were new faces; some didn't speak English. Everyone smiled and said hello, sending out and receiving those invisible yet unbreakable tendrils of connection.

SEVEN
PACE

> My life as a walking person ended at thirteen. . . . My mind-body relationship changed in an instant—the time it took for my back to break. But the changing relationship between mind and body is a feature of everyone's life. We are all leaving our bodies—this is the inevitable arc of living.
>
> —Matthew Sanford, yoga teacher and author

THE HUMAN FOOT HAS TWENTY-SIX BONES. OUR ANKLES CAN sprain and twist. We get collapsed arches, shin splints, plantar fasciitis. "Everyone has foot problems," wrote paleoanthropologist Jeremy DeSilva in an article for the Leakey Foundation, "and if you don't yet, just wait."

Our spines are equally vulnerable. The American Academy of Pain Medicine says that back pain is the leading cause of disability for adults under forty-five years of age. Living with chronic and sometimes severe back pain myself after several car crashes, twenty years of sitting in front of computers for work, and an untreated tailbone fracture as a child, I'm well-acquainted with this statistic. Our long lumbar region and unconstrained vertebrae give us flexibility and mobility that aren't available to animals like chimpanzees, and two other curves in the upper chest and neck help keep our trunk stabilized over our hips. These features, exacerbated by the amount of sitting we do, also make us highly susceptible to lower back pain, and the construction of our vertebrae makes slipped disks and brittle bones probable later in life. Bipedality, unfortunately, makes the human body particularly prone to disability.

But humans adapt to injury, age, illness, and changes in mobility in more ways than we can imagine. Our capacity to compensate for impairments or limitations can sometimes be as miraculous as our bipedal walking in the first place. From broken foot bones to losing a limb to suffering from long-term vertigo, we become acutely aware, often suddenly and unexpectedly, of how our bodies move, what their constraints are, and how they might surprise us.

AS THE PACE of change increases, news headlines sometimes pose the question of how much technology we can integrate onto or into our bodies before we stop being "human" and become something else. But the truth is our lives are already deeply intertwined with technology. We've always used, worn, and depended on our tools. In some cases, this has benefited humanity greatly: Disability and illness are no longer always verdicts of restriction or death. Millions of us have some sort of technology attached to our bodies that help us function in the world or keep us alive: heart stents, IUDs, hearing aids, prosthetic arms and legs, titanium joints. Eyeglasses. Bicycle helmets. Shoes. The difference between these technologies and, say, cars is that these devices allow us to exist more fully *in* our bodies rather than abandon them.

And the fact that those tools are now increasingly digital might be less of a shift than it feels like. For centuries, our minds have moved in and out of technology without our conscious awareness: brain studies have shown that being utterly absorbed in a good book is like running a virtual reality scenario in our heads (without the attendant motion-induced nausea). Once we learn to ride a bike, we pedal and steer and brake almost as if the vehicle is part of our body; we develop similar relationships with tools like knives and hammers. We become addicted to social media because it's designed to tap into our evolutionary need for connection and approval. Every time you look at a computer screen or use a cell phone device, says cyborg anthropologist Amber Case, "you're a cyborg."

A cyborg, though, no matter what form it takes—we take—is still an embodied creature. *We* are embodied creatures. We sit too much, we diet, we go to the gym, we consume food we know isn't good for us, we slouch in front of Facebook even after our eyes have grown tired and our brains have stopped registering our friends' posts; we abuse and neglect and attempt to control our bodies in countless ways. Until, that is, we're involved in an accident or contract an illness or achieve an age at which our bodies no longer have the mobility they once did. It is only then that most of us realize the gift we've been scorning.

Lynn K. Hall, an ultra-runner, mountaineer, and writer, was forced to leave the Air Force Academy after an initially untreated meningitis infection left her in such severe chronic pain that she was throwing up several times a day while pushing herself through the grueling military training. "For years," she wrote in her memoir *Caged Eyes: An Air Force Cadet's Story of Rape and Resilience*, "I was resentful at my body for becoming ill, for breaking, for ending my dreams. Running and hiking have taught me how to work *with* my body, not against it. I'm most capable when I harness my body's strength rather than demanding its compliance."

To better direct where our walking will take us, we all need to rediscover this kind of relationship with our bodies. And we need to reestablish our understanding of technology as a tool that is there to serve us, even if it's in futuristic ways we can't foresee.

Matthew Sanford, a yoga teacher and paraplegic specializing in adaptive yoga, probably put our capacity for adaptation best: "Life force isn't completely determined by your ability to flex muscles." We are all better off facing the reality of our varied abilities. Any individual can at any moment become disabled. In fact, if we live long enough the possibility that we'll remain free of some kind of mental or physical limitation is almost zero. I've met or talked with people who've lost legs due to bomb blasts, car crashes, and infection; people who've started using wheelchairs due to degenerative diseases like multiple sclerosis; and people who became paralyzed from any number of illnesses or accidents. One woman, Rachelle Friedman, became paralyzed after a friend playfully pushed her into a swimming pool at her bachelorette party, resulting in a broken neck. Matthew Sanford became a paraplegic at the age of thirteen due to a car crash that also killed his father and sister.

When I started forming the ideas for this book, and was contemplating disability in the context of the idea that walking makes us human, I received an email from Edie Clark, the author of several memoirs who'd been a professor in my graduate program and had remained a mentor and friend. "Start with longing," she wrote of disability. Those words haunted me for over a year. They still do. *Start with longing*.

I first met her in 2002, when Clark was the fiction editor of *Yankee* magazine and wrote a regular column for them titled "The View from Mary's Farm," which she later turned into a book, about the farm she lived on near Mount Monadnock in New Hampshire. She was teaching a travel writing class I'd signed up for and had also, incidentally, recently recovered from a bout of Lyme disease. Her Lyme has flared up repeatedly over the years; in 2016, her illness and two strokes left her temporarily blind and in a wheelchair, unable to walk.

Clark's "Mary's Farm" columns are a rich catalogue of her ongoing relationship with a piece of the New Hampshire landscape that she came to know intimately over many years. They are full, too, of her presence among those hills. Her foot-bound connection with that land, her love for it, is why, when we spoke about walking and the realities of disability, I found her words "start with longing" so haunting.

Juliette Rizzo, Miss Wheelchair America 2005, reminded the audience at the 2017 National Walking Summit in St. Paul, Minnesota, that "Walking is a way to get from A to B, and I do that." Beginning in childhood, Rizzo acquired three different auto-immune diseases but didn't find herself in a wheelchair until she was thirty-one. She talked hopefully of once again getting to the point of walking on her own two feet; at the same time, she pressed able-bodied people, especially walkability advocates, to expand their understanding of what "walking" means.

Acknowledging the longing articulated by Clark while admitting that striding forward might not be within a person's means or desire—not everyone who can't or doesn't walk longs to do so—is a delicate and necessary balance, not least of all for the individual herself. Rachelle Friedman, who chronicled her paralysis in a memoir titled *The Promise*, maintains an upbeat Instagram feed that challenges widespread assumptions about disability. She shares her family's life, her love of the ocean, her chic sense of style, and her wheelchair rugby team. Very rarely does she speak of her wish for a cure or her desire to walk and use her hands, but when she does, the longing is palpable. In a post that shows Friedman bound in what looks like duct tape, pinned in her wheelchair with her mouth covered, she reminded her over forty thousand followers of her disability: injured at the C6 level of the spine, she's paralyzed from the chest down and can't move her fingers. She is, she wrote under the photo, like others with disabilities, "smart, beautiful, sexual, loving and more" and she will continue to fight misconceptions about people with disabilities. But a cure "would change our world. What I'd give to walk with my little girl and to hold my husband's hand."

An accident or illness leading to disability, leaving our lives changed and our physical selves perhaps dependent on others, could happen to any of us at any time. Even those of us who reach old age without impairment can develop gait problems due to neuropathy or diseases like Parkinson's. And any disability requires adaptation.

Serious vertigo, which can be caused by crystals in the inner ear's vestibular system shifting out of place, can take a year to treat. Some sufferers never recover at all, limiting their ability to trust their body's upright movement in this unpredictable world. Pain can cause severe disability by its simple presence. Lynn K. Hall eventually underwent a series of surgeries to implant a peripheral nerve stimulator, which reduced her pain enough to allow her to take up running and mountain climbing.

My mother-in-law has several titanium joints due to an arthritic condition she was born with, and when he was little my son liked to think of his Granny as part robot. But prosthetics are nothing new; they've been around since long before humans learned such complex metalworking. The oldest known prosthetics were replacements for toes and are nearly three thousand years old: the Greville Chester toe, dated to 600 BCE and possibly older, was made from cartonnage (a mixture of linen, glue, and plaster) in the unmistakable shape of a right big toe and part of the foot. Another toe, known as the Tabaketenmut toe for its owner, Tabaketenmut, a priest's daughter, was made of wood and leather and dates to between 950 and 710 BCE. Both of the toes show significant signs of wear, indicating that their owners walked around in them, either barefoot or in traditional Egyptian sandals. The Capua Leg, one of the most well-known ancient prosthetics, was found in Naples in 1910. Dating from around 300 BCE and made of wood with a hollowed-out bit at the top, possibly for padding against the remaining limb, the leg was covered in bronze sheeting, similar to the metal pieces once shaped to cover the shins of soldiers, and had rods and straps designed to hold the prosthetic in place.

"If you're living in East Africa two million years ago and you get a stress fracture, you're going to get eaten," I quoted Jeremy DeSilva as saying in Chapter 1. To a large extent this is true. And historical records predominantly portray society's relationship to those with disabilities as tolerant at best, deadly at worst—even into modern times. In both the United States and the UK, those with disabilities, including children, were for much of the twentieth century institutionalized, living in conditions that were often brutal. The Nazi regime openly practiced eugenics by killing people with disabilities, but those policies were far from unique. Canada sterilized people classified as disabled throughout most of the twentieth century. Many American states practiced forced sterilization of women with disabilities until very recently; California did away with the practice only in 1979.

But not every ancient hominin who broke a bone or grew old or frail turned into leopard food. In his online course on bipedalism (which I took in October 2017), DeSilva displayed a remarkable collection of fossils millions of years old that showed evidence of fractures that had healed, and of hominins who had lived with often painful and debilitating disabilities. These include the famous fossil Lucy, of the species *Australopithecus afarensis*. According to DeSilva, Lucy had a spinal deformation called Scheuermann's disease that causes severe pain in the lower, middle, and upper back, as well as the neck. The Nariokotome skeleton, popularly known as Turkana Boy, of the species *Homo erectus*, shows indications of trauma-related injuries to the spine, and possibly scoliosis. DeSilva displayed another *Australopithecus* who had a broken and healed ankle, a femur from an uncertain species that had also broken and healed, and two other skeletons with evidence of severe infections that probably would have affected both their survival and how easily they walked. An anthropological dig at the Qafzeh site in Israel unearthed evidence of a Paleolithic child living around 100,000 years ago who suffered from blunt-force trauma to the front of the skull, likely leaving him or her suffering from personality and neurological changes and in need of a significant amount of care. The skull showed that the child was six or seven years old at the time of the injury but didn't die until he or she was twelve or thirteen. He or she was also buried carefully, the grave including funerary objects like deer antlers, suggesting that the child was a valued member of the community.

What these injuries and others imply is that we evolved not from species of hominins in which only the ablest survived, but from creatures of community and mutual support, and that our interdependence is one of our most powerful adaptations. Even before humans were human we relied on one another. "If you're a two-legged creature and you have no legs," said paleoanthropologist Richard Leakey, "you don't go very far." Leakey was speaking from experience. He lost both legs after a plane crash in 1993, and he links the discussion about disability and bipedalism to his interest in the question of when human compassion came about. "When did we start worrying," he wondered aloud, "about the survival of an individual?"

In *Loneliness*, John Cacioppo wrote that it might even be bipedality that made our interdependence necessary. A mother monkey can climb trees with a baby clinging to her neck, but a human baby is far more helpless. A bipedal hominin mother looking to gather fruit from a high tree branch and encumbered by a baby on her hip would have had to pass her child on to someone else. Someone she'd have to trust to care for the baby as well as she would.

Being upright walkers has benefited humans immensely, and while there is no actual evidence that bipedalism led to compassion, it is a logical explanation for why we find fossils millions of years old with evidence of healed breaks. Someone had to care for those individuals while they recovered, to bring them food and protect them from predators. Bipedalism may have ensured the human traits that make for strong communities. "It is just possible," said DeSilva, "that the development of care and compassion in our human ancestors—qualities we hold so dear and regard as so human-like—may have developed in the context of our imperfect 'design.' Bipedalism may have only worked as an evolutionary innovation in a lineage that was already caring to some degree for the sick and injured."

"START WITH LONGING." Edie Clark, Rachelle Friedman, my mother-in-law—every one of these people has mentioned, at least once, the longing to be upright, to be mobile, to move bipedally through the world. But deeper even than the desire to walk is the craving for independence. When we first learn to walk, as toddlers, we discover ourselves anew as independent beings. We can run away from our parents, run toward toys, move through the world entirely on our own beyond the pace of a crawl. We remain interdependent, but we feel giddily free because our bodies allow us to go wherever we wish.

The loss of independence, not just the longing to walk, is something that comes up again and again in reading and talking about disability, and it is here that our evolutionary capability to care for one another can truly take modern form. With the technologies we have today, it's not only possible to make better prosthetics and pursue research into cures for conditions like Rachelle Friedman's; it's also more than possible to build our larger infrastructures to accommodate all users, whether they get around on their feet, with a wheelchair, or somewhere in between.

As Dr. Ashley Shew, a technology professor at Virginia Tech who also has a prosthetic leg, wrote in a short blog post about cyborg bodies, glamorizing prosthetic technology "imagines that there will be a solution to the problem of body—with the idea that bodies are problems. But the problems are often surfaces, environments, interfaces, places, and others."* Millions of years ago, hominins began evolving to care for one another while recovering from injuries and illnesses; today, we can use that same evolutionary capability to build our shared spaces so that everyone can access them. We need only make a commitment to accessible infrastructure, or what's known as universal design.

Universal design is a concept that's been making its way around urban planning circles for years, although not necessarily quickly enough to serve the people it's meant to help. Cities, as we've seen repeatedly, are riddled with barriers to accessibility, from sidewalks that don't exist or stop abruptly, to public transportation that lacks elevators and wheelchair on-ramps. Sunday Parker, a transit advocate who works in sales and gets around San Francisco in a wheelchair, pointed out in an interview that "sidewalks . . . are completely paramount to me being able to navigate through a city."

Parker runs a Twitter feed under the handle @sundaytakesbart, where she chronicles her experiences taking the BART public transportation system in the Bay Area. She's logged broken elevators and elevators that rarely get cleaned, inaudible intercom announcements that clearly can't serve riders who are hard of hearing, and more. Of a trip to New York City, she wrote on Twitter that "NYC is amazing, but unless you can walk a flight of stairs I could never live there" following a series detailing her efforts using the New York City subway, only to find that the station she needed to exit near the World Trade Center had no working elevator. Parker is a big fan of public transit, and shows a lot of affection for San Francisco's BART system. But, she pointed out, BART was built in the 1960s; the Americans with Dis-

---

*Shew also included the interesting point that moving to Mars would entail becoming disabled, as humans didn't evolve in tandem with that planet's gravity or atmosphere. Science fiction writer Kim Stanley Robinson, in his 2015 book *Aurora*, made a related question key to the novel's plot, and this reality is central to the science fiction show *The Expanse*, as mentioned in Chapter 1. Fantasies of colonizing other planets generally neglect the fact that our bodies evolved on this specific planet with its specific air, gravity, microbes, and perhaps other qualities we aren't even yet aware of.

abilities Act was implemented only in 1991, which means the system has decades of embedded infrastructure to either revamp or rebuild.

Universal design spans not just elevators and smoother, wider sidewalks but also wheelchair ramps that aren't too steep (and that aren't, as so many are, placed at some obscure, hard-to-find side or rear door of a building); "kneeling buses" that allow easy accessibility on and off, whether it's for wheelchairs, baby strollers, walkers, or simply for people whose balance is unsteady; sloped sidewalk corners at intersections; information signs in Braille and raised alphabets; and much, much more. For universal design to truly be universal, property owners must clear snow, ice, and leaves from sidewalks and municipalities must ensure that signs are placed so that people with limited mobility can get around them easily (including road construction signs, which are often placed in the middle of sidewalks so as not to impede drivers). In addition, bus and train services need to make it convenient to get around without a car, which involves more than just frequent service. Many people, including some with vision problems like my now-deceased grandmother with macular degeneration, or others with illnesses like epilepsy, can't drive a car, leaving them dependent on someone else driving them around if public transportation isn't easily accessible.

As Heidi Johnson-Wright, an attorney specializing in disability law, and journalist Steve Wright wrote for the American Planning Association, "Despite good intentions, planners and architects tend to design for the mythical five-foot-10, 175-pound, nondisabled male." Accessibility is added afterward as a "necessary evil."

But to repeat what Race Forward's Glenn Harris said at the 2017 National Walking Summit, "If we fix what is most harmful to those in the community who are the most vulnerable, then we will fix our communities for the benefit of everyone." Designing cities, towns, buildings, and transit for all users from the outset is not only more equitable and often cheaper, it's also, in the end, easier and benefits all sorts of underserved people, even if unintentionally.

In 2017, Portland, Oregon, widened the scope of its bike share program Biketown after listening to residents with disabilities, who have different needs than able-bodied users. The city added better access to bike rentals, for example, adaptive bikes and tricycles for people with balance problems, and ways to protect assistive devices while riding. In England, Transport for London posts the location and variety of accessible access points in its various Tube stations, which is useful information but also highlights the scarcity of accessible transit. In a 2017 article, *The Guardian* mapped where transit is truly accessible all across the city and came up with sketchy lines that are sadly anemic compared to the entirety of the system, a reality that is partly due to its age. The Underground opened in 1863, and by 2017 only seventy-one out of two hundred and seventy stations were wheelchair accessible. In Paris, only fifteen out of nearly three hundred were, whereas in Barcelona nearly every station is accessible. While wheelchair user John Morris, quoted in the same *Guardian* article, said that he tells people to avoid the subway in downtown Manhattan "at all costs," citing a haphazard system that is uninformative and difficult to navigate, Washington, D.C., has a fully accessible transit system that includes emergency intercoms with instructions in Braille and raised alphabet, and a reputation for keeping people informed of any power outages that might affect elevators.

Like so many other advances, universal design requires the dedication of engaged residents who recognize that our communities work best when they work for everyone.

ACCESSIBLE DESIGN IS just one aspect of our adaptive strategy. Assistive devices also play a large and growing role. They exist on a spectrum of tools that have enabled and enhanced human mobility for thousands of years, from shoes to pacemakers to canes to Fitbits.

Prosthetics have changed drastically since the bronze-covered wooden leg of Capua. While headlines do often, as Shew pointed out, glamorize technological advances, the nitty-gritty details behind them are the result of decades of research in engineering, biomechanics, and the human body, often by people who have lost limbs and who direct their work in an effort to increase their own mobility.

Several labs around the world are developing ever more sensitive prosthetics, called neuroprosthetics, that use the brain neurons responsible for muscle control to control the prosthetic devices in much the same way we control the limbs we're born with. These devices have become possible because of advances in technology and materials, as well as neuroscience's uncovering of the deep links between the brain's activity and physical movement.

Much of the research into advanced prosthetics has been born out of the decades-long struggle to develop a walking robot like the University of Michigan's MARLO. The development of walking robots—more to the point, the failure to do so despite getting incrementally closer—has exposed, layer by layer, the intricacy involved in human walking.

While robots are developed for a variety of reasons, many significant advances in this particular area of robotics are actually pursued with the intention of making more functional prosthetics for humans. Dr. Ayanna Howard, a professor of bioengineering at the Georgia Institute of Technology and a former scientist at NASA's Jet Propulsion Laboratory, sees prosthetics as the most exciting future for robotics. Devices like neural-linked prosthetics, she told me, "show the first step in human-robotic technology." The future will move toward seamless integration, where we tap into signals from eyes, muscles, and so on "to make our lives better."

⁂

THERE ARE MANY prosthetics, just as effective as those developed through neural linkages and other advances, and in many cases far more suited to a person's needs, that are also simpler, learning from the designs of nature and often avoiding complex computer linkages entirely.

Some of these less electronically complex prosthetics perform so much better than the human body that they beg the question: why didn't we evolve that way in the first place? Take the blade form of a leg prosthetic, often used by athletes. The designer of the blade prosthetic, Van Phillips, became a below-the-knee amputee after a water-skiing accident in 1976. Phillips had been an athlete, and after he was given a standard prosthetic leg made of wood and rubber, he said that it "felt like a sentence from hell." Prosthetics, he found out, hadn't changed much since World War II, and were based on the idea that people wanted a limb that looked normal, not one that functioned with the springy elastic energy found in the human body. Instead of focusing on prosthetics modeled on the human foot, Phillips turned to other animals to work out how they moved. He studied "ligaments that store muscle energy, observing the tendons of porpoises, kangaroos and cheetahs, noting how the cheetah's hind leg landed and compressed, and the elastic nature of it."

There is actually a nonhuman animal equivalent of the blade prosthetic. Ostriches walk with their ankle bones and the soles of their feet are "fused together in a single rigid structure called the tarsometatarsus," said Jeremy DeSilva. An ostrich foot has only eight bones compared to humans' twenty-six, and the "blade" structure stores more elastic energy than the human foot does, while the rigid base gives ostriches a powerful propulsion method.

Humans don't have this kind of foot because we evolved from a different lineage—apes, not feathered creatures. "Evolution does not create perfection," wrote DeSilva. "It molds previous structures to produce anatomies just good enough to survive." The wonderful thing about being a human being is that, when our anatomy becomes damaged, we have these inventive, curious brains that try to figure out how we can adapt.

BUT PROSTHETICS, HOWEVER advanced or useful, can also be painful. No matter what kind of padding is used between a leg cup and a person's remaining limb, the device can chafe and bruise, and it sometimes breaks, leaving users to become expert tinkerers as they repair their limbs. "Keeping technologies in and on one's body actually takes a lot of work," wrote Shew. She sometimes ends up gluing her prosthetic leg back together, and has found herself sitting on the floor of a hardware store trying to find the right-sized screw to repair it. The technologies used to assist people in mobility tend to get idealized, ignoring, Shew has said, issues like maintenance. "Cyborg bodies aren't these shining examples of human 'overcoming' and technological triumph," she wrote on a Twitter thread about assistive devices. "I use stuff because I need it."

News stories about athletes sprinting on blade prosthetics tend to leave out details about jarring, impact, deadened senses, infections, and irritated, raw skin. When Boston Marathon bombing survivor Rebekah Gregory ran part of that same race two years later on a blade prosthetic, news stories focused on the uplifting statement she wrote on Facebook after crossing the finish line: "I got my life back today." She talked about being an inspiration, about the pleasure she took in walking again. But few reporters asked her or her trainer, Artis Thompson III, about the amount of pain they were in. In response to one reporter, Thompson said his pain in general ranged from mild to "feeling like my leg is getting crushed." The two also had to worry about their prosthetics slipping in the rain. Ashley Shew told me that there's too much attention given to that first moment a person stands up on a prosthesis and not enough given to what follows. Not only will it hurt, a lot, but "that first year your legs will change, and you'll have to be in your prostheticist's office all the time, complaining."

Much of the progress being made in prosthetics now is focused on reducing that pain and discomfort and improving a person's ability to receive physical sensations that closely mimic those we receive through our organic bodies. The ability to feel the world, in other words. Haptics, the study of enhancing or replacing the sense of touch, is being used not just to give amputees the feeling of touch, but also to improve the ways in which we interact with the world. A prosthetic hand can help a person manipulate objects, but until recently it couldn't help him *feel* them; a prosthetic foot can help a person walk, but it couldn't help her feel the ground underfoot. Prosthetics that involve haptic design can begin to fill that sensory gap. Many people who've never faced a disability at all have interacted with haptic design: before Apple did away with the home button on its iPhone X, previous versions, starting with the iPhone 7, had a haptics-enabled button; when you pressed it, it *felt* like you were pushing a button, but there was no actual button. What you felt was a small vibration.

Haptics can mimic touch for those who have lost a limb or sensory perception—through paralysis, spinal cord damage, or neuropathy, for example. Igor Spetic, a young father who lost his right arm in an industrial accident, tested out a haptics-enabled prosthetic hand created by a biomedical engineering team at Case Western Reserve University in Ohio. Spetic and a second amputee fitted with the sensors were able to pull a stem off a cherry and put toothpaste on a toothbrush with enough control not to squish the objects. A haptic feedback system developed in 2008 for lower-limb prosthetics gave wearers the ability to detect force and movement with over 90 percent accuracy. The information that our feet read from the ground is vital for our balance and stability; getting back some of that information helps enormously in being able to walk confidently in a varied world, though it still doesn't erase the pain of wearing a device.

In "Robot Awakening," a *Science News* article on embodied robots, Dr. Alice Wu talked about her dream of giving robots a sense of touch that can help them "sense the surface they're on and adjust their walk accordingly." Those efforts, like the development of prosthetics, run into some hard real-world barriers: if you're able-bodied, think about the force of your heel when it hits the ground; most engineered sensors can't take that kind of impact, meaning that Wu can't just stick the same sensors on the bottom of the robot's feet that she uses on its hands.

Meghan Rosen, the author of that article, wrote of efforts to give robots a more refined sense of touch, "The crux is embodiment . . . or the robot's awareness that each of its actions brings on an ever-shifting kaleidoscope of sensations." That's a lyrical summation, too, of the nature of human existence. In our interactions with others as well as with every physical motion, no matter what our abilities, our bodies and our brains absorb and translate a universe of information, informing our choices and the steps we take next.

WHILE NOT EVERYONE who spends all or most of their time in a wheelchair longs to walk again, many do, and one of them, Amit Goffer, who became a quadriplegic after an ATV crash, invented a device that can help them do so. Goffer's invention is called the ReWalk exoskeleton, and it looks like what it sounds like: a system of joints, bars, padding, and motors attached to a person's body. Goffer invented the exoskeleton with the intention of helping people like himself walk under their own power, although he can't yet make use of his own invention—ReWalk works only for people who can control their arms, and Goffer is a quadriplegic.

Exoskeletons are also being used in tandem with virtual reality to treat people with paralysis, in studies that could eventually have far-reaching effects. Working initially with only eight patients with spinal cord injuries, Duke University neuroscientist Dr. Miguel Nicolelis and his team found that combining a brain-machine interface with wearing an exoskeleton led to unexpected sensory input below the levels of people's spinal cord injuries. The technique involved extensive training with the equipment, but in interviews about the research Nicolelis said that the results might mean patients with paralysis actually have some spinal nerves left intact that have simply "gone quiet" through lack of communication between the brain and muscles. The changes seen in Nicolelis's study were profound. All eight patients involved in the study "experienced a significant improvement in tactile, proprioceptive, vibration, and nociceptive* perception," the only exception being no change in the ability to sense temperature. A thirty-two-year-old woman who'd been paralyzed for thirteen years, and who'd been unable to stand, became "capable of walking using a walker, braces and the assistance of one therapist."

At the University of Melbourne, Dr. Thomas Oxley and his team have been testing brain stents on a small group of people with quadriplegia. These are implanted devices that might, with training, allow them to control an exoskeleton and begin walking. Other labs around the world are following suit, revisiting our assumptions about paralysis and perceived limitations, and what we expect of the human body's capabilities. Does this mean the future of humans is robotic, a more fully integrated and self-directed cyborg? Perhaps, with all the devices we use in our daily lives, we're already so far down that road that the baseline definitions of "human" and "robot" no longer apply.

AS SHEW WARNED, it's easy to get caught up in the dazzling technological advances aimed at making mobility possible for people with disabilities. But not every technological answer fits the needs of every person. Rose Eveleth, a science and technology writer who specializes in covering advances in prosthetics and exoskeletons, pointed out that some of the most state-of-the-art prosthetics are useless for many of the people they're aimed at. Farmers, for example, don't get much

*Nociceptive reception allows us to feel pain that is causing bodily damage to bone, muscle, or skin and connective tissue, such as exposure to toxic chemicals and extreme temperatures. Neuropathic pain, by contrast, is caused by other factors, such as nerve damage or diabetes.

use out of prosthetics that can't get wet or dirty, and some farmers, Eveleth learned, find that prosthetics can actually be dangerous on the job. Shew said that her own prosthetic is pretty low-tech, no computerized parts, and she's come to love not the kind of technology captured in news headlines, but Velcro.

Even for people who want these devices, and who can afford them or have insurance that will cover the cost, the technology simply might not give them what they seek. The best candidates for advanced prosthetics that assist with walking, wrote Eveleth, are the 15 percent of amputees who are trauma victims and cancer survivors. A full 80 percent of amputations are the result of diabetes and other vascular diseases. "Weight gain, cardiovascular issues and general immobility make it hard for amputees with vascular diseases to get up and walking again at all after an amputation," she wrote, "let alone running around on a myoelectric leg."

What's far more important, and what Eveleth has written about several times in her articles covering these technologies, is "understanding each patient and what makes them most independent. . . . The measure of success for a patient isn't how state-of-the-art their legs or arms are, but how well they can live their lives."

This, it seems to me, is the true goal of adaptation, whether it's individual devices or how we design our cities and towns: to allow each of us to live our lives as well as we can in the ways we choose.

THERE ARE ALL sorts of devices that assist in the mobility of even the most able-bodied people. Fitbits and Apple Watches have prompted stronger pushback against our sedentary culture, and our relationships with these devices are themselves evolving. Many people use them as an incentive to walk more, exercise regularly, and get better sleep, while others have reported the need to go through a "Fitbit breakup." (One journalist said in a Facebook group that she had to get rid of her

Fitbit because she found herself refusing to move while it charged, unwilling to give up the recording of her steps.) My own spouse, who has heard me go on a hundred times about how he should stand up and walk around more often while he's on conference calls, didn't start doing it until he got an Apple Watch that tapped him with regular haptic reminders. If we need these tools to keep our bones and hearts strong, then we should probably use them. After all, very few of us would walk outside our doors without shoes.

While headlines about exoskeletons focus on how people with paralysis can gain greater mobility, it shouldn't surprise anyone that the military backs a large portion of that research in order to develop devices that will allow soldiers to carry much heavier loads while in the field. How might those advances translate into the civilian world? Might we someday see a tiny exoskeleton assist a parent carrying a surprisingly heavy, sleeping five-year-old home? Or groceries? Or helping nurses shift temporarily immobile patients in a hospital?

How, in other words, might technology be carefully and deliberately designed to improve human existence, without rushing headlong into a wholesale rewriting of it? How do we avoid making the same mistakes with assistive technology that we made with automobiles?

In 2017, Facebook CEO Mark Zuckerberg made a lengthy announcement of an initiative to create a truly global online community that would somehow lead to a new world order formed around (one supposes) peaceful and progressive shared values. Historian Yuval Noah Harari wrote a sharp critique of this vision in the *Financial Times*, noting that "online giants" like Facebook tend to "view humans as audiovisual animals—a pair of eyes and a pair of ears connected to 10 fingers, a screen and a credit card," disregarding almost the entirety of the human body and its experience. To their detriment and to ours.

An increasing number of researchers would probably agree with Harari's criticism, as their work cracks open the reality that embodiment, being in a body, is part and parcel of having a human mind at all. "We think with our whole body, not just with our brain," wrote

Ben Medlock, the creator of the predictive texting app SwiftKey, in an essay about the flaws in artificial intelligence research. The world that our minds interpret is revealed through our "evolved, embodied needs as an organism," one formed through billions of years of changing biology.

These long, swinging limbs, this upright posture, these expressive faces and miraculous balance—these are what at least six million years of evolution have given us. Everything we know about our world, everything that we perceive, interpret, reason, create, *all* of it comes through our bodies. There is nothing about the human experience that isn't related in some way to how our bodies exist and move. Our minds, what we think of as our "selves," exist within and around our bodies, and are shaped by our bodies' experiences.

When we lose connection to those bodies, wrote Harari in his critique of Zuckerberg, we become "alienated and disoriented. Pundits often blame such feelings on the decline of religion and nationalism, but losing touch with your body is probably more important. . . . If you don't feel at home in your body, you will never feel at home in the world."

What if we treated this physical form as the glorious, miraculous thing it is? What if we paid attention, for once, not to our bodies' drawbacks and limits, but to their potential? What if true freedom isn't freedom *from* our bodies, but the freedom to fully inhabit our bodies, to roam where we will, to exist completely in the physical world, and to revel in it?

OUR BODIES GET us from A to B, but they also contain and release our sorrow, harbor our heartaches and longings and joy, introduce us every day to the miracle of ourselves and the world. Our bodies' abilities are infinite, greater than we know and more varied than we acknowledge.

Technologies like prosthetics or devices that bring us closer to the cyborg brink do not need to change what it means to be human. At their best they are, as Rose Eveleth wrote, about helping people live their best lives. Combined with an inclusive approach to urban design, prosthetics can allow many more people to participate, if they wish, in the activity of walking and so much more, continuing a dialogue we've had with our bodies and one another for millions of years. There is no perfect body and there is no perfect mind; there is just a relationship built on trust and self-knowledge, and a willingness to care for ourselves and one another.

"I never forget about my disability," wrote poet and essayist Molly McCully Brown, who has cerebral palsy, in an opinion essay for *The New York Times*. "It's not just that I'm often in pain, or that I have to think about my body almost all the time, although both of these things are true. It's that *I don't exist* without my body. . . . My body isn't standing apart from me holding my life in a vise grip: It is *making* my life, indivisible from the rest of me. We are walking together through the world, as odd and slow as it looks."

EIGHT

MEANDER

The Appalachian Trail was the longest conversation I'd ever had with my body, both where I fit in it and where it fits in the world.

—Rahawa Haile, "Going It Alone," *Outside* magazine, 2017

"WHEREABOUTS IS IT YOU'RE GOING?"

"Happisburgh." I held up a piece of paper on which a woman at the train station's information desk had written the destination and bus information: "x11 to Martham, get off at post office, 2 minutes' walk to Happisburgh." All of which had turned out to be wildly incorrect, but I kept the paper because I feared that my American accent would mangle the village's name enough to send me off with instructions to a completely different part of Norfolk.

This was the second day I'd tried to get to Happisburgh (pronounced HAZE-bur-uh) from Norwich, from a city of over 145,000 people served by major train lines to a village of 1,400 served—at least it seemed to be served—by a bus. This was my last chance before leaving England to head back to Montana. The previous Saturday, the day I'd acquired the misleading piece of paper in my hand, I'd run a gauntlet of wrong answers, "no idea" answers, and one "I used to do that run, it's lovely. Just ask the other driver when he comes by," which he never did. I texted my husband a summation of the struggles, to make him laugh, and he texted back his usual answer: just get an Uber. But despite the many difficulties I'd had with buses in Denver, the Twin Cities, and my own little Montana town, places that ostensibly have some public transportation but seem to be under the assumption that nobody uses it, or that the needs of people who do use it are unimportant, I had never yet taken an Uber.

I'd given up on Saturday. As far as I could tell, it was possible I'd get to Happisburgh, or somewhere nearby, but there was little assurance I'd get back. Today, a Tuesday, the bus to the village was looking likely but the return maintained its Schrödinger's cat–like quality.

I took the 10, not the x11, which went somewhere else, from Norwich to Stratham, where the bus driver stopped at the far end of the village and told me this was where I wanted to get off. He paged through a thick book of timetables. "You'll have to the catch the 34 around the corner. But you can't go that way because that's the road." "The road," I'd learned years ago when driving my in-laws around the UK, did not mean just any old road. It meant a road with no shoulder and no sidewalk, often one lane, and a lot of high-speed traffic. "You'll have to walk back into the village and turn right by the Tesco, walk straight through to the other side and then around." I turned myself around and bent my hand right, imitating and then repeating his directions because getting lost is one of the things I'm best at, something I'd come to enjoy when I'd traveled more in my twenties, but just this once I couldn't spare the time. "You want one of these?" he asked, lifting a basket of timetable booklets toward me.

"Oh my gosh, *thank you*," I said. There were the answers to the questions I'd been asking all day. *Which* bus, *where*, *what time*? Answers all locked away on a website that assumed a detailed knowledge of local geography, and bus stop signage (or lack thereof) that assumed people knew exactly which bus they wanted and when. The timetable was like a Rosetta Stone, complete with every bus route this company ran and a map of them on the back cover. I'd looked everywhere for a timetable, for a map of the bus routes, for something to orient myself, and found nothing. I held it tight as I walked back into the village of Stratham, toward the Tesco. My phone had lost connection some time ago; the timetable was now my lifeline.

Twenty minutes or so later, the 34 bus came roaring up to the stop and I went through a similar routine. Going to Happisburgh, yes, but the question is, can I get back today? The timetable, like the Rosetta Stone, still held some unanswered questions. Some buses ran only on school days, some only on non-school Mondays-through-Fridays, some stops at certain times were only by request, and some villages seemed to get passed over completely at certain times of day. Happisburgh was one of them. The driver scratched his head and ran a finger down the timetable. "The last one's at—no, there's no more today." He paused. "There's that one," pointing down. "It doesn't stop in Happisburgh but I do that run and I could pick you up there and get you to Sea Palling." Which was kind of him but did me little good. Sea Palling had no buses going anywhere else, and I had to get back to London that night to catch my flight home in the morning.

I pointed down at the timetable to the next village after Happisburgh, which had one extra stop. "Do you know how far Ostend is from Happisburgh? Could I walk from one to the other?" It couldn't be far, I figured, since the bus stop times were only six minutes apart. He hesitated.

"About three, four miles." I could do that, easily. "But it's on the road." "The road," in this case, was so narrow that drivers had to reverse into pullouts to let someone go the opposite direction. Hemmed in by hedges and berms, the road held no place for a walker to step off quickly.

As we talked for a few more minutes and I apologized to the other passengers for the delay, I could see the driver had the same question that the driver of the 10 bus had, the same question everyone, from the information desk clerk in Norwich to my mother-in-law in Nottingham, had wondered: why on earth do you want to go to Happisburgh?

In 2013, on the beach below the claggy dirt cliffs that make up Happisburgh's eastern boundary, researchers who'd been working on an archaeological site nearby for the Pathways to Ancient Britain project stumbled across the oldest fossilized hominin footprints found outside Africa.

Fossilized hominin footprints are rare. The oldest and most famous are the Laetoli footprints, first discovered in Tanzania in 1978 by paleontologist Mary Leakey's team. Seventy hominin footprints were preserved in volcanic ash about 3.6 million years ago, most likely left by *Australopithecus afarensis*, the species represented by the famous fossilized partial skeleton we know as Lucy. Footprints are uniquely valuable pieces of information in our evolutionary story, and they can't be preserved in caves or buried in hillsides in quite the same way that bones can. Footprints are an absence, yet proof of a presence. A whisper of a life left behind.

The prints in Tanzania tell us that this long-gone species had *Homo sapiens*–like feet, with a big toe in line with the foot rather than off to the side as chimps' big toes are, and that Lucy and her relatives walked the way we do, striking the ground with the heel and pushing off from the toes, the swaying choreography of balance that makes our bipedality distinctive.

Footprints in Kenya found in 2007, about a million and a half years old, show similar features, as well as the arched foot that gives us our springiness. And in Crete in 2017 researchers found human-like footprints over five and a half million years old that bring into question our story of human origins, though far more research is needed to study the hominins' gait, or if the creatures who left them by the banks of a river were in fact hominins rather than gorillas, which is equally likely. As with all new discoveries in science, more questions are raised by this find than answers.

The Happisburgh footprints had a similar effect. The team led by Dr. Nick Ashton, an archaeologist and curator at the British Museum, faced a unique challenge after coming across the footprints on the Norfolk coast. Happisburgh hangs right on the edge of the coastal cliffs, but at the time it was founded nearly nine hundred years ago, another entire village sat between it and the sea. The coast erodes at an alarming rate—residents lose about five meters of land per year—so Ashton and his team had to act fast. The Laetoli footprints were left in volcanic ash that had been rained on, making the material harden like cement, but the Happisburgh footprints were left in mudflats, which can feel like rock if you touch them, but are in fact fragile. Subject to any kind of force, such as heavy waves or a shovel, they crumble and come apart, like shale.

Ashton and his colleagues tried to lift out one footprint for study, but they had to dig out a huge block of hardened mud, which ended up weighing about fifty kilograms (about a hundred and ten pounds), and haul it up a cliffside. It was still too fragile to work with.

Over the two weeks after their discovery, then, the team worked through driving wind and rain and against the tide to take 3-D images of the footprints using a process called photogrammetry, a technique that is also used to make topographical maps. Photogrammetry feeds quantities of images and other information into computational analysis to produce highly accurate 3-D images. Once the images from Happisburgh had been analyzed—by Dr. Isabelle De Groote, a paleoanthropologist at Liverpool University, who confirmed that they were hominin footprints—Ashton and his team used a variety of techniques to date the surrounding sediment. Boreholes gave them pine and birch pollen, plant seeds, animal bones, and beetles. Work at the nearby archaeological site had revealed species like red deer, giant elk, certain species of horse, and a form of mammoth that had become extinct about 800,000 years ago. Using paleomagnetism* allowed them to place the date of the prints between 850,000 and a million years ago.

At that period, during the Calabrian stage of the Pleistocene Epoch, England was still connected to Europe by a wide land bridge. While Ashton's archaeological work in Happisburgh shows definitive early hominin existence through the presence of Paleolithic tools made of stone, and fossilized animal remains showing cut marks, indicating that the meat was cut off the animal, not just torn by predatorial teeth, the footprints showed something different. They showed, very likely, long-term habitation. "The footprints weren't in a straight line," Ashton told me when we met at his British Museum office. Not being in a straight line was a criticism other researchers had leveled at the find. But to him, the wandering nature of the footprints made complete sense. Because the Happisburgh footprints included children. This wasn't just a temporary hunting party, a group moving through seasonally. These people were living there.

The Laetoli footprints are in a straight line, and it's easy to imagine those hominins some three or four million years ago walking across the savannah, heading . . . where? The Happisburgh footprints, though, give us movement and life, images of children veering off to poke in the mud, chase some small animal or crustacean, or peer at a plant, just as my children did at that age. Just as the infants in Karen Adolph's lab do, roaming around in the most inefficient manner possible because that is how we grow and explore and learn.

The questions these footprints brought up for Ashton will provide a wealth of research and speculation for many years to come. The

*Every several hundred thousand years or so, Earth's poles reverse their polarity. Our compasses point north, but if the poles reversed, they would point south. Scientists don't know enough about this process to understand why it happens, but the most recent research ties the reversals to instability in the molten metal boundary between Earth's core and mantle, which controls the planet's magnetic field. The magnetic field affects metals like iron on the planet surface. For the Happisburgh site, researchers studied the orientation of iron particles within the sediment, which allowed them to place the date of the site between two pole reversals that took place 780,000 and 950,000 to a million years ago, respectively.

most likely hominin to have made them, *Homo antecessor*, was living in Europe at the time, having moved north from the tropics. But why did they migrate farther, to this remote coast? They were unlikely to have been in competition with other hominins; there were simply too few. But with other carnivores, possibly. They might have been looking for new resources. Europe at that time, as a friend of Ashton's described it, was like a pinball machine, with pockets of hominins pinging around. Changes in climate had them moving around a bit more, searching for resources, and at some point one of the pinballs popped into Britain, leaving traces that would lead Ashton to excavate the oldest known human habitation in northern Europe. It still would have been cold on that part of the planet, similar to present-day Scandinavia. Were they able to make skins and fur into clothes? Did they have shelter? What about fire? Were they active hunters or still just scavengers of other predators' kills? Questions to chase, to walk down, to dig for, to ponder.

For at least another 400,000 years the land bridge to Europe remained intact. The original route of the River Thames led it out to sea near Happisburgh, some ninety-three miles north of its present location. At that time, the geography of Dover, those iconic white cliffs, stretched all the way to Europe. There was no English Channel. But over time, ice began to creep down from the north, swallowing up the North Sea and the outlets of any rivers it came across, pushing any freely flowing water into the territory of a vast glacial lake dammed by bedrock at the Strait of Dover. More water poured in, forced by rock and soil in Europe and England and ice elsewhere, and one day the dam did what any dam does when pushed to its limits. It broke.

The quantity of water released, and the havoc it wreaked, is almost impossible to imagine. The flood, which took place around 425,000 years ago, together with another about 200,000 years later, scraped out the English Channel and severed the island from mainland Europe. The original hard Brexit, my mother-in-law and I joked ruefully when I explained to her why I was going to Happisburgh. The flood has been compared to the release of Glacial Lake Missoula, an even larger flood that formed much of the geography of the northwestern United States, including my home ground of Montana. The hominins that had left their traces on what was once the Thames estuary and what is now the coast of Norfolk would have been wiped out by such a cataclysmic event. But they were there, once. We don't know exactly how they lived, but we know that they did.

THE FOOTPRINTS ARE no longer in Happisburgh. Two weeks after Ashton and his colleagues discovered them, the rough North Sea had washed them away. But I still wanted to see that coastline, to feel the soil and walk the sand that held its own chapter of our shared human story.

The driver of bus 34 whipped around corners and curves and pulled over for oncoming traffic at such speeds that I wondered for a minute if he was trying to prove to me how unwalkable the roads were. I didn't need any proof. We passed two bicyclists and I thought they were some of the bravest people I'd met all year. There's no room for error on those roads, and I hoped mightily that not a single driver was glancing down at their phone.

Norfolk is full of Norman churches. It's famous for them, around six hundred all over the county. Everywhere you look, there's another one coasting along, square-towered and built of local flint stone. I wondered idly what the Normans had been thinking, if they were bored or truly that pious, or if churches were kind of like the Walmart of nine hundred years ago, built as if nobody could live without one within a twenty-minute commute.

Eventually, we got to the tiny seaside village of Ostend, rows of brick houses bordered by fields of hay and potatoes. "I'll be driving the route back," the driver said. "I'll pick you up right here about half-three. If you get bored, walk up to the café in the next village. I stop there, too." I said thank you and that I would be in one or the other place, and started walking away from the closest Norman church toward the coast, sniffing at the familiar, unexpected tang of burning slash. The bus driver drove forward a few feet, then stopped and opened his door. "Up there's the beach," he told me, stepping off the bus and pointing. "If you want something to do."

After he left, I strolled forward, mindful of the dropping daylight and thankful that Ashton had reminded me to check the tide tables before I went. I walked past a few small brick houses and over a small rise to look down, abruptly, on the pounding sea. A ramp led down to the sand-and-gravel beach, empty except for a couple walking their dog. "Is it possible to walk to Happisburgh from here?" I asked them. "I mean safely," I added, referring to the tide.

"Sure," they said. "It's only about two miles, and you can always scramble up the cliff. High tide's not until about four." Not completely reassuring for a landlubber who couldn't even remember to check the tides until someone reminded her, but promising. Since giving up walking on the road, I'd counted on being able to walk either on a public footpath* or along the shore. I wiggled my heels into the sand, pointed my feet south, and began to walk. The sea boomed unceasingly, crashing against rotting wooden reinforcements that had been built in 1953 after catastrophic floods, and the light was soft, hushed with gray, reminding me unexpectedly of St. Petersburg on a winter's day when the light is brief and the air is eyelash-freezing cold.

My boots sh-shd into the sand, barely audible above the roaring of the sea, the sand-walking sound like the little sister of crunch-crunch snow-walking. I ran my hands along the black mounds hunched under the silt-and-clay-packed cliffs. Knocking on them, they felt solid,

---

*England is laced with ancient rights-of-way in the form of footpaths all over private land, and in 2000 the country passed a Right to Roam law that further opened up access: you are legally allowed to walk on and through a great deal of private land, such as moors, heaths, and mountains. Scotland's Right to Roam, passed in 2003, is even broader, allowing walking and activities like paddleboarding on all private land in the country, as long as users behave responsibly.

like rock, but I wiggled a piece of flint that was sticking out from the side of one, and the black mud cracked and crumbled. Above, the cliffs exposed different shades of brown, pocked with holes that looked like the workings of some small vole-like animal, but were probably caused by water when the tide came up. A fringe of farmland peeked over the top, but the smell of burning slash had given over to the scent of a cold sea.

IN HIS OFFICE the day before, Ashton had handed me a hefty block of resin, flat on the bottom and sides and lumpy everywhere else, reminding me, once again, of one of my mother's topographical maps. Rises and hills and little curls and inlets. And in the middle, pressed deep into the recreated mudflat, the shape of a foot.

I felt around the deep heel indentation, the rise where an arch lifted, the impression left by the big toe digging in as a hominin took that pendulum-like swing, trusting her upright stride to the fine-tuned balance of her body, and stepped forward. I could almost, just, make out the outline of the second toe. Ashton showed me a picture of another print with a full set of toes more clearly defined.

The feet were probably about a British size eight—an American ten or European forty. I've never held anything more thrilling in my life, including the dinosaur fossils tens of millions of years old that I dug out of the hard-baked Montana soil myself. This footprint hit me harder than the ancient cave paintings left in places like France and Utah, haunting and beautiful and created by humans tens of thousands of years ago. This footprint and its companions were never intended to leave a trace. They weren't planted or crafted in that lonely cry to the universe, that "Here I am!" that we wish could live for eternity. It's just a step, and then another, a few minutes of everyday life for an everyday family—possibly a family—living over 800,000 years ago. Ashton had found footprints of women, probably, and men, likely, and children, most certainly. They were walking south, along an estuary edge, putzing around, being human. They gathered, walked, and looked, and they left, unintentionally, this moment of their lives for us to meditate upon.

They were here.

WHEN I WAS twenty, I traveled to Turkey with some friends. We spent a day at Ephesus, walking three-thousand-year-old ruins of a once-vibrant city. My travel companions and I couldn't let go of the thrill of walking down the harbor road, which was still mostly intact, although the sea's shoreline was now miles off. "Imagine the people who used to walk down here flirting," said one of my friends, and we all stopped, caught by the image of those long-dead footsteps leaving behind traces of lives very much like our own. At twenty, setting my foot down on a track worn by feet that have been dust for millennia sparked a thrill akin to religious ecstasy.

"Touch is a reciprocal action, a gesture of exchange with the world," wrote essayist and author Robert Macfarlane in his widely acclaimed book *The Old Ways*, in which he followed ancient pathways on sea and land. "To make an impression is also to receive one, and the soles of our feet, shaped by the surfaces they press upon, are landscapes themselves with their own worn channels and roving lines." Where our feet land leaves a story for those who can read it, whether it's a tracker in the woods following a few hours behind, an archaeologist studying fossilized footprints millions of years old, or the rest of us ordinary humans, drawn to the magic of old pathways, the reminder of people who were once alive and laughing and loving and walking.

"A walk is only a step away from a story," wrote Macfarlane, "and every path tells."

There are paths all over the world, seen and unseen, that draw us to them. Even newer ones have this power. As Robert Moor wrote in

On Trails, paths are shaped by those who walk them. Without footsteps, human trails wouldn't exist; the walking of a path gives it meaning that lasts long past its use in daily life; we return to these trails in later years because we crave the visceral reality of stories told through the million-plus-year conversation between our bodies and the earth we walk.

The Oregon Trail, named for the thousands of wagon-pulling pioneers drawn out to the promise of land and a better life in the American West, is still identifiable from deep wagon ruts, and graffiti carved by those same pioneers as they passed Register Cliff, a sandstone cliff in Wyoming that the settlers used to navigate themselves past more deadly mountainous terrain. "The fact that you're literally walking in the footsteps of pioneers is kind of mind-blowing," wrote Anna Hider for the Roadtrippers website, on visiting the Register Cliff and walking the rutted sandstone. The power of memory and history rise from the ground we walk, story intertwined with grief and hardship. This is even more true for lines like the Trail of Tears, the path west followed by several Native American tribes after being forced off their lands, but in particular the people of the Cherokee Nation, who were driven east of the Mississippi after the discovery of gold in Georgia. Thousands of people died as they walked west, from starvation, cold, or murder by white settlers. "The Cherokee Removal was the cruelest work I ever knew," wrote one Georgian soldier of participating in the removal. Today there are few better ways to get close to understanding that suffering than walking the parts of the trail that remain accessible.

The older the trail, the more attractive humans find it. Nazca Lines, the iconic images sketched out on plateaus in Peru, fascinated travelers and researchers for centuries before it was discovered in 2015 that they may have been the pathways for religious ceremonies. The same is true of the Mayan *sacbeob*: these roads were built by pre-Columbian Mayan cultures and were sometimes used for transportation but, judging by accounts left from the mid-1800s, may have been used more often for a religious purpose. Western writers told of local people saying a prayer every time they crossed a *sacbe*, but the true purpose and significance of these roads will probably never be known to most of us. Their power over our imaginations and their draw for our feet, though, will only grow as time moves forward and their creators dwindle further into the past.

ONLY TWENTY MILES from Happisburgh, but a world apart in atmosphere and access to bus services, a cathedral towers over the East Anglian city of Norwich. It's nine hundred years old, and the nearby Norman castle is over a thousand. Built, like the churches floating all over the Norfolk landscape, of local flint and faced with imported limestone, these imposing, intricate buildings seep with human history. The cathedral has seen the peaceful comings and goings of Benedictine monks, singing lauds and vespers and tending to the medicinal herb garden. And it has seen far less peaceful times. It survived the dissolution of churches during the Reformation by the simple expedient of changing allegiance to the Church of England. It stood through the battle for power between King Stephen and Empress Matilda (also known as Empress Maud) in the 1100s, and the War of the Roses in the 1400s, and the English Civil War in the 1600s. It endured the assault of the Industrial Revolution's caustic pollution clinging to its sides, and escaped German bombers during World War II even as much of the city burned, and, finally, withstood the twentieth century's slow loss of interest in the centuries-old faiths that have shaped life for much of the Western world.

Walking through the cathedral, you can feel this charged history. In these ancient buildings it's easy to remember that they were once the central gathering places for villages, towns, and growing cities. People have walked to places of worship from time out of mind, whether it's to a mosque in answer to the call to prayer, to synagogues on Saturday, to a Hindu or Buddhist temple, or to church on Sunday. Even I have spent years walking to services, though I am no longer a person of faith. When I was little, maybe eight, I used to get up while the rest of the house slept, put on my baggy tights and a hand-me-down dress, and walk across town to the Presbyterian Church on the other side of the tracks where, if I was lucky, it would be my turn to pull the bell-rope after Sunday school.

I exited Norwich Cathedral up a few stone steps leading to a court-yard, where I craned my neck to see the top of the church spire, the second tallest in England at over three hundred feet. Looking down again, I realized that visitors weren't just wandering in aimless paths around the courtyard; they were following a labyrinth built of stone set flush against the grass.

Although I'd read as much as I could about labyrinths, including Reverend Lauren Artress's *Walking a Sacred Path*, I had never actually seen one. And I hadn't, to be honest, been all that interested. As a person who is even less spiritual than she is religious, if that's possible, I tend to be skeptical of any spiritual or religious practice that claims to put us in touch with the divine, much less with ourselves. Walking a labyrinth, I thought, might contribute to my research but wouldn't actually *do* anything.

I believed that, that is, until I walked one.

There weren't many people at Norwich Cathedral that day. I joined four or five milling about the labyrinth, but instead of walking straight into it, I felt compelled, and I still have no idea why, to cir-cumambulate the outside first. While walking, I began to form a ques-tion, one drawn from a personal existential struggle I'd been caught up in over the previous year or two.

I wasn't prepared for what happened when I entered the labyrinth. I carried my question in with me, and as I began walking responses came—not direct answers, just thoughts—pulled from somewhere deep inside, a psychological place that I have looked into only at cer-tain points in my life when all other answers have failed. A place of the heart but also of the soul. And as these responses rose up to meet my conscious mind, my feet slowed down of their own accord. I didn't choose to slow down, not in the way we usually understand choosing—my feet dragged, as if being drawn down by the ground, as if responding directly to the gravitational pull involved in each footfall. I became acutely aware of how each lift of the foot and step forward related to the grass and dirt and rocky crust and molten core beneath.

I tried walking faster, as an experiment, but each time was pulled back, so I let my feet take the lead and examined the responses of darkness and light that came up to meet me.

I don't believe in these things, any of them. But my body clearly did, and that is not something I can explain. This part of who I am as a person, a human, knows that this connection to the ground is real. It feels the thin places of the world, the shiver of being closer to some kind of otherness. What do we mean by "sacred" if not this—something unknowable that acts on us with unconscious force? For all our research into dark matter and string theory, for all our detection of gravitational waves and the hidden lives of trees and the communication of animals, for all our prayers and meditations and faiths, existence—our existence—is still an utter mystery.

I took a long time to walk into and out of the labyrinth. People passed me going each direction. I stepped around a woman crouched on the ground taking photos, and two kids leapt from stone to stone around me, and still I walked, stuck with my questions and responses and the pace my feet insisted on. When I finally exited, it was with an eerie feeling of having been knitted back together, not just within myself, but with far more than I could fathom.

PEOPLE WALKED TO Norwich Cathedral for centuries, on Sundays, for harvest festivals, for the pagan-turned-Christian rites of Winter Solstice-turned-Christmas. They walked, they gathered, they prayed and were instructed and rebelled and fought and took revenge and gathered again. The church, like all public spaces, held the tension and trust of public life. Its stones now hold the weight of tourists in Merrells and Converse sneakers and my own boots, passing fashions on a floor worn smooth by generations beyond reckoning.

The floor of this church, too, has a story to tell, one of community and connection and the binding power of simple human trust. Places of worship were the focal points of this trust building, this community fabric, for centuries. The call of faith may be waning, but the place of the church or the synagogue or the mosque or the temple hasn't yet been filled by anything else. These are the places where people see one another on a regular, frequent basis, where they meet and get to know one another in a context of assumed shared values.

Neighborhoods build similar fabric, if they're allowed to. If people can see one another face-to-face on a regular basis, walk the same sidewalks, engage in the organic daily activities of work, life, child-rearing, food, education, leisure. In *The Death and Life of Great American Cities*, Jane Jacobs addressed directly the assumption that a neighborhood or community needed to be "ethnically cohesive" in order to be stable. It doesn't. Neighborhoods that work, that have high levels of social capital, "contain," Jacobs wrote, "many individuals who stay put." Communities with strong social capital, especially in cities, tend to be sticky. People stay put, even at different stages of life and through changes in careers. They build trust over many years and countless interactions.

I find this in my own town, where people from a variety of backgrounds, and different faiths and ethnicities, perform the hard work year in and year out of guiding the community, step-by-step, into a future shaped by common, though not uncontentious, choices. People have moved away, gone to college, lived overseas, married foreigners, and come back. In Jacobs's terms, despite leaving for a time, they've stayed put. "This, I think, more than sheer ethnic identity, is the significant factor" in a strong neighborhood, she wrote.

Someday, perhaps, far-off generations will walk the sidewalks of my town and the wilderness trails we've built up and connected over years of negotiation and persuasion—because no matter how well you know people, every change brings a need and opportunity to know one another better—and sheer physical labor, and wonder about the people whose footsteps made these paths.

My town is young, barely a hundred years old. It has a bubbling fresh-spring American quality I'm reminded of every time I go to Britain or mainland Europe. Norwich Cathedral's history has heft and richness and stories a person could spend the rest of her life exploring, yet the nine hundred years of human history it's soaked in are literally nothing compared to the 850,000 or more years those footprint fossils rested on the coast at Happisburgh. And even that 850,000 years is only a sliver in the long hominin history that stretches into the millions.

The French writer Marcel Proust, made famous by the publication of his four-thousand-plus-page novel *In Search of Lost Time*, is less famous himself than a singular scene he placed toward the beginning of the book. Biting into a madeleine, a small seashell-shaped baked item loosely related to a muffin, the unnamed narrator of Proust's book reels in memory, sent back to his aunt's house when he was younger. Not immediately—first he is gripped by a feeling of joy, and gropes around trying to understand its cause, his long, flowing sentences drawing the reader along like a child who has grasped you by the hand and taken you into the woods to show you something amazing they've found.

The flavor of the madeleine dipped in tea has become an iconic reference in literature, a touchstone for memory. Lesser known, though (simply because, I'd guess, fewer people have read the whole book than know about the madeleine bite) is a scene toward the far end of the book in which the narrator finds himself encountering a similar flood of memories, only this time they were brought about by something far different: after stumbling in a Venice courtyard, he catches himself and steps from one flagstone to another set slightly lower than the one next to it. "All at once, I recognized that the Venice which my descriptive efforts and pretended snapshots of memory had failed to recall; the sensation I had once felt on two uneven paving slabs in the Baptistry of St. Mark had been given back to me and was linked with all the other sensations of that and other days which had lingered expectant in their place among the series of forgotten years from which a sudden chance imperiously called them forth. So too," wrote Proust, "the taste of the little madeleine had recalled Combray."

This happens to be my favorite scene in *In Search of Lost Time*, because the book is like the story of a river, wide and meandering and fed by innumerable tributaries hidden high in the mountains. And in this moment, Proust proves that he hasn't just been fiddling around showing us his favorite rapids runs and stretches of calm, floatable water; in this moment, he shows the reader that he knows exactly where he's been headed, and while the story is full of distinct floodplains and gravel beds, in the end he leaves us with a bird's-eye view of the entire thing, a satisfying sense of knowing a story wholly and deeply, a rare feeling even with the best of novels.

In that footstep, as in the madeleine scene, Proust also demonstrates an understanding of something we have only recently shown scientifically: memory and knowledge come from the body. A flavor can send us back to childhood, and a footstep can send signals, like an electric charge, all the way up the legs, sizzling up the spine and to the brain, where they fire neurons of memory and emotion, snapping connections we've yet to fully comprehend.

The places our ancestors have walked are part of the stories of our lives, of the communities we've built and the connections that have always sustained human societies. These pathways bring the past to life for us, as if echoes of bygone lives swirl near ground level, along with the dust left by our own footsteps. As we slow down and turn away from our cars and our commutes, we come back to our bodies, ushering in a new world reshaped around our ability and desire to stride, stroll, and meander. A world that welcomes, as it always did even underneath the vast pavements we've pressed upon it, our footprints.

ONE LAST STORY before we return to Happisburgh and then home and I leave you to walk your own paths. And although my own personal interest gravitates most toward deep time, toward evolution and the mysteries of the human story, as befits someone who as a child most wanted to be a paleontologist when she grew up, I think that the following story is the most important one I encountered in my research.

ONE OF THE better-known healing walks to go mainstream in modern times is the Warrior Hike, organized by Warrior Expeditions, a non-profit founded by military vets from the Iraq War. It helps vets deal with PTSD carried back from the battlefield. Stories from the first Warrior Hike along the Appalachian Trail repeated over and over the refrain "walking off the war."

A little-known endeavor along similar lines was launched by two young Iraq War vets in 2016. Based in Great Falls, Montana, Luke Urick and Scott Moss lead small groups of Marine Corps veterans, especially those suffering from PTSD, on days-long treks covering over a hundred miles into Montana's iconic wilderness areas through an initiative called Montana Vet Program, or MVP.

Theirs is a journey with an even more specific focus than that of Warrior Hike. Initially, when Moss, who like Urick was a Marine sniper, came back from the war, he had a hard time adjusting to civilian life. Then by chance he was posted to a wilderness area in California. "We were mountain guides in uniforms," he said of his time in the Marine Corps Mountain Warfare Training Center, which borders Yosemite National Park and ten miles of National Forest Service land.

They had to become proficient in navigating different terrain and varying weather—rocks, ice, snow, rain. For Moss, the reintroduction to wilderness life came as a huge relief, and it also made clear one of the drawbacks of military training. Wilderness training provided by the military is, in his words, miserable. "The saying is, 'If it ain't rainin', we ain't trainin'.' If there's an organization that can ruin being in the outdoors for people, it's the US military."

The Mountain Warfare Training Center rescued his relationship with nature and led him to eventually get behind the idea of the Montana Vet Program. "It was a really good way to exit the military because you have this long decompression period," he said. Ninety-eight percent of military personnel get no such thing. There is no adjustment to civilian life, no transition from the deep camaraderie and brotherhood formed on the battlefield, no true understanding of the scars that war veterans carry, both physical and psychological. "They just get off a plane and get back to waiting tables or whatever."

The Mountain Warfare Training Center was where he met Urick, who is from Great Falls, Montana, and they began hiking and backpacking on their own. One day, they and some other friends, including Charlie Beard, one of Moss's closest friends, set off into the woods, hiking forty miles to Hetch Hetchy and then back to the office. The oldest of the group at twenty-nine, Moss said he felt like a kid again. "I got back to the house, had some beers, and wrote up a constitution and charter for our group. I had fun."

That was in 2008. In 2009, Charlie was killed in Iraq.

THE LOSS OF his friend and a feeling akin to guilt was a weight Moss carried with him that he didn't know how to shift. But he'd always loved the outdoors and wanted to rekindle his relationship with nature as he nursed his grief. "Hiking is walking meditation," he said, unknowingly echoing countless people I've read about and interviewed, from backcountry hunters to religious leaders to some of history's best-known scientists, composers, and poets. "It gets your blood flowing; you view the world differently" when you're hiking.

So he moved to Montana, where Urick was living and working with vets through Eagle Mount, a counseling center in Great Falls. They brainstormed a wilderness-focused plan for vet-to-vet healing. They wanted to reteach war vets what it can mean to be out in nature. But Urick and Moss didn't want it to be solely about walking off the war. They and their fellow Marines carry intense grief, not just the war traumas most of us hope never to face, but the scarring, debilitating loss of close friends, people as close as brothers, to combat.

These scars and the lack of any supportive transition into civilian life are causing more American deaths than combat itself has: twenty veterans kill themselves in the United States every day. We need to learn, Urick believes, from the mistakes made with returning Vietnam War veterans, for whom these statistics hit the hardest. "We can't turn to isolation," he pressed when we met up over lunch in Great Falls. "We can't turn to alcohol." The two men wanted a new way to address the suffering of returning veterans, one that faces that pain head-on, in part because they have learned not to accept the conventional wisdom that PTSD can just go away. Maybe part of treating it is learning how to live with the knot of sorrow, anxiety, fear, guilt, and anger that causes the suffering. And to do that, they didn't want to have veterans just sitting in a room talking about their pain. They didn't want to rely on counselors or prescription drugs. They wanted to return, as many of us do when hit with grief, before depression immobilizes us, to their bodies.

So Moss and Urick decided to bring something else with them on their hikes, something to represent Charlie's absence: they decided to bring his dog tag. And not just his dog tag, but thousands of others. Six thousand eight hundred and thirty-nine, to be exact, dog tags etched with the names of those killed in Operation Iraqi Freedom and Operation Enduring Freedom.

While trekking into the landscapes of Montana's vast wilderness areas, places like the nearly million-acre Absaroka-Beartooth Wilderness with its craggy mountains of granite and volcanic rock, Urick and Moss and the Marines they guide carry a seventy-five-pound bag with them, called a "pig egg," filled with dog tags representing all the American men and women who have died in the wars in Iraq and Afghanistan. The term "pig egg" comes from the Marine Corps sniper community. When a new Marine passes sniper training, he's termed a PIG, a professionally instructed gunman. The PIG then has to prepare his own pig egg, a sandbag that from that day forward never leaves the pack he carries during training, and judge what weight he thinks he can handle. It's similar, Moss said, to when he was a kid and his grandmother would make him go out to cut his own switch: "It can't be too small, but you don't want it to be too big."

The pig egg they carry on their healing hikes is almost the inverse of that used by Marine Corps snipers: the weight is predetermined by the quantity of loss. The vets have no choice over the number of dog tags they carry, just as they have no control over the mental and emotional scars they bring back from the wars. And as Moss pointed out, chances are, if you were deployed, you know somebody in that bag.

Through the pig egg, the MVP hikes bring together the pain of war and the weight of grief. "You're literally wearing the weight of the war on your back, and you're feeling it through your whole body," said Chad Russell, a Marine vet who participated in the Absaroka-Beartooth trek. The burden, said Moss, is a reminder that you're still alive, "and you're still alive for a reason."

These walks aren't meant to be easy. MVP's motto is "Suffer Well," which Urick explained to me is an acknowledgment that the suffering is not only present, but also useful. It might not be healed and it might not go away, but through the hardship of the walks—dealing with poor weather, wildlife, sleeping in the dirt, whatever comes along—a veteran might form a different kind of relationship with their pain.

While we talked, I thought of several people who had told me stories of walking through mourning, people like Katherine Davies, who found that shifting grief required weeks of walking. She wasn't the only person who described grief as a physical, bodily presence, one that required motion and intense use of the body to understand and cope with. And I thought of former Air Force cadet Lynn K. Hall, who wrote in *Caged Eyes* of running her first, exhausting ultramarathon that "in completing this journey I will reclaim a tiny piece of myself that I lost at the Academy. It will be a reminder that my physical pain—and the memories of the trauma that caused it—don't hold me hostage anymore. But both are still there, and I carry them with me every mile I travel." In abandoning pain as a tool, Urick told me, we as humans have lost something essential. "Suffering is part of evolution," and it can serve us.

The reason I say that this is the most important story in the book is that the Montana Vet Program isn't just about walking or healing or nature or grief or even suffering. It encompasses the full spectrum of what walking gifts us as human beings: the ways in which walking, pushing our bodies to see what they're capable of, especially in natural spaces like America's unmatched public lands, can bring us back from even the most extreme individual brinks, but also how walking nourishes our vital connections to one another. Suffering well and suffering together are both essential to MVP's mission: "In relying on each other and suffering with each other," Urick said, "we can open up those lines of communication with other veterans." Through the journey, the pain, the shared laughter, and their mutual trust and support, the veterans who participate in the program are changed. With the pig egg, the veterans' losses have shape and weight, something they carry with them, bending their backs to honor the war's losses still present in their hearts. But they are also reminded of their value as individuals. They remember, to use Urick's words, that they're badasses.

At the time I met with Urick in December 2017, MVP's pig egg held 6,894 dog tags.

I ONCE TOLD this story to a German violinist who lived in Berlin. She'd watched as Syrian refugees fled their country's war, carrying their children and little else, to finally land in Germany, one of the few countries to initially welcome them. The final endpoint of a long journey during which some of those people might have passed BBC reporter Bethany Bell on their way through Nickelsdorf.

She had been in a church one time, the violinist said, which was playing host to a display of sand and a weighted sack. She didn't know quite what its purpose was, but anybody could come, pick up or drag the sack, and crunch their footsteps along the sand-covered floor.

A boy came in, a refugee maybe nine or ten years old. He was too small to lift the sack whole, but hauled its end over his shoulder. And then he dragged it along the floor, walking in slow circles for over an hour. "I don't know what his pain was," said the violinist, "but he needed this, needed something about the walking and the weight."

In leaving his country and his home, what horrors had that boy walked away from? How many times had he stumbled on the way to the Hungarian border, where so many refugees were held up before Germany sent a train for them? What grief was he carrying inside that little-boy heart that needed such a weight to find relief? I wonder if, in his heavy tread, he found a way to move forward, to begin to comprehend the pain his body carried, and to take the next step into a new life.

CURVING AROUND NORFOLK'S knobbly coast, I came near to Happisburgh and wandered the ground that had for so many eons husbanded the remains of some forgotten hominins' long-gone lives. They had walked and wandered, perhaps hunted, and eaten. Loved, raised children. So many questions about who they were and where they'd come from and how they'd lived, questions that electrified paths wandering all over Europe and North America, down to Africa and the tip of South America, paths full of story and depth, sunken deeper into the ground the further back in time we look. Paths full of branches and abrupt ends, wanderings and U-turns, and one unbroken line, just barely traceable, that our ancient ancestors walked to lead to us.

Homo antecessor or some other long-gone hominin species left flint blades and stone tools in Happisburgh, and those beautiful footprints that shouted of life. What stories will *Homo sapiens* leave for future generations?

THE VILLAGE OF Happisburgh is sliding into the sea. Local residents are lobbying the government to build defenses and save their homes and farms, but as with all cash-strapped governments, this one is loath to spend the millions of dollars it would take to defend the coastline from the relentless forces of nature. A story tells of a farmer who ploughed a twelve-acre field one night in 1845 and woke to find the sea had replaced it entirely. Perhaps apocryphal, but tumbling soil on the cliffs exposes their fragility to the climbing ocean, and the coast is already dwindling at a rate of about fifty meters per decade. As climate change raises sea levels and exacerbates the problem, residents might find themselves in a managed retreat, similar to coastal communities in Alaska and Louisiana whose homes are disappearing beneath the rising waters.

Before my father was old enough to walk the streets of Leningrad, before he was even born, his parents, too, had been refugees, his mother and siblings sent off to the Ural Mountains with thousands of others as Germany's Army Group North closed in for what would become the 900-day Siege of Leningrad. His father joined them later after nearly starving to death in the siege and together, after my father was born, they returned to a city changed and devastated, full of the dead, and their communal apartment rooms taken over by a shifty Communist Party bureaucrat.

For all the things we create for ourselves, the homes we build, the lives, sometimes we just have to walk away, carrying the new burden of a broken heart and a lost homeland.

It was October 31, Halloween, the day I walked to Happisburgh. Also known, I'd learned from Robert Macfarlane's Instagram feed that morning before I lost cell phone service, as the date of Samhain, an ancient Gaelic festival marking summer's end and the start of the darkness of the year. I turned back from the sea and headed up to firmer ground, toward Ostend and the bus that would provide the first link in a circuitous route back to the paths my feet know best, the land I call home.

INVITATION

> If you told me I had only twenty-four hours to live, I would spend it outside. I would walk around and admire the world in all its beauty and wonder. . . . I would spend it just walking around looking at the trees, the birds, the snowfall, and the skies.
>
> —Jack Turner, "Conversations: Brooke Williams and Jack Turner—On Wildness"

OUR WORLD IS CHANGING SO RAPIDLY THAT WE CAN BARELY keep up, in many ways enabling new modes of connection, empowerment, and health. At the same time, though, much of this change is being wrought with very little thought of the long-term consequences, and the revelations in 2017 and 2018 about the roles of bots and fake news pervading social media and gaming YouTube's algorithms, not to mention screen and social media addiction, are probably just the tip of the iceberg. Facebook's motto for years was "Move Fast and Break Things," and it's clear by now that it might have broken fewer things so badly if it had moved just a little bit more slowly and with a greater understanding both of human ethics and of human failings.*

But the ways in which digital technology has taken over our lives are not going to disappear, nor are they going to stop at the Apple Watches and smartphones that could comprise any dictionary's entry for "love-hate relationship." There will be more, and much of that emergent technology already exists, such as the computers that a human, or a lab monkey, can control with her mind.

One of the blind spots of technology developers has been to assume that these creations will eventually replace many aspects of the human experience and, crucially, that that replacement is desirable. Theoretical physicist Michio Kaku, though, in his 2011 book *Physics of the Future*, pointed out that inventors and engineers near the beginning of the Internet era thought that activities like online shopping and cybertourism would spell the death of tourism, in-person shopping, and live music and theater performances. The opposite has happened, he wrote, in large part because humans have a biological need to connect with one another, and crave real, visceral, touchable experiences over simulacra. "One medium," he wrote, "never annihilates a previous one but coexists with it."

The choice, then, between living with hyper-connected digital technology and living without it is a false one. It's here. It's not going to disappear, no matter how often I imagine stamping a boot heel decisively on my headache-inducing smartphone, not unless I choose to live completely off-grid, and the vast majority of us will never make that choice, or even have the option.

Nor should we necessarily want to. Technological advances have enabled us not just to Skype with far-flung relatives, but to understand both human motion and infrastructure design so that more people

*The company's new motto, revealed in 2014, was "Move Fast with Stable Infra," referring to the company's aim to continue to produce technology quickly but with fewer bugs in the computer code. Whether a later version might include some version of "Move Thoughtfully and Don't Encourage People to Hate on Each Other" remains to be seen.

can traverse the world as they wish, and those particular technologies will continue to improve. The future before us requires us to face the realities of our world full-on, and to figure out both what we want from our most cutting-edge inventions, and how they can serve us better, how we can reclaim our physical world, our physical selves, and the time and attention to appreciate both. We cannot lose sight of what technologies are for: human potential does not refer only to the brain or to efficiency and productivity, but to the entirety of the human experience.

"What I want from technology is not a new world," wrote technology and culture writer Nicholas Carr. "What I want from technology are tools for exploring and enjoying the world that is—the world that comes to us thick with 'things counter, original, spare, strange,' as Gerard Manley Hopkins once described it." The true aim of progress is about our abilities to connect with one another authentically, both online and across the street, and to listen to what our bodies have to tell us about emotion, faith, movement, the physical world, and who we are.

ONE OF MY favorite things to do is to get in my car, alone, and drive north fast on the empty roads toward Glacier National Park and uncluttered skies where you can see the stars in all their immensity. Get in late at night, in winter, shut the door, turn on the radio or the Ramones, head to the highway. Keep going until I get to where there are no houses and then turn the engine off and get out. Wait until the music stops ringing in my ears, and soak in the silence and the darkness and the utter dizzying divine beauty of this complex, amazing planet.

I loved doing this as a teenager, and I love doing it now. But driving for pleasure, for a treat, is very different from living a car-dependent life. From being forced into a community or society where the car is the only option. From a life where our finances and infrastructure and expectations bend toward the automobile, and a walking life, all our walking lives, are stolen out from under our feet. This gift of evolution is slipping away from us, but we can save it before it's gone. We start by falling in love with walking again.

While writing this book, I traveled to many cities and averaged, while I was in them, about ten miles a day of walking. (I do live in a walkable town, but generally average closer to three or four—a mother with young children and a job and the never-ending pile of laundry simply doesn't have that many hours in the day.) At some point I stopped being conscious of it, stopped checking my phone to see how many miles I'd managed to clock chasing research and places and people to interview and getting lost. Even before that, I woke up once in my hotel in Denver feeling something Katherine Davies had once described happening after she'd already been walking for days, if not weeks: "Every morning I would wake up and feel this energy up and down my legs saying, 'Okay, let's walk!'" She said it was like she was turning into a walking machine. That morning in Denver, I felt the same electricity in my legs, something vital and alive shouting at me before I'd even had any coffee. *Walk*, it said, like when my kids were little and jumped on my bed far too early in the morning. *Let's get walking!*

Once you start to pay attention to the press of your foot on uneven ground, the pleasure becomes conscious. Sensations tingle up from nerves and senses most of us haven't been aware of since childhood. Once I started noticing my steps, instead of brisk-striding them wherever I needed to go as efficiently as possible, the shift in my awareness and in my tension was palpable.

It reminded me of watching my children, my daughter in particular, jump in puddles when they were smaller, two or three years old. My son stamped and stomped in the water, but my daughter would jump, wait for the splashes and ripples to subside, and then jump again, over and over, all the time intently watching her yellow rain boots. She would never, now, be able to put into words an answer to my question, but I wonder anyway: did she feel the same consuming, nerve-pulsing delight that I became aware of as I relearned to pay attention to my steps?

"It's an odd feeling: being aware of the Earth rotating beneath your feet," wrote Out of Eden walker Paul Salopek in an essay sent from Azerbaijan. He felt it, he said, for the first time near the Turkish city of Tarsus. He walked through olive groves, on red soil, past lakes, and one day, "I felt it: The burning horizons were creaking up to meet me. I was walking, effortlessly, atop a gigantic ball. . . . I feel it now all the time: a kind of hyper-attentive trance. When it overcomes me, I feel capable of walking to the edge of the world where the water falls off."

I found myself envious when reading this dispatch. Having found my own pace, the walking body hidden in the one I've lived with for over forty years, I yearn now for the gift of time that Salopek has, time to walk this Earth every day. But I take whatever chances I can, delight in every hike into the mountains, jaunt to the mailbox, stroll with a friend.

"Start with longing," said my friend and teacher of walking and losing it. Start with longing.

Jump in a puddle today. Meander across town. Go for a stroll. Roll among the world. Pace off your frustrations. Tread, stomp, skip, press those feet on the earth wherever you can find it. Walk alone; walk with a friend. Walk to think and to grieve. And then look outward and find ways to give those denied it the freedom to walk. Step together. Walk barefoot on grass. Stride down the sidewalk. Keep walking, even if you've nowhere to go. Step in a puddle again. Watch the ripples you're capable of creating. Leave a story in your footprints.

ACKNOWLEDGMENTS

THIS BOOK WOULD NEVER HAVE MADE ITS WAY INTO THE WORLD if my early writing hadn't had the encouragement and support of editors like *Full Grown People*'s Jennifer Niesslein, who originally published my essays in *Brain, Child* and was the first to teach me how to rewrite, revise, and dig for the heart of what I'm trying to say; Brigid Hains and Pamela Weintraub, who taught me to plunge in deep for the big ideas at *Aeon*; Ross Anderson at *The Atlantic*, who reminded me that curiosity can always lead somewhere new, even for a seemingly careworn subject; and Tim Leffel at *Perceptive Travel*, where I spent four very fun years writing about travel and travel literature.

I'm particularly grateful to the editors of *Aeon*, *Orion* magazine, and the literary journal *Lunch Ticket* for first publishing my essays about walking ("The End of Walking," "Follow Your Feet," and "Wander, Lost," respectively). A few paragraphs from those pieces found their way into this book, and the book itself originally grew out of the ideas explored in "The End of Walking."

Without my incredible agent, Sarah Levitt, I might have still written a book about walking but would have spent much more time treading well-worn paths, lacking the vision that Sarah brought to the subject. I truly could not, and probably would not, have done this without you.

The same is true for Renée Sedliar, my editor at Da Capo Press, who from the first time we talked understood what I was trying to do and worked constantly to help me do it better. I am so, so grateful for her conversation, guidance, problem solving, and passion. Thanks go to Kerry Rubenstein for truly knocking the cover design out of the park, and to Linda Mark for the interior design that brought the whole thing together. Also to Michael Clark, project editor at Perseus, for clearing brambles out of my path and being a steadfast companion through the later part of the publishing process. And Beth Partin, a jewel among copy editors, for her excellent editing and probing questions.

Many scientists and researchers gave generously of their time and knowledge so that I could make this book happen. Thank you especially to Alexander Claxton for fact-checking the paleoanthropology sections, and to Karen Adolph for correcting me on the infant research. These experts worked hard and patiently to help me understand their research, and if in the end I still didn't grasp the scope and meaning of their work, that is entirely down to my own inadequacy: Karen Adolph, Ayanna Howard, Nick Ashton, Jeremy DeSilva, Steve Cummings, Herman Pontzer, Patrick MacAlpine, Ashley Shew, Peter Norton, and Mike Upchurch, who took the time to explain the 1906 video of San Francisco to me. I'm extremely grateful for the time many others took to walk and talk with me about their experiences, including Katherine Davies, Jonathon Stalls, Pam Jiner, Paul Kashmann, Don Nelson—who first told me about Mount Kailash and is very much missed in our community—Danny Grassrope, and Scott Moss and Luke Urick of the Montana Vet Program. And my dear friend Bethany Bell, who painstakingly walked me through her reporting experiences on Syrian refugees finally making it to Austria.

I have been fortunate throughout my life to have worked under some of the world's best teachers—in my opinion—going all the way back to high school, when Mrs. Sullivan first sparked my interest in writing creatively. Somewhere in the back of my mind, Jael Prezeau is still my first reader, and Klaus Heinrich's history lessons have had an impact on me for decades. As my debate coach and physics teacher, Bruce Tannehill taught me to research and constantly critique my own assumptions about what I think I know. Thank you and Gail for your years of friendship.

Joel Baer and the late Alan Greenberg gave me much-needed encouragement at Macalester College, and never tried to persuade me to abandon my home in the math department, where Karen Saxe and David Bressoud refined my mind and my values. At Emerson College, Doug Whynott and Edie Clark first showed me what it means to take writing seriously. And I'm particularly grateful to Alan Weisman, Tom Swick, and Pico Iyer for their later teaching, mentorship, and kindness.

I have always believed that writing is a community act; my own work would never have improved without constant feedback, support, and commiseration from the friends and colleagues I have met over the years. Jill Neimark and Rebecca Gasior Altman, I love the conversations that spring up out of the blue, and how my work is influenced by your acute minds and sensitivity; Sara Bir, Sarah Buttenweiser, Powell Berger, Meredith Fein Lichtenberg, Shaun Anzaldua, and Karen Dempsey, I don't know where I'd be without our writing group. Carolyn McCarthy, I hope we get to reschedule that long walk someday. Abbie Gascho Landis and Jeanine Pfeiffer, I'm grateful for your friendship and your models of what truly excellent science and nature writing look like. Sarah Boon, Melissa Sevigny, Rebecca Boyle, Lené Gary, Kim Moynahan, Erin Zimmerman, and Kim Steuterman Rogers, I feel privileged every time we talk books and hash out research and science writing hurdles together. Julie Schwietert Collazo, thank you a hundred times over for always being generous in all walks of life. Anita August and Ellen Goldstein, you always make me laugh and ponder in equal measure. And here's to the Freds, my first true writing community: Fred Osuna, Stephanie Austin, Chelsea Biondolillo, Jo Deurbrouck, Dewi L. Faulkner, E. Victoria Flynn, Raymond Gibson, Jane Hammons, Kate Moseley, Ericka Schenck, Kellie M. Walsh, Karrie Higgins, and the late William Bradley.

I was fortunate enough to find a literary home at the very beginning of this process via a residency at the Banff Centre for Arts and Creativity, under the visionary literary director Devyani Saltzman. I can't imagine a better place to nurture a creative project.

While none of this would have been possible without teachers, editors, and colleagues, there is so much more that I could never accomplish without my community and my friends. Erica Mortensen (in some ways this entire book is conversations we've had on the ski lift, even if only in my head; we'll always have the Big), Courtney Erickson, Louise Larimore, Sarah Harding, Francine Roston, Alec and Jean Galli, Annie Kloer, Tessa Pitman, Kendra Hope, Candy and Randy Mills, and Amy Chisholm. Scott Larimore, for giving me the confidence to shoot straight and giving my family the will and knowledge to venture further into the wilds, and Aaron Pitman, for always being there for my family. Zabyn Towner and Katie Shriver, I wish we lived closer but look forward to every visit. Amy Tavano, thank you for helping me keep it together. Wendy McFadden, Koan Mercer, Alison and Bill Thompson, Nikki Wessel, Paul Cantrell, Skye Drynan, and Laurie Cheung—we always, somehow, carry our oldest friends with us.

And my family, whom I love more than I'll ever be able to show. Thanks to Sasha for stepping into the editor's role and constantly steering me closer to truth and accuracy; Papa, thank you for reading this manuscript far too many times and never letting me get away with sloppy thinking. Mama, thank you for always encouraging me to keep writing, and Jessie, I'll share a home with you again any day (just kidding). That we can spend our lives near each other makes me happier than I ever could have imagined.

My children have put up with so much during this process, while continuing to learn and grow and being a joy to know and love every single day. And Ian, with whom I share the greatest gift, to be able to walk together in silence and trust and be at peace. Thank you for always believing in me.

REFERENCES

SELECTED BIBLIOGRAPHY FOR *A WALKING LIFE*

THE RESEARCH PAPERS, ARTICLES, ESSAYS, INTERVIEWS, VIDEOS, AND PODcasts listed here are not an exhaustive list of the research used to inform this book. These references are only the ones that relate directly to facts stated within the manuscript. The links to research papers will in some cases lead to abstracts rather than complete papers, as many of them are behind a paywall.

BOOKS

Artress, Lauren. *Walking a Sacred Path: Rediscovering the Labyrinth as a Spiritual Practice.* New York: Riverhead, 1995.

Brown, Brené. *Braving the Wilderness: The Quest for True Belonging and the Courage to Stand Alone.* New York: Random House, 2017.

Cacioppo, John T., and William Patrick. *Loneliness: Human Nature and the Need for Social Connection.* New York: W. W. Norton, 2008.

Commager, Henry Steele, and Richard B. Morris, editors. *The Spirit of 'Seventy-Six: The Story of the American Revolution as Told by Participants.* Indianapolis: Bobbs-Merrill, 1958.

Elkin, Lauren. *Flâneuse: Women Walk the City in Paris, New York, Tokyo, Venice, and London.* New York: Farrar, Straus and Giroux, 2017.

Francis, John. *Planetwalker: 22 Years of Walking. 17 Years of Silence.* Washington, D.C.: National Geographic Books, 2009.

Friedman, Rachelle. *The Promise: A Tragic Accident, a Paralyzed Bride, and the Power of Love, Loyalty, and Friendship*. Guilford, CT: Taylor Trade Publishing, 2014.

Gros, Frédéric. *A Philosophy of Walking*. Translated by John Howe. London: Verso, 2014.

Hall, Lynn K. *Caged Eyes: An Air Force Cadet's Story of Rape and Resilience*. Boston: Beacon Press, 2017.

Harari, Yuval Noah. *Homo Deus: A Brief History of Tomorrow*. New York: Harper, 2017.

______. *Sapiens: A Brief History of Humankind*. London: Harvill Secker, 2014.

Herzog, Werner. *Of Walking in Ice: Munich–Paris, 23 November–14 December 1974*. Translated by Martje Herzog and Alan Greenberg. Minneapolis: University of Minnesota Press, 2015.

Jacobs, Jane. *Dark Age Ahead*. New York: Random House, 2004.

______. *The Death and Life of Great American Cities*. New York: Random House, 1961.

Junger, Sebastian. *Tribe: On Homecoming and Belonging*. New York: Hachette Book Group, 2016.

Kaku, Michio. *Physics of the Future: How Science Will Shape Human Destiny and Our Daily Lives by the Year 2100*. New York: Doubleday, 2011.

Laing, Olivia. *The Lonely City: Adventures in the Art of Being Alone*. New York: Picador, 2016.

Levine, James A. *Get Up! Why Your Chair Is Killing You and What You Can Do About It*. New York: St. Martin's Press, 2014.

Lieberman, Daniel E. *The Story of the Human Body: Evolution, Health, and Disease*. New York: Pantheon Books, 2013.

Macfarlane, Robert. *The Old Ways: A Journey on Foot*. New York: Penguin, 2012.

Moor, Robert. *On Trails: An Exploration*. New York: Simon and Schuster, 2016.

Norton, Peter D. *Fighting Traffic: The Dawn of the Motor Age in the American City*. Cambridge: MIT Press, 2008.

Putnam, Robert. *Bowling Alone: The Collapse and Revival of American Community*. New York: Simon and Schuster, 2000.

Reader, Ian. *Pilgrimage: A Very Short Introduction*. Oxford: Oxford University Press, 2015.

Roberts, Alice. *The Incredible Unlikeliness of Being: Evolution and the Making of Us*. London: Heron Books, 2015.

Rothstein, Richard. *The Color of Law: A Forgotten History of How Our Government Segregated America*. New York: W. W. Norton, 2017.
Rubinstein, Dan. *Born to Walk: The Transformative Power of a Pedestrian Act*. Toronto: ECW Press, 2015.
Sadik-Khan, Janette, and Seth Solomonow. *Streetfight: Handbook for an Urban Revolution*. New York: Penguin Books, 2016.
Smith, Adam. *The Theory of Moral Sentiments*. London: Penguin Classics, 2010. (Original publication date 1759).
Solnit, Rebecca. *Wanderlust: A History of Walking*. New York: Penguin, 2001.
Speck, Jeff. *Walkable City: How Downtown Can Save America, One Step at a Time*. New York: Farrar, Straus and Giroux, 2012.
Strayed, Cheryl. *Wild: From Lost to Found on the Pacific Crest Trail*. New York: Alfred A. Knopf, 2012.
Tufekci, Zeynep. *Twitter and Tear Gas: The Power and Fragility of Networked Protest*. New Haven: Yale University Press, 2017.
Vanderbilt, Tom. *Traffic: Why We Drive the Way We Do (and What It Says About Us)*. New York: Alfred A. Knopf, 2008.
Vernikos, Joan. *Sitting Kills, Moving Heals: How Simple Everyday Movement Will Prevent Pain, Illness, and Early Death—and Exercise Alone Won't*. Fresno: Quill Driver Books, 2011.
Williams, Florence. *The Nature Fix: Why Nature Makes Us Happier, Healthier, and More Creative*. New York: W. W. Norton, 2017.
Wilson, Frank. *The Hand: How Its Use Shapes the Brain, Language, and Human Culture*. New York: Pantheon Books, 1998.

ARTICLES, ESSAYS, VIDEOS, AND INTERVIEWS

The First Step

Bell, Bethany, in conversation with the author, May 19, 2017.
Salopek, Paul. "Setting Out." *National Geographic*, January 21, 2013. https://www.nationalgeographic.org/projects/out-of-eden-walk/blogs/lab-talk/2013-01-setting-out.

Chapter 1: Toddle

Blaxland, Beth. "Hominid and Hominin—What's the Difference?" Australian Museum. February 5, 2016, https://australianmuseum.net.au/hominid-and-hominin-whats-the-difference.

Boardman-Pretty, Freya. "Humans Learn to Walk Like Rats." *New Scientist*, November 17, 2011. https://www.newscientist.com/article/dn21186-humans-learn-to-walk-like-rats/.

"Cascade." *The Expanse*, season 2, episode 10, SyFy, March 28, 2017. Amazon Prime, https://www.amazon.com/Safe/dp/B01MSZILS5/ref=sr_1_2?s=instant-video&ie=UTF8&qid=1536253591&sr=1-2&keywords=the+expanse.

Faridi, Sophia. "Happy Teaching, Happy Learning: 13 Secrets to Finland's Success." *Education Week*, June 24, 2014. https://www.edweek.org/tm/articles/2014/06/24/ctq_faridi_finland.html.

Fye, Bruce W. "Profiles in Cardiology: Ernst, Wilhelm, and Eduard Weber." *Clinical Cardiology* 23, no. 9 (September 2000): 709–710. (This article no longer seems to be online; only the basic abstract information is available through the NIH: https://www.ncbi.nlm.nih.gov/pubmed/11016024.)

Hancock, LynNell. "Why Are Finland's Schools Successful?" *Smithsonian Magazine*, September 2011. https://www.smithsonianmag.com/innovation/why-are-finlands-schools-successful-49859555/.

HUMᐯNS, season 2, episode 5, AMC, Channel 4, and Kudos, March 12, 2017. Amazon Prime, https://www.amazon.com/Episode-1-Original-UK-Version/dp/B01MR9Y1WM/ref=sr_1_3?s=instant-video&ie=UTF8&qid=1536252988&sr=1-3&keywords=humans.

LaFrance, Adrienne. "What Is a Robot?" *The Atlantic*, March 22, 2016. https://www.theatlantic.com/technology/archive/2016/03/what-is-a-human/473166/.

"MARLO Walks Elegantly on 'Stilts.'" University of Michigan College of Engineering Robotics blog, September 10, 2015. https://robotics.umich.edu/marlo-walks-elegantly-on-stilts/.

Nagourney, Eric. "Aging: Sharper Minds with Bustling Feet." *The New York Times*, September 28, 2004. https://www.nytimes.com/2004/09/28/health/aging-sharper-minds-with-bustling-feet.html.

"*Sahelanthropus tchadensis*." Smithsonian Museum of Natural History. http://humanorigins.si.edu/evidence/human-fossils/species/sahelanthropus-tchadensis.

Salopek, Paul. "To Walk the World: Part I of a Series." *National Geographic*, December 2013. https://www.nationalgeographic.com/magazine/2013/12/out-of-eden/.

Sharp, Levi. "Two-Legged Robot with Human Feet Can Now Walk Independently." *Popular Science*, July 10, 2015. https://www.popsci.com/two-legged-robot-people-feet-can-walk.

Teaching handout on robot sensors, optics, motion, etc., from the University of Edinburgh's School of Informatics course titled "Introduction to Vision and Robotics," 2007. http://www.inf.ed.ac.uk/teaching/courses/ivr/lectures/handout4.pdf.

"Treating Parkinson's Disease by Solving the Mysteries of Movement." *Neuroscience News*, January 28, 2016. https://neurosciencenews.com/optogenetics-parkinsons-bg-3517/.

Van Deusen, Amy. "Bombing Survivor Rebekah Gregory on Marathon: 'I Took My Life Back Today.'" *ESPN*, April 20, 2015. http://www.espn.com/espnw/athletes-life/article/12729607/bombing-survivor-rebekah-gregory-runs-boston-marathon.

Villarica, Hans. "A Rat's First Steps: How Humans and Other Animals Learn to Walk." *The Atlantic*, November 17, 2011. https://www.theatlantic.com/health/archive/2011/11/a-rats-first-steps-how-humans-and-other-animals-learn-to-walk/248601/.

Chapter 2: March

Abramović, Marina, interview by Manoush Zamarodi. "Come and Sit with Marina Abramović." *Note to Self* podcast, WNYC, October 25, 2016. https://www.wnycstudios.org/story/marina-abramovic-walk-through-walls/.

Blakeley, Edward J. "In Gated Communities, Such as Where Trayvon Martin Died, a Dangerous Mind-Set." *The Washington Post*, April 6, 2012. https://www.washingtonpost.com/opinions/in-gated-communities-such-as-where-trayvon-martin-died-a-dangerous-mind-set/2012/04/06/gIQAwWG8zS_story.html?utm_term=.a69556031580.

Blakeley, Edward J., and Mary Gail Snyder. "Divided We Fall: Gated and Walled Communities in the United States." In *Architecture of Fear*, edited by Nan Ellin, 85–99. New York: Princeton Architectural Press, 1997.

Conradt, Stacy. "How Photos of Tank Man Were Smuggled out of China." *Mental Floss*, June 4, 2012. https://www.youtube.com/watch?v=SACHK-W4o1E.

Cullen, Dave. "'The News Forgets. Very Quickly.': Inside the Marjory Stoneman Douglas Students' Incredible Race to Make History." *Vanity Fair*, March 7, 2018. https://www.vanityfair.com/news/2018/03/inside-the-marjory-stoneman-douglas-students-race-to-make-history.

Drew, Edward J., and Jeffrey M. McGuigan. "Prevention of Crime: An Overview of Gated Communities and Neighborhood Watch." International

Foundation for Protection Officers website. Undated. http://www.ifpo.org/resource-links/articles-and-reports/crime-prevention-physical-security-training-and-risk-management/prevention-of-crime-an-overview-of-gated-communities-and-neighborhood-watch/. Accessed December 5, 2017.

Elbein, Saul. "The Youth Group That Launched a Movement at Standing Rock." *The New York Times Magazine*, January 31, 2017. https://www.nytimes.com/2017/01/31/magazine/the-youth-group-that-launched-a-movement-at-standing-rock.html.

Evans, Ieshia. "I Wasn't Afraid. I Took a Stand in Baton Rouge Because Enough Is Enough." *The Guardian*, July 22, 2016. https://www.theguardian.com/commentisfree/2016/jul/22/i-wasnt-afraid-i-took-a-stand-in-baton-rouge-because-enough-is-enough.

Fontaine, Tim. "Standing Rock Protest Grows with Thousands Opposing North Dakota Pipeline." CBC News, September 8, 2016. https://www.cbc.ca/news/indigenous/standing-rock-camps-grow-1.3752623.

Grassrope, Danny, in conversation with the author, March 20, 2018.

Hague v. Committee for Industrial Organization, 307 US 496 (1939). US Supreme Court Justia case syllabus: https://supreme.justia.com/cases/federal/us/307/496/.

Isiksel, Turkuler. "Prepare for Regime Change, Not Policy Change." *Dissent Magazine*, November 13, 2016. https://www.dissentmagazine.org/blog/trump-victory-regime-change-lessons-autocrats-erdogan-putin.

Klinenberg, Eric. "Adaptation." *The New Yorker*, January 7, 2013. https://www.newyorker.com/magazine/2013/01/07/adaptation-2.

———. "Want to Survive Climate Change? You'll Need a Good Community." *Wired*, October 25, 2016. https://www.wired.com/2016/10/klinenberg-transforming-communities-to-survive-climate-change/.

Leakey, Richard, interview by Dr. Sanjay Gupta. "Human Evolution and Why It Matters: A Conversation with Leakey and Johanson." YouTube video from the American Museum of Natural History, May 9, 2011. https://www.youtube.com/watch?v=pBZ8o-lmAsg.

Long Soldier, Layli. "Women and Standing Rock." *Orion Magazine*, 35th anniversary issue (Fall 2017). https://orionmagazine.org/article/women-standing-rock/.

Neuborne, Burt. "Reading the First Amendment as a Whole." National Constitution Center. Undated. https://constitutioncenter.org/interactive-constitution/amendments/amendment-i/assembly-and-petition-neuborne/interp/34.

Popova, Maria. "The Lonely City: Adventures in the Art of Being Alone." *Brain Pickings*. Undated. https://www.brainpickings.org/2016/07/11/the-lonely-city-olivia-laing/.

Racine, Eliza. "Native Americans Facing Highest Suicide Rates." Lakota People's Law Project, May 12, 2016. https://www.lakotalaw.org/news/2016-05-12/native-americans-facing-highest-suicide-rates.

Reese, Hope. "Margaret Atwood Explains How to Know If You're Living in a Totalitarian State." *Vox*, April 26, 2017. https://www.vox.com/conversations/2017/4/26/15435378/margaret-atwood-handmaids-tale-interview.

Sagar, Paul. "The Real Adam Smith." *Aeon*, January 16, 2018. https://aeon.co/essays/we-should-look-closely-at-what-adam-smith-actually-believed.

Simon, Evan. "Meet the Youths at the Heart of the Standing Rock Protests Against the Dakota Access Pipeline." ABC News, February 25, 2017. http://abcnews.go.com/US/meet-youth-heart-standing-rock-protests-dakota-access/story?id=45719115.

Starbird, Kate (@katestarbird). "Recently, Our Lab Published a Paper [Titled] 'Frame Contests' Within the #Blacklivesmatter and #Bluelivesmatter Conversations on Twitter in 2016. Not Surprisingly, Those Conversations Often Had a Very Divisive Tone." Twitter thread, January 20, 2018, 11:48 a.m. https://mobile.twitter.com/katestarbird/status/954802718018686976?p=v.

"US Protest Law Tracker." The International Center for Not-for-profit Law (Information is as of latest update on August 22, 2018). http://www.icnl.org/usprotestlawtracker/?location=&status=enacted&issue=&date=&type=legislative.

Van Gelder, Sarah. "At Standing Rock, a Sense of Purpose: 'This Is How We Should Be Living.'" *Huffington Post*, December 26, 2017. https://www.huffingtonpost.com/sarah-van-gelder/at-standing-rock-a-sense_b_12249332.html.

Widener, Jeff, interview by *BBC Newsnight*. "Tank Man: The Amazing Story Behind THAT Story." *BBC Newsnight*, June 5, 2014. https://www.youtube.com/watch?v=SACHK-W4o1E.

Woodman, Spencer. "Update: Lawmakers in Ten States Have Proposed Legislation Criminalizing Peaceful Protest." *The Intercept*, January 23, 2017. https://theintercept.com/2017/01/23/lawmakers-in-eight-states-have-proposed-laws-criminalizing-peaceful-protest/.

Yoder, Traci. "Conservative-Led Anti-Protest Legislation Already Doubled Since Last Year." National Lawyers Guild, February 15, 2018. https://www.nlg.org/conservative-led-anti-protest-legislation-already-doubled-since-last-year/.

Chapter 3: Stumble

Badger, Emily. "Why Highways Have Become the Center of Civil Rights Protest." *The Washington Post*, July 13, 2016. https://www.washingtonpost.com/news/wonk/wp/2016/07/13/why-highways-have-become-the-center-of-civil-rights-protest/?utm_term=.170417961f6d.

Brown, Cat. "Law Enforcement: Partners in Safety and Engagement." Panel, National Walking Summit, Thursday, September 14, 2017.

Dark City. Directed by Alex Proyas. New Line Cinema, 1998.

Domonoske, Camila. "Pedestrian Fatalities Remain at 25-Year High for Second Year in a Row." NPR, February 28, 2018. https://www.npr.org/sections/thetwo-way/2018/02/28/589453431/pedestrian-fatalities-remain-at-25-year-high-for-second-year-in-a-row.

Garfield, Leanna. "This Ingenious Illustration Reveals How Much Space We Give to Cars." *Business Insider*, April 28, 2017. http://www.businessinsider.com/car-illustration-karl-jilg-2017-4.

Gottfried, Mara H. "Black Lives Matter Protesters Claim MLK's Legacy with Roving St. Paul March." *Twin Cities Pioneer Press*, January 18, 2015. https://www.twincities.com/2015/01/18/black-lives-matter-protesters-claim-mlks-legacy-with-roving-st-paul-march/.

Kudler, Adrian Glick. "Los Angeles Might Finally Do Something About the Dumbest Jaywalking Tickets." *Curbed Los Angeles*, May 5, 2015. https://la.curbed.com/2015/5/5/9963892/los-angeles-might-finally-do-something-about-the-dumbest-jaywalking.

Levick, M. B. "The Confusion of Our Sidewalkers: And the Traffic Problem of the Future in the Erratic Pedestrian." *The New York Times*, August 3, 1924, p. 6.

Lopez, Steve. "Here's a Jaywalking Ticket That's Nonsense." *The Los Angeles Times*, August 19, 2007. http://articles.latimes.com/2007/aug/19/local/me-lopez19.

Miles Brothers. "A Trip Down Market Street, 1906—with Sound!" April 14, 1906. YouTube video uploaded by Mike Upchurch January 6, 2014 (further details verified via email exchange with Upchurch). https://www.youtube.com/watch?v=8Q5Nur642BU&t=156s. Also "A Trip Down Market Street, 1906: W/ New Footage!!!" https://www.youtube.com/watch?v=8YRbMMqj0qw.

Misra, Tanvi. "How Early White Flight Drove Racial Segregation." *CityLab*, March 18, 2016. https://www.citylab.com/equity/2016/03/how-early-white-flight-drove-racial-segregation/474057/.

"Mom Granted New Trial in Death of Son Struck by Driver." CNN, July 27, 2011. http://www.cnn.com/2011/CRIME/07/27/georgia.mother.new.trial/index.html.

Mosher, Dave, and Skye Gould. "How Likely Are Foreign Terrorists to Kill Americans? The Odds May Surprise You." *Business Insider*, January 31, 2017. http://www.businessinsider.com/death-risk-statistics-terrorism-disease-accidents-2017-1.

Norton, Peter, email message to author, July 19, 2018.

Peters, Adele. "These Beautiful Maps Show How Much of the U.S. Is Paved Over." *Fast Company*, January 17, 2015. https://www.fastcompany.com/3039983/these-beautiful-maps-show-how-much-of-the-us-is-paved-over.

Plumer, Brad. "Cars Take Up Way Too Much Space in Cities. New Technology Could Change That." *Vox*, September 26, 2016. https://www.vox.com/a/new-economy-future/cars-cities-technologies.

Rossi, Tony. "Dorothy Day, the San Francisco Earthquake and the Aftermath of 9/11." *Patheos*, September 11, 2013. http://www.patheos.com/blogs/christophers/2013/09/dorothy-day-the-san-francisco-earthquake-and-the-aftermath-of-911/.

Sanders, Topher, and Kate Rabinowitz. "Walking While Black." *ProPublica* and *Florida Times-Union*, November 16, 2017. https://features.propublica.org/walking-while-black/jacksonville-pedestrian-violations-racial-profiling/.

Stromberg, Joseph. "Highways Gutted American Cities. So Why Did They Build Them?" *Vox*, March 11, 2016. https://www.vox.com/2015/5/14/8605917/highways-interstate-cities-history.

Studley, Joe, and Kelly Goff. "Complaint Filed After Rough Jaywalking Arrest Video Goes Viral." NBC, September 17, 2015. https://www.nbclosangeles.com/news/local/Complaint-Filed-After-Rough-Arrest-Video-Goes-Viral-328148691.html.

"Traffic Safety Facts: Pedestrians." National Highway Transportation Safety Administration. DOT HS 812 493. March 2018. https://crashstats.nhtsa.dot.gov/Api/Public/ViewPublication/812493.

Vanderbilt, Tom. "Learning to Walk." *Slate*, April 13, 2012. http://www.slate.com/articles/life/walking/2012/04/walking_in_america_how_we_can_become_pedestrians_once_more_.html.

Wood, Jeff. "Talking Headways Podcast: Ghosts of Motordom's Past and Future." *Streetsblog USA's Talking Headways* podcast, episode 104. June 17, 2016. https://usa.streetsblog.org/2016/06/17/talking-headways-podcast-ghosts-of-motordoms-past-and-future/.

Chapter 4: Lurch

Amos, Heather. "Poor Air Quality Kills 5.5 Million Worldwide Annually." *UBC News*, February 12, 2016. http://kutv.com/news/local/doctor-says-utahs-air-pollution-leading-to-premature-death-of-thousands.

Associated Press. "Chicago Kids Crossing Gang Boundaries Escorted to School." *USA Today*, August 26, 2013. https://www.usatoday.com/story/news/nation/2013/08/26/chicago-schools-violence/2700373/.

"Attention-Deficit/Hyperactivity Disorder." Centers for Disease Control and Prevention, March 20, 2018. https://www.cdc.gov/ncbddd/adhd/data.html.

Blair, Leonardo. "Father Arrested for Walking to School to Pick Up His Children Instead of Driving a Car." *Christian Post*, November 26, 2013. https://www.christianpost.com/news/father-arrested-for-walking-to-school-to-pick-up-his-children-instead-of-driving-a-car-watch-video-109600/.

boyd, danah, interview by Krista Tippett. "The Internet of the Good, the Bad, and the Ugly." *On Being*. July 27, 2017. https://onbeing.org/programs/danah-boyd-the-internet-of-the-good-the-bad-and-the-ugly-jul2017/.

Brown, Brené. "Brené Brown at TEDxHouston." TEDx Talks, October 6, 2010. https://www.youtube.com/watch?v=X4Qm9cGRub0.

Cadogan, Garnette. "Walking While Black." *Literary Hub*, July 8, 2016. https://lithub.com/walking-while-black/.

Carrington, Damian. "Three-Quarters of UK Children Spend Less Time Outdoors Than Prison Inmates—Survey." *The Guardian*, March 25, 2016. https://www.theguardian.com/environment/2016/mar/25/three-quarters-of-uk-children-spend-less-time-outdoors-than-prison-inmates-survey.

______. "Toxic Air Pollution Particles Found in Human Brains." *The Guardian*, September 5, 2016. https://www.theguardian.com/environment/2016/sep/05/toxic-air-pollution-particles-found-in-human-brains-links-alzheimers.

Chabria, Anita. "'I Have Nightmares': Black Man Beaten by Officer for Jaywalking Filing Federal Suit." *Miami Herald*, April 24, 2017. http://www.miamiherald.com/news/nation-world/national/article146332444.html.

Chaney, Rob. "Timber Wars Inspired Missoula's Environmental Movement." *The Missoulian*, December 2, 2016. https://missoulian.com/news/local

/timber-wars-inspired-missoula-s-environmental-movement/article_64225300-2d2d-5fae-8cdd-578e6865b8c2.html.

Dart, Tom. "Houston's Health Crisis: By 2040, One in Five Residents Will Be Diabetic." *The Guardian*, February 11, 2016. https://www.theguardian.com/cities/2016/feb/11/houston-health-crisis-diabetes-sugar-cars-diabetic.

Devlin, Sherry. "Scientists Say Cars Still Main Culprit in Pollution." *The Missoulian*, February 4, 2001. https://missoulian.com/uncategorized/scientists-says-cars-still-main-culprit-in-pollution/article_30077172-a531-53bd-bdf0-47f6dab10357.html.

Donnelly, Laura. "Air Pollution Stunting Children's Lungs, Study Finds." *The Telegraph*, October 25, 2015. https://www.telegraph.co.uk/journalists/laura-donnelly/11953613/Air-pollution-stunting-childrens-lungs-study-finds.html.

Grady, Denise. "Obesity-Linked Diabetes in Children Resists Treatment." *The New York Times*, April 29, 2012. https://www.nytimes.com/2012/04/30/health/research/obesity-and-type-2-diabetes-cases-take-toll-on-children.html.

Gumbrecht, Jaimie. "Chicago's $8 Million Push to Protect Students from Gangs." CNN, April 10, 2014. https://www.cnn.com/2014/04/10/us/chicagoland-safe-passage/index.html.

Hampton, Elizabeth. "When Walking to School Is Unsafe." *Huffington Post*, May 25, 2011. https://www.huffingtonpost.com/elizabeth-hampton/when-walking-to-school-is_b_785805.html.

Harris, Sarah. "Nearly a Third of Four-Year-Olds Are Too Unfit to Start School: Sedentary Lifestyles Mean Some Youngsters Cannot Walk in a Straight Line." *Daily Mail*, September 1, 2016. http://www.dailymail.co.uk/news/article-3770013/Nearly-four-year-olds-unfit-start-school-Sedentary-lifestyles-means-youngsters-walk-straight-line.html.

Harvey, Chelsea. "Even Before They Start Breathing, Babies Can Be Harmed by Air Pollution, Scientists Say." *The Washington Post*, March 29, 2016. https://www.washingtonpost.com/news/energy-environment/wp/2016/03/29/even-before-they-start-breathing-babies-are-harmed-by-air-pollution-scientists-say/?utm_term=.dce4bd252105.

Knapton, Sarah. "Loneliness Is a Public Health Epidemic Which Raises Risk of Stroke and Heart Disease." *The Telegraph*, April 19, 2016. https://www.telegraph.co.uk/science/2016/04/19/loneliness-is-public-health-problem-which-raises-risk-of-stroke/.

Lahey, Jessica, and Tim Lahey. "How Loneliness Wears on the Body." *The Atlantic*, December 3, 2015. https://www.theatlantic.com/health/archive/2015/12/loneliness-social-isolation-and-health/418395/.

Leech, Nick. "Walking in Abu Dhabi: A Matter of Life and Death?" *The National*, August 5, 2017. https://www.thenational.ae/lifestyle/comment/walking-in-abu-dhabi-a-matter-of-life-and-death-1.616940.

Kennedy, Merrit. "300 Million Children Are Breathing 'Extremely Toxic' Air, UNICEF says." *NPR*. October 31, 2016. https://www.npr.org/sections/thetwo-way/2016/10/31/500048135/300-million-children-are-breathing-extremely-toxic-air-unicef-says.

Malley, CS et. al. "Preterm birth associated with maternal fine particulate matter exposure: A global, regional and national assessment." *Environment International 101* (April 2017): 173–182. https://www.ncbi.nlm.nih.gov/pubmed/28196630.

Miller, Chris. "Doctor Says Utah's Air Pollution Leading to Premature Death of Thousands." KUTV Salt Lake City. (Undated, but reports on journal article released February 12, 2016.) http://kutv.com/news/local/doctor-says-utahs-air-pollution-leading-to-premature-death-of-thousands.

"Newark Kids Choking on Port Authority's Diesel Exhaust." NJ.com, May 15, 2016. http://www.nj.com/opinion/index.ssf/2016/05/newark_kids_choking_on_port_authoritys_diesel_exha.html.

O'Brien, Edward. "Missoula Air Lands on List of Most Polluted." *Montana Public Radio*, April 18, 2018. http://www.mtpr.org/post/missoula-air-lands-list-most-polluted.

Penrod, Emma. "Utah Doctors: Air Pollution Harms Unborn, Lowers Fertility." *The Salt Lake Tribune*, February 15, 2016. http://archive.sltrib.com/article.php?id=3534955&itype=CMSID.

Renn, Aaron M. "Are We Still Bowling Alone?" *Governing*, September 2017. http://www.governing.com/columns/eco-engines/gov-broken-communities-bowling-alone-social-capital.html.

Sample, Ian. "Air Pollution Now Major Contributor to Stroke, Global Study Finds." *The Guardian*, June 9, 2016. https://www.theguardian.com/science/2016/jun/09/air-pollution-now-major-contributor-to-stroke.

Sandeman, George. "6 Million Middle-Aged People Take No Exercise." *The Guardian*, August 24, 2017. https://www.theguardian.com/lifeandstyle/2017/aug/24/around-6-million-middle-aged-english-people-take-no-exercise.

Sanders, Sam. "To Make Children Healthier, a Doctor Prescribes a Trip Through the Park." *NPR*, July 14, 2014. https://www.npr.org/sections/health-shots/2014/07/14/327338918/to-make-children-healthier-a-doctor-prescribes-a-trip-to-the-park.

Schmitt, Angie. "It's Not Rocket Science: If Streets Are Safe, More Kids Walk or Bike to School." *Streetsblog USA*, May 5, 2016. https://usa.streetsblog.org/2016/05/05/its-not-rocket-science-if-streets-are-safe-more-kids-walk-or-bike-to-school/.

Solnit, Rebecca. "If I Were a Man." *The Guardian*, August 26, 2017. https://www.theguardian.com/lifeandstyle/2017/aug/26/rebecca-solnit-if-i-were-a-man.

Strauss, Valerie. "Why So Many Kids Can't Sit Still in School Today." *The Washington Post*, July 8, 2014. https://www.washingtonpost.com/news/answer-sheet/wp/2014/07/08/why-so-many-kids-cant-sit-still-in-school-today/?utm_term=.4c48d5afb802.

Taibel, Ella. "Link Between Air Pollution and Diabetes Grows Stronger." *Geographical*, July 13, 2017. http://geographical.co.uk/places/cities/item/2321-link-between-air-pollution-and-diabetes-grows-stronger.

Talbot, Margaret. "The Disconnected; Attachment Theory: The Ultimate Experiment." *The New York Times*, May 24, 1998. https://www.nytimes.com/1998/05/24/magazine/the-disconnected-attachment-theory-the-ultimate-experiment.html.

Twenge, Jean M. "Have Smartphones Destroyed a Generation?" *The Atlantic*, September 2017. https://www.theatlantic.com/magazine/archive/2017/09/has-the-smartphone-destroyed-a-generation/534198/.

Vinther, Dann. "Children Who Walk to School Concentrate Better." *ScienceNordic*, November 30, 2012. http://sciencenordic.com/children-who-walk-school-concentrate-better.

Wabuke, Hope. "My Father Could Have Been Killed by Police." *STIR-Journal*, April 22, 2016. http://www.stirjournal.com/2016/04/22/my-father-could-have-been-killed-by-police/.

Wallace, Carvell. "How to Parent on a Night Like This." *Huffington Post*, November 26, 2014. https://www.huffingtonpost.com/carvell-wallace/how-to-parent-on-a-night-like-this_b_6225132.html.

Watkins, Andrea. "School's New Policy Bans Parents From Walking to School." Fox, April 5, 2016. http://www.fox26houston.com/news/schools-new-policy-bans-parents-from-walking-children-to-school.

"White Christmas." *Black Mirror*, season 2, episode 4, Channel 4, December 16, 2014. Netflix. https://www.netflix.com/watch/80073158?trackId=14277283&tctx=0%2C3%2C2b813822-6e9f-4791-8bef-02a92499cca2-32237452%2C%2C.

Yeung, Peter. "Toxic Air Pollution Hits Record Levels." *The Times*, April 15, 2017. https://www.thetimes.co.uk/article/toxic-air-pollution-hits-record-levels-d3fl56xng.

Zarr, Robert. "'Why I Prescribe Nature': In D.C., Pioneering Pediatricians Offer New Help and Hope through Parks Rx." Children & Nature Network. November 5, 2013. https://www.childrenandnature.org/2013/11/05/why-i-prescribe-nature-in-d-c-pioneering-pediatricians-and-park-rx-offer-new-hope-and-health/.

Zhou, Jiang et. al. "Time-Series Analysis of Mortality Effects on Fine Particulate Matter Components in Detroit and Seattle." *Environmental Health Perspectives* 119, no. 4 (April 2011): 461–466. https://www.ncbi.nlm.nih.gov/pmc/articles/PMC3080926/.

Chapter 5: Quest

Brighton, Carol. "The Great Mountain—Kailash Memories." *YoWangdu*, December 14, 2012. https://www.yowangdu.com/tibet-travel/images-of-kailash.html.

Brown, Derek (dbderekbrown). *Sand Creek Massacre Spiritual Healing Run/Walk*. 2011. https://vimeo.com/23782202.

Bullard, Chelsi. *Nine-Story Mountain*. 2014. https://vimeo.com/96321633 (30-minute excerpt from full film).

Campbell, Alexander Chapman. "Songs of Open Spaces." *Resurgence and Ecologist*, no. 308 (May–June 2018): 53.

"CNN Hero Dr. David Sabgir: Walk with a Doc." CNN. (Undated.) https://www.cnn.com/videos/tv/2015/09/03/cnnheroes-sabgir-extra.cnn.

Davies, Katherine, in conversation with the author, April 15, 2017.

Franklin, Deborah. "How Hospital Gardens Help Patients Heal." *Scientific American*, March 1, 2012. https://www.scientificamerican.com/article/nature-that-nurtures/.

Ghose, Tia. "Mysterious Nazca Line Geoglyphs Formed Ancient Pilgrimage Route." *LiveScience*, May 1, 2015. https://www.livescience.com/50699-nasca-lines-ritual-procession.html.

Graham, Latria. "Paulette Leapheart Walked from Biloxi to Washington." *ESPN*, June 30, 2016. http://www.espn.com/espnw/culture/feature/article

/16593240/paulette-leaphart-walked-topless-biloxi-washington-talk-realities-cancer-survivors.

Grant, Cole. "Salish Walkers Retrace Exodus from the Bitterroot." *Montana Public Radio*, October 13, 2016. http://mtpr.org/post/salish-walkers-retrace-exodus-bitterroot.

Hauser, Christine. "Climate Change Activist's Barefoot Walk Across America Ends in Tragedy." *The New York Times*, January 24, 2017. https://www.nytimes.com/2017/01/24/us/mark-baumer-killed-climate-change-activist.html?nytmobile=0.

Hillman, James. "Walking in Paradise." *Resurgence*, July–August 1988. https://www.resurgence.org/magazine/article4599-walking-in-paradise.html.

Iyer, Pico, email message to the author, September 4, 2018.

Jacobs, Tom. "Teenagers Surrounded by Green Are Less Aggressive." *Pacific Standard*, June 30, 2016. https://psmag.com/news/teenagers-surrounded-by-green-are-less-aggressive.

Khazan, Olga. "How Walking in Nature Prevents Depression." *The Atlantic*, June 30, 2015. https://www.theatlantic.com/health/archive/2015/06/how-walking-in-nature-prevents-depression/397172/.

Kumar, Satish. "My Life on the Move." *Resurgence and Ecologist*, March/April 2016. https://www.resurgence.org/magazine/article4604-my-life-on-the-move.html.

Mathieson, S. A. "Into the Woods: How Walks Are Improving Mental Health." *The Guardian*, June 14, 2016. https://www.theguardian.com/healthcare-network/2016/jun/14/woodland-walks-mental-health-forestry-commission-scotland-health-boards.

Maxmen, Amy. "Stress: The Privilege of Health." *Nature*, March 29, 2016. https://www.nature.com/articles/531S58a.

"More Than 100 Attend 18th Annual Sand Creek Massacre Spiritual Healing Run." *Indian Country Today*, December 1, 2016. https://indiancountrymedianetwork.com/history/events/more-than-100-attend-18th-annual-sand-creek-massacre-spiritual-healing-run/.

Rushby, Kevin. "Mountains of the Mind: 'I've Become Part of the Landscape and It's Become Part of Me.'" *The Guardian*, May 5, 2017. https://www.theguardian.com/society/2017/may/05/mountains-of-the-mind-sion-jair-lake-district-fell-walking-dementia.

Sander-Palmer, Sharon. "Walking the Water." *Minnesota Women's Press*. (Undated.) http://www.womenspress.com/Content/Features/Features/Article/Walking-the-water/1/1/4337.

Stabler, David. "Steve Jobs, Beethoven Knew Walking Increases Creativity; Stanford Study Says They Were Right." *The Oregonian*, April 30, 2014. https://www.oregonlive.com/performance/index.ssf/2014/04/walking_increases_your_creativ.html.

Upham, Lailani. "Walking Home." *Char-Koosta News*, October 20, 2016, p. 1.

Yeo, Lara Koerner. "Travel Memoir: The Power of Pilgrimage." *Elle Canada*, March 4, 2015. http://www.ellecanada.com/culture/travel/article/travel-memoir-the-power-of-pilgrimage.

Chapter 6: Stride

"AAPM Facts and Figures on Pain." The American Academy of Pain Medicine. (Undated.) http://www.painmed.org/patientcenter/facts_on_pain.aspx.

Achenbach, Joel. "Life Expectancy Improves for Blacks, and the Racial Gap Is Closing, CDC Reports." *The Washington Post*, May 2, 2017. https://www.washingtonpost.com/news/to-your-health/wp/2017/05/02/cdc-life-expectancy-up-for-blacks-and-the-racial-gap-is-closing/?utm_term=.547c1777be55.

Arellano, Megan. "Obese Children Tend to Get Worse Sidewalks in Denver." *Denverite*, May 25, 2017. https://www.denverite.com/denver-neighborhoods-high-childhood-obesity-worse-sidewalks-36417/.

Barnes, Zahra. "8 Health Conditions That Disproportionately Affect Black Women." *Self*, March 30, 2017. https://www.self.com/story/black-women-health-conditions.

Barr, Emilie. "Walking Toward Equity." *Salud America!* June 8, 2017. https://salud-america.org/walking-toward-equity/.

Berg, Sven. "Boise Sees a Whole New Way of Thinking About Transportation." *The Idaho Statesman*, March 25, 2016. http://www.idahostatesman.com/news/local/community/boise/article68389437.html.

"City and County of Denver Pedestrian Master Plan." August 2004. https://www.denvergov.org/content/dam/denvergov/Portals/705/documents/PolicyPlanning/PMPAugust04.pdf.

Formby, Brandon. "Counting Trees? Downtown Dallas Taking Steps to Be More Pedestrian-Friendly." *Dallas News*, July 2016. https://www.dallasnews.com/news/transportation/2016/07/28/make-downtown-dallas-walkable-urban-researchers-count-every-tree-bench-business.

Garrison, Vanessa, and T. Morgan Dixon. "The Trauma of Systemic Racism Is Killing Black Women. A First Step Toward Change . . ." TED2017, April 2017. https://www.ted.com/talks/t_morgan_dixon_and_vanessa_garrison_walking_as_a_revolutionary_act_of_self_care.

Hassan, Carma. "California Police Buy Walk-to-Work Teen a Bicycle." CNN, October 1, 2016. https://www.cnn.com/2016/10/01/us/california-police-bike-teen-trnd/index.html.

Holywell, Ryan. "Houstonians Want to Live in Walkable Communities. Often, That Doesn't Happen." Kinder Institute Research, April 25, 2016. https://kinder.rice.edu/2016/04/25/half-of-houstonians-want-to-live-in-walkable-communities/.

Jiner, Pam, in conversation with the author, August 8, 2017.

Kashmann, Paul, in conversation with the author, August 8, 2017.

Kauffman, Bill. "The Real Buffalo Rises." *The American Conservative*, October 5, 2017. http://www.theamericanconservative.com/articles/the-real-buffalo-rises/.

Locantore, Jill, in conversation with the author, August 7, 2017.

Madwar, Samia. "A Healing Walk on Ice." *Hakai Magazine*, June 6, 2016. https://www.hakaimagazine.com/features/healing-walk-arctic-ice/.

"Millennials Favor Walkable Communities, Says New NAR Poll." National Association of Realtors, July 28, 2015. https://www.nar.realtor/newsroom/millennials-favor-walkable-communities-says-new-nar-poll.

Mortimer, Caroline. "Paris Bans Cars for a Day in a Bid to Tackle Pollution." *The Independent*, October 3, 2017. https://www.independent.co.uk/news/world/europe/paris-car-ban-day-pollution-climate-change-a7981196.html.

Schaff, Libby, Bill Peduto, and Michael Hancock, interviewed by Jeff Wood. "Talking Headways Podcast: The Mayors of Innovation." *Talking Headways* podcast (rebroadcast of live panel at Rail~Volution 2017), November 1, 2017. https://usa.streetsblog.org/2017/11/01/talking-headways-podcast-the-mayors-of-innovation/.

Stalls, Jonathon, in conversation with the author, June 9, 2017.

Talton, Jon. "Companies Rediscover the Allure of Cities." *Seattle Times*, April 2, 2016. https://www.seattletimes.com/business/companies-rediscover-the-allure-of-cities/.

"Valley Hi Healthy Eating Active Living (HEAL) Zone." Health Education Council. Fact sheet, undated.

van der Kolk, Bessel, interview by Krista Tippett. "Bessel van der Kolk: How Trauma Lodges in the Body." *OnBeing*, March 9, 2017. https://onbeing.org/programs/bessel-van-der-kolk-how-trauma-lodges-in-the-body-mar2017/.

Vaughan, Adam. "Nearly 9,500 People Die Each Year in London Because of Air Pollution — Study." *The Guardian*, July 15, 2015. https://www

.theguardian.com/environment/2015/jul/15/nearly-9500-people-die-each-year-in-london-because-of-air-pollution-study.

Walljasper, Jay. "The Movement to Make Every American Community Walkable." Project for Public Spaces, November 12, 2015. https://www.pps.org/article/the-movement-to-make-every-american-community-walkable.

Willsher, Kim. "Paris Mayor Heralds 'Reconquest of Seine' as Riverbank Traffic Banned." *The Guardian*, September 26, 2016. https://www.theguardian.com/cities/2016/sep/26/paris-council-approves-ban-vehicles-right-bank-seine-road.

Yancey-Bragg, N'dea. "Alabama College Student Walks Almost 20 Miles Overnight to First Day of Work; CEO Gives Him His Car." *USA Today*, July 17, 2018. https://www.usatoday.com/story/news/nation-now/2018/07/17/alabama-man-walks-14-miles-work-ceo-gifts-him-car/792519002/.

Yehuda, Rachel, interview by Krista Tippett. "Rachel Yehuda: How Trauma and Resilience Cross Generations." *OnBeing*, November 9, 2017. https://onbeing.org/programs/rachel-yehuda-how-trauma-and-resilience-cross-generations-nov2017/.

Chapter 7: Pace

Brignell, Victoria. "When America Believed in Eugenics." *The New Statesman*, December 10, 2010. https://www.newstatesman.com/society/2010/12/disabled-america-immigration.

Brown, Molly Mccully, and Susannah Nevison. "Explaining Our Bodies, Finding Ourselves." *The New York Times*, November 15, 2017. https://www.nytimes.com/2017/11/15/opinion/explaining-diabled-bodies-friendship.html?nytmobile=0.

Case, Amber. "We Are All Cyborgs Now." TEDWomen 2010. https://www.ted.com/talks/amber_case_we_are_all_cyborgs_now#t-79291.

Chapman, Rachelle (@rachelles_wheels). "There Are So Many Stereotypes and Misconceptions About People with Disabilities." [Post] Instagram, August 17, 2017. https://www.instagram.com/p/BX628f0h2fi/?utm_source=ig_web_button_share_sheet.

Collins, Nick. "Evolution to Blame for Bad Backs, Dropped Arches and Impacted Wisdom Teeth, Say Scientists." *The Telegraph*, February 15, 2013. https://www.telegraph.co.uk/news/science/evolution/9873352/Evolution-to-blame-for-bad-backs-dropped-arches-and-impacted-wisdom-teeth-say-scientists.html.

Deamer, Kacey. "3,000-Year-Old Wooden Toe Prosthetic Discovered on Egyptian Mummy." *LiveScience*, June 22, 2017. https://www.livescience.com/59581-ancient-prosthetic-toe-found-in-egyptian-grave.html.

DeSilva, Jeremy. "Why Walk on Two Legs?" Leakey Foundation, March 6, 2015. https://leakeyfoundation.org/2015why-walk-on-two-legs/.

______, in conversation with the author, November 9, 2017.

"Dizziness Can Be a Drag: Coping with Balance Disorders." *NIH News in Health*, August 2012. https://newsinhealth.nih.gov/2012/08/dizziness-can-be-drag.

Dvorsky, George. "Paralyzed Patients Learn to Walk Again Using Virtual Reality." *Gizmodo*, November 11, 2016. https://gizmodo.com/paralyzed-patients-learn-to-walk-again-using-virtual-re-1785162361.

Eveleth, Rose. "When State-of-the-Art Is Second Best." *Nova*, March 5, 2014. http://www.pbs.org/wgbh/nova/next/tech/durable-prostheses/.

Ghose, Tia. "100,000-Year-Old Case of Brain Damage Discovered." *LiveScience*, July 23, 2014. https://www.livescience.com/46955-ancient-brain-damage-unearthed.html.

Harari, Yuval Noah. "Yuval Noah Harari Challenges the Future According to Facebook." *Financial Times*, March 25, 2017. https://www.ft.com/content/ac0e3b20-0d71-11e7-a88c-50ba212dce4d.

Howard, Ayanna, in conversation with the author, August 4, 2016.

Klein, Alice. "Brain Stent to Let Five Paralysed People Control Exoskeleton." *New Scientist*, May 17, 2017. https://www.newscientist.com/article/mg23431261-600-brain-control-via-blood-vessel-stent/.

MacDonald, James. "A Brief History of Prosthetic Limbs." *JSTOR Daily*, July 21, 2017. https://daily.jstor.org/a-brief-history-of-prosthetic-limbs/.

Medlock, Ben. "The Body Is the Missing Link for Truly Intelligent Machines." *Aeon*, March 14, 2017. https://aeon.co/ideas/the-body-is-the-missing-link-for-truly-intelligent-machines.

Parker, Sunday. "I have never been so happy to be on BART. NYC is amazing, but unless you can walk a flight of stairs, I could never live there." Twitter thread, May 9, 2017. https://twitter.com/sundaytakesbart/status/862007692000362496.

______, interview by Jeff Wood. "100% Universal Design with Sunday Parker." *Talking Headways* podcast, October 9, 2016. http://theoverheadwire.blogspot.com/2016/10/podcast-100-universal-design-with.html.

Pennisi, Elizabeth. "Prosthetic Hands Endowed with a Sense of Touch." *Science*, October 8, 2014. http://www.sciencemag.org/news/2014/10/prosthetic-hands-endowed-sense-touch.

Pogash, Carol. "A Personal Call to a Prosthetic Invention." *The New York Times*, July 2, 2008. https://www.nytimes.com/2008/07/02/sports/olympics/02cheetah.html.

Rosen, Meghan. "Robot Awakening: For Robots, Artificial Intelligence Gets Physical." *Science News*, November 2, 2016. https://www.sciencenews.org/article/robots-artificial-intelligence-gets-physical.

Sanford, Matthew, interview by Krista Tippett. "Matthew Sanford: Compassion for Our Bodies." *OnBeing*, April 4, 2016. https://onbeing.org/programs/compassion-bodies-matthew-sanford/.

Shew, Ashley. "Technoableism, Cyborg Bodies, and Mars." *Technology and Disability* blog. November 11, 2017. https://techanddisability.com/2017/11/11/technoableism-cyborg-bodies-and-mars/.

Talaty, Mukul. "Step by Step—the ReWalk Motorised Exoskeleton." Medical Device Developments, November 24, 2014. http://www.medicaldevice-developments.com/features/featurestep-by-step—the-rewalk-motorised-exoskeleton-4447524/.

Van Mead, Nick, Harvey Simons, and Aghnia Adzkia. "Access Denied: Wheelchair Metro Maps Versus Everyone Else's." *The Guardian*, September 21, 2017. https://www.theguardian.com/cities/2017/sep/21/access-denied-disabled-metro-maps-versus-everyone-elses.

Wilson, Robert A. "Eugenics Never Went Away." *Aeon*, June 5, 2018. https://aeon.co/essays/eugenics-today-where-eugenic-sterilisation-continues-now.

Wright, Steve, and Heidi Johnson-Wright. "Designing for Everybody." *Planning*, March 2016. https://www.planning.org/planning/2016/mar/designforeverybody/.

Zuckerberg, Mark. "Building Global Community." Facebook, February 16, 2017. https://www.facebook.com/notes/mark-zuckerberg/building-global-community/10154544292806634/.

Chapter 8: Meander

Ashton, Nicholas, in conversation with the author, October 30, 2017.

"Fossil Footprints Challenge Established Theories of Human Evolution." *Phys.org*, August 31, 2017. https://phys.org/news/2017-08-fossil-footprints-theories-human-evolution.html.

"Getting On by Getting Out." Montana Vet Program (video). https://www.facebook.com/pg/MTvetprogram/videos/?ref=page_internal.

Haile, Rahawa. "Going It Alone." *Outside*, April 11, 2017. https://www.outsideonline.com/2170266/solo-hiking-appalachian-trail-queer-black-woman.

Hider, Anna. "You Can Actually Walk in the Footsteps of Pioneers at Oregon Trail Ruts and Register Cliff." *Roadtrippers*, October 9, 2014. https://roadtrippers.com/stories/oregon-trail-ruts-and-register-cliff.

Hilts, Carly. "Earliest Human Footprints Outside Africa Found—in Norfolk." *Archaeology*, February 7, 2017. https://www.archaeology.co.uk/articles/news/earliest-human-footprints-outside-africa-found-in-norfolk.htm.

Moss, Scott, in conversation with the author, August 26, 2016.

Rowell, Jenn. "Montana Veterans Find Healing Through Nature, Camaraderie." *Great Falls Tribune*, June 30, 2016. https://www.greatfallstribune.com/story/news/local/2016/06/30/montana-veterans-find-healing-nature-camaraderie/86571138/.

Shew, Ashley, in conversation with the author, December 4, 2017.

"Trail of Tears." Georgia Tribe of Eastern Cherokee. Undated. http://www.georgiatribeofeasterncherokee.com/TrailofTears.htm.

Urick, Luke, in conversation with the author, December 14, 2017.

Invitation

Carr, Nicholas. "The World Wide Cage." *Aeon*, August 26, 2016. https://aeon.co/essays/the-internet-as-an-engine-of-liberation-is-an-innocent-fraud.

Eisenberg, Christina. "Conversations: Brooke Williams and Jack Turner on Wildness." *Whitefish Review* 6, no. 1 (summer 2012): 113.

Salopek, Paul. "The Case for Xenophilia." *The New York Times*, May 19, 2017. https://www.nytimes.com/2017/05/19/opinion/paul-salopek-the-case-for-xenophilia.html?nytmobile=0.

______. "Exploring the World on Foot." *The New York Times*, December 12, 2015. https://www.nytimes.com/2015/12/13/opinion/exploring-the-world-on-foot.html.

______. "What I'm Learning from Walking 21,000 Miles Around the World." *National Geographic*, April 6, 2016. https://news.nationalgeographic.com/2016/04/160406-national-walking-day-out-of-eden-walk-paul-salopek-migration/.

RESEARCH PAPERS

Abu El-Haj, Tabatha. "Defining *Peaceably*: Policing the Line Between Constitutionally Protected Protest and Unlawful Assembly." (July 30, 2015). 80 MO. L. REV. 961 (2015); Drexel University Thomas R. Kline School of

Law Research Paper No. 2015-A-03. https://papers.ssrn.com/sol3/papers.cfm?abstract_id=2638092##.

______. "The Neglected Right of Assembly." *UCLA Law Review* 56 (2009): 543–589. http://www.uclalawreview.org/pdf/56-3-1.pdf.

Adolph, Karen E., et al. "How Do You Learn to Walk? Thousands of Steps and Dozens of Falls Per Day." *Psychological Science* 23, no. 11 (October 19, 2012): 1387–1394. http://journals.sagepub.com/doi/10.1177/0956797612446346.

Adolph, Karen E., and Catherine S. Tamis-LeMonda. "The Costs and Benefits of Development: The Transition from Crawling to Walking." *Child Development Perspectives* 8, no. 4 (2014): 187–192. http://psych.nyu.edu/adolph/publications/AdolphTamisLeMonda-2014-CostsAndBenefits.pdf.

Beauchet, Olivier, et al. "Poor Gait Performance and Prediction of Dementia: Results from a Meta-Analysis." *Journal of the American Medical Directors Association* 17, no. 6 (June 1, 2016): 482–490. https://www.ncbi.nlm.nih.gov/pmc/articles/PMC5319598/.

Berman, Mark G., et al. "The Cognitive Benefits of Interacting With Nature." *Psychological Science* 19, no. 12 (December 1, 2008): 1207–1212. http://journals.sagepub.com/doi/abs/10.1111/j.1467-9280.2008.02225.x.

Brave Heart, Maria Yellow Horse. "Historical Trauma and Unresolved Grief: Implications for Clinical Research and Practice with Indigenous Peoples of the Americas." (Undated presentation.)

______. "*Wakiksuyapi*: Carrying the Historical Trauma of the Lakota." *Tulane Studies in Social Welfare* (2000): 245–266.

Buckley, J. P., et al. "The Sedentary Office: An Expert Statement on the Growing Case for Change Towards Better Health and Productivity." *British Journal of Sports Medicine* 49 (2015): 1357–1362. https://bjsm.bmj.com/content/49/21/1357.

Clark, David J. "Automaticity of Walking: Functional Significance, Mechanisms, Measurement and Rehabilitation Strategies." *Frontiers in Human Neuroscience* 9 (May 5, 2015): 246. https://www.ncbi.nlm.nih.gov/pmc/articles/PMC4419715/.

Collins, Denis. "Adam Smith's Social Contract: The Proper Role of Individual Liberty and Government Intervention in 18th Century Society." *Business and Professional Ethics Journal* 7, nos. 3–4 (1988): 119–146. http://dcollins.faculty.edgewood.edu/pdfdocuments/AdamSmith.pdf.

Dominici, Nadia, et al. "Locomotor Primitives in Newborn Babies and Their Development." *Science* 334, no. 6058 (November 18, 2011): 997–999. https://www.ncbi.nlm.nih.gov/pubmed/22096202.

Feigin, Valery L., et al. "Global Burden of Stroke and Risk Factors in 188 Countries, During 1990–2013: A Systematic Analysis for the Global Burden of Disease Study 2013." *The Lancet Neurology* 15, no. 9 (August 2016): 913–924. https://www.thelancet.com/journals/laneur/article/PIIS1474-4422(16)30073-4/abstract.

Franco, Eloisa Sartori, and Ivone Panhoca. "Vestibular Function in Children Underperforming at School." *Brazilian Journal of Otorhinolaryngology* 74, no. 6 (November–December 2008): 815–825. https://www.sciencedirect.com/science/article/pii/S1808869415301415?via%3Dihub.

Gibbar, Philip. "Europe Cut Adrift." *Nature* 448 (July 19, 2007): 259–260. http://www.readcube.com/articles/10.1038/448259a.

Gomez-Panilla, Fernando, et al. "The Influence of Exercise on Cognitive Abilities." *Comprehensive Physiology* 3, no. 1 (January 1, 2013): 403–428. https://www.ncbi.nlm.nih.gov/pmc/articles/PMC3951958/#R109.

Harcourt-Smith, W. E. H., and L. C. Aiello. "Fossils, Feet and the Evolution of Human Bipedal Motion." *Journal of Anatomy* 204, no. 5 (May 2005): 403–416. https://doi.org/10.1111/j.0021-8782.2004.00296.x.

Hidaka, Brandon H. "Depression as a Disease of Modernity: Explanations for Increasing Prevalence." *Journal of Affective Disorders* 140, no. 3 (November 2012): 205–214. https://www.sciencedirect.com/science/article/pii/S0165032711007993.

Inazu, John D. "The Forgotten Freedom of Assembly." *Tulane Law Review* 84 (2010): 565–612. https://scholarship.law.duke.edu/faculty_scholarship/2116/.

Kühn, Simone, et al. "In Search of Features That Constitute an 'Enriched Environment' in Humans: Associations Between Geographical Properties and Brain Structure." *Nature: Scientific Reports* 7, article 11920 (September 20, 2017): 1–8. https://www.nature.com/articles/s41598-017-12046-7.

Leavitt, Rachel A., et al. "Suicides Among American Indian/Alaska Natives—National Violent Death Reporting System, 18 States, 2003–2014." *Centers for Disease Control and Prevention Morbidity and Mortality Weekly Report* 67, no. 8 (March 2, 2018): 237–242. https://www.cdc.gov/mmwr/volumes/67/wr/pdfs/mm6708a1-H.pdf.

McDonald, Noreen C. "Active Transportation to School: Trends Among U.S. Schoolchildren, 1969–2001." *American Journal of Preventive Medicine* 32, no. 6 (2007): 509–516.

McKlean, K. "There's Nothing Here: Deindustrialization as Risk Environment for Overdose." *International Journal of Drug Policy* 29 (March 2016): 19–26. https://www.ijdp.org/article/S0955-3959(16)00032-3/fulltext?code=drupol-site.

Mitchell, Richard, and Frank Popham. "Effect of Exposure to Natural Environment on Health Inequalities: An Observational Population Study." *The Lancet* 372, no. 9650 (November 8, 2008): 1655–1660. https://www.thelancet.com/journals/lancet/article/PIIS0140-6736(08)61689-X/abstract.

Moobela, Cletus, et al. "Investigating the Physical Determinants of Social Capital and Their Implications for Sustainable Urban Development." *The International Journal of Environmental, Cultural, and Economic Sustainability* 5, no. 2 (2009): 255–265. http://eprints.lincoln.ac.uk/8307/.

______. "Gated Communities: Violating the Evolutionary Pattern of Social Networks in Urban Regeneration?" Paper presented at the conference Gated Communities: Building Social Divisions or Safer Communities?, University of Glasgow, September 18–19, 2003. http://citeseerx.ist.psu.edu/viewdoc/download?doi=10.1.1.197.7083&rep=rep1&type=pdf.

Oppezzo, Marily, and Daniel L. Schwartz. "Give Your Ideas Some Legs: The Positive Effect of Walking on Creative Thinking." *Journal of Experimental Psychology: Learning, Memory, and Cognition* 40, no. 4 (2014): 1142–1152. http://www.apa.org/pubs/journals/releases/xlm-a0036577.pdf.

Pirker, Walter, and Regina Katzenschlager. "Gait Disorders in Adults and the Elderly." *Wiener klinische Wochenschrift* 129, nos. 3–4 (February 2017): 81–95. https://link.springer.com/article/10.1007/s00508-016-1096-4.

Proulx, Michael J., et al. "Where Am I? Who Am I? The Relation Between Spatial Cognition, Social Cognition and Individual Differences in the Built Environment." *Frontiers in Psychology* 7 (February 11, 2016). https://www.frontiersin.org/articles/10.3389/fpsyg.2016.00064/full.

Shaw, Ben, et al. "Children's Independent Mobility: An International Comparison and Recommendations for Action." Policy Studies Institute, July 2015. http://www.psi.org.uk/docs/7350_PSI_Report_CIM_final.pdf.

Stewart, Leo G., et al. "Drawing the Lines of Contention: Networked Frame Contests Within #BlackLivesMatter Discourse." *PACM on Human-Computer Interaction* 1, no. CSCW, Article 122 (November 2017): 23 pp.

http://faculty.washington.edu/kstarbi/Stewart_Starbird_Drawing_the_Lines_of_Contention-final.pdf.

Sunyer, Jordi, et al. "Association Between Traffic-Related Air Pollution in Schools and Cognitive Development in Primary School Children: A Prospective Cohort Study." Ed. Bruce P. Lanphear. *PLoS Medicine* 12, no. 3 (2015). https://www.ncbi.nlm.nih.gov/pmc/articles/PMC4348510/.

Voss, Michelle W., et al. "Plasticity of Brain Networks in a Randomized Intervention Trial of Exercise Training in Older Adults." *Frontiers in Aging Neuroscience* 2 (August 26, 2010): 32. https://www.ncbi.nlm.nih.gov/pmc/articles/PMC2947936/.

Wei, Yongjie, et al. "Chronic Exposure to Air Pollution Particles Increases the Risk of Obesity and Metabolic Syndrome: Findings from a Natural Experiment in Beijing." *The FASEB Journal* 30, no. 6 (June 2016): 2115–2122. https://www.fasebj.org/doi/full/10.1096/fj.201500142.

Wiener-Vacher, Sylvette R., et al. "Vestibular Activity and Cognitive Development in Children: Perspectives." *Frontiers in Integrative Neuroscience* 7, no. 92 (11 December 2013): 1–13. https://www.frontiersin.org/articles/10.3389/fnint.2013.00092/full.

Yee, Eunice Y., et al. "Traffic-Related Air Pollution and Telomere Length in Children and Adolescents Living in Fresno, CA: A Pilot Study." *Journal of Occupational and Environmental Medicine* 59, no. 5 (May 2017): 446–452. https://journals.lww.com/joem/Abstract/2017/05000/Traffic_Related_Air_Pollution_and_Telomere_Length.4.aspx.

Younan, Diana. "Environmental Determinants of Aggression in Adolescents: Role of Urban Neighborhood Green Space." *Journal of the American Academy of Child and Adolescent Psychiatry* 55, no. 7 (July 2016): 591–601. https://jaacap.org/article/S0890-8567(16)30172-1/fulltext.

Young, Simon N. "The Neurobiology of Human Social Behavior: An Important but Neglected Topic." *Journal of Psychiatry and Neuroscience* 33, no. 5 (September 2008): 391–392. https://www.ncbi.nlm.nih.gov/pmc/articles/PMC2527715/.

Zoorob, M. J., and J. L. Salemi. "Bowling Alone, Dying Together: The Role of Social Capital in Mitigating the Drug Overdose Epidemic in the United States." *Drug and Alcohol Dependence* 173 (April 1, 2017): 1–9. https://www.ncbi.nlm.nih.gov/pubmed/28182980.

ABOUT THE AUTHOR

ANTONIA MALCHIK has written essays and articles for *Aeon*, *The Atlantic*, *Orion*, *GOOD*, and *High Country News*, among others. She spent several years as a travel writer after living in Moscow, Vienna, Sydney, and Boston, and eventually returned to her native Montana, where she lives with her family.